THE EPIC OF
Latin American
LITERATURE

ARTURO TORRES-RÍOSECO

UNIVERSITY OF CALIFORNIA PRESS
Berkeley and Los Angeles
1967

University of California Press
Berkeley and Los Angeles, California

Cambridge University Press
London, England

© 1942 by Arturo Torres-Ríoseco
Sixth printing, 1967
Originally published by Oxford University Press
Printed in the United States of America

PREFACE

ᴧᴧᴧᴧᴧᴧᴧᴧᴧᴧ

THE FIRST EDITION OF THIS BOOK, published sixteen years ago, is now out of print. The author, therefore, believes that a new printing is called for. He has received many letters from colleagues and students requesting him to reissue the book, and if possible, bring it up to date. However, editorial circumstances make it impossible to supplement the first edition, with, for example, a chapter on the literary essay covering the work of José Enrique Varona, Baldomero Sanín Cano, Carlos Vaz Ferreira, Alfonso Reyes, Francisco Romero, José Carlos Mariátegui, and others; or a chapter on contemporary writers. In the past twenty years there has been an upsurge in literary production in all the countries of Latin America. Many new names have appeared: distinguished poets such as José Gorostiza, Carlos Pellicer, Octavio Paz, León de Greiff, Ricardo Molinari, Vicente Barbieri, Herib Campos Cervera, Augusto Roa Bastos; outstanding novelists such as Agustín Yáñez, José Revueltas, Juan Rulfo, Miguel Angel Asturias, "Salarrué," Alejo Carpentier, Lino Novás Calvo, Adolfo Bioy Casares, Ernesto Sábato; gifted essayists such as Jorge Mañach, Mariano Picón Salas, Ezequiel Martínez Estrada, Victoria Ocampo, Germán Arciniegas, Leopoldo Zea. Their work is so important that the author feels they deserve a book to themselves, and he promises one in the near future.

In the 1942 edition the author wrote, and he still holds it to be true, that

The literature of Latin America is entering its Golden Era. The days of simple imitation are over; Spanish American and Brazilian writers have realized that only an earth-born conscience could save them from superficial and artificial thinking. They have discovered their true continent in the realm of the spirit, and they are creating new values

v

in this realm. Yet they have not forgotten their European
ancestry, their classic tradition. For this reason the literature of Spanish America possesses the stark realism of
Spanish literature without being Spanish; it has the elegance of French models, but is not French; it has a cosmopolitan horizon, but retains the flavor of its own earth.
It is time, then, to attempt the definition and study of this
vast literary production, which has been hitherto neglected
or ignored even among critics of the Spanish language.

That essential element of artistic creation known as form is
what gives the literature of Spanish America its cosmopolitan
contour. It is through form that our writers break through
their geographical limitations and acquire universal meaning:
thus Gabriela Mistral wins the Nobel Prize, Pablo Neruda,
the Stalin Prize; Alfonso Reyes becomes a symbol of Hispanic
culture; Alejo Carpentier and Jorge Luis Borges are translated
into many foreign languages. Yet each remains authentically
Spanish American.

The author wrote in the Foreword to the first edition—and
reiterates today—that

This book, written from a literary point of view, acquires
at present a truly political significance. Once the people
of the United States understand the intensity of Latin
American ideals, they will be prouder of their southern
neighbors.

In the interim the author has become aware of the North
American students' interest in the literature of Latin America.
It is his hope that this interest will deepen, and that it will
extend to leaders of thought and culture of the North, for
the peoples of both Americas, although of different race and
language, face a common future.

The purpose of this book is to allow Latin American idealism to speak for itself through its masterworks of literature.

The author wishes to express his thanks to Professor Joseph
Gillet of Bryn Mawr—to whom this book is cordially dedicated—for his interest in Latin American culture which made
possible the conception and development of this work; to

President Marion Park of the same institution, for her inspiring interest; to Helen Rand Parish, for assistance in rounding out the manuscript; to the translators whose names appear in the notes; to Mr. A. Rodríguez Ramón, for preparing the index, and to the many friends and colleagues who generously gave of their time and advice.

Acknowledgment is gratefully made for permission to reprint selections from the following books: Rivera's *The Vortex*, translated by Earle K. James, G. P. Putnam's Sons; Rodo's *Ariel*, translated by F. J. Stimson, Houghton Mifflin Company; *Martín Fierro*, translated by Walter Owen, Farrar and Rinehart; *Rousseau in the Spanish World Before 1833*, by J. R. Spell, University of Texas Press; *Hispanic Studies*, by E. C. Hills, Stanford University Press; *The Modernist Trend in Spanish-American Poetry*, by G. Dundas Craig, University of California Press; "Colonial Society" in *Colonial Hispanic America*, by Irving A. Leonard, George Washington University Press; and *Remarks on the Occasion of the Dedication of the Hispanic Room in the Library of Congress*, by Archibald MacLeish.

                                                    A. TORRES-RÍOSECO

Berkeley, California
May, 1958

CONTENTS

ⱭⱭⱭⱭⱭⱭⱭⱭⱭⱭⱭⱭⱭ

THE EPIC OF LATIN AMERICAN LITERATURE

The Colonial Centuries

THE HEROIC SIXTEENTH CENTURY

FOR Spain, the sixteenth century was the age of conquistadors. When Columbus discovered America in 1492—eight years before the beginning of the new century—the unification of Spain had at last been achieved, largely through the efforts of Ferdinand and Isabella. The power of the barons had been destroyed. The same year that saw the boats of Columbus sail the rough waters of the Atlantic saw too, in the fall of Granada, the close of the long struggle to reconquer Spain from the Moors. A great country had been created, perhaps the greatest since the Roman Empire, a nation of conquerors and heroes.

'Every man a King!' seems to have been the motto of the Spaniards of that time. There was no limit to imagination, adventure, or ambition. The Spaniard conquered in the realm of the spirit as well as in the physical world. While Cortés, Pizarro, and Balboa discovered and claimed new lands for the crown of Castile, San Ignacio de Loyola organized his order of Jesuits, the soldiers of Christ; Santa Teresa explored the mystic world; and Don Quixote (springing into symbolic life before the next century was fairly started) travelled the dusty roads of La Mancha in search of wrongs to redress and injustices to right. This, the sixteenth century, was the beginning of Spain's Golden Age. Painters, musicians, novelists, poets, playwrights, scholars, historians, and scientists contributed to the intellectual brilliancy of the Empire. It was a great moment in history: Spain was creating a new type of culture, and at the same time she was changing the face of the known world.

Truly, at the start of the sixteenth century the Spaniards had the spiritual make-up of conquerors: The Iberian Peninsula was just arriving at the period of the greatest literary splendor that any country has ever known. The Italian school of poetry in Spain, with Boscán and Garcilaso, was preparing the way for great lyric writers like Fray Luis de León and San Juan de la Cruz; the Spanish theatre had been founded with Juan del Encina and Torres Naharro, worthy precursors of Lope de Vega; the romances of chivalry were in vogue, and the picaresque novel was about to dominate the entire field of fiction. Under the influence of humanism, a generation of Neoplatonic philosophers sprang up; the new conception of documented history made its way with Florián de Ocampo and Gerónimo Zurita; and modern theories of international law were being developed. All this was conquest in the spiritual field and it was the revelation of the Spanish individuality. Outlets for the enormous energy of the race were needed. Thought, on the one hand, and the New World, on the other, were the proper channels for the welling forth Spanish genius.

For just this auspicious moment came the miracle of discovery, conquest, and settlement—events which partake of the dramatic, the epic, and the lyric. Spain poured her very life blood into the new lands. She gave freely of herself, of her greatness and her weakness. The heroic navigators went forth, on the pretext that they were searching for a new way to the Indies, but there was a vision of fantastic discovery in the air; cartographers, cosmographers, shipbuilders, students, sailors, and adventurers entrusted their fate to the unknown and mysterious ocean. Destiny challenged, and the conqueror of the seas took up the gauntlet. He defeated ignorance, doubt, opposition, and hatred; he mastered the waves; he discovered a

New World. After him followed the conqueror of the land: daring explorers and captains, bearded and mail-clad, forging nails from their sword-hilts and making their own gunpowder; plunging into the conquest of native empires, the dominating of millions of men, the opening of uncharted continents.

The material conquest of Spanish America had started, and the spiritual conquest followed almost immediately. Padres came in the footsteps of the soldiers, and sometimes outstripped them, seeking to convert the multitudes of Indians 'sunk in gentilism.' Scholars, scientists, philologists, descended upon the colonies and began their works of erudition. Printing presses were set up in rapid succession after new conquests—18 years after Cortés, fifty years after Pizarro. Great universities opened their doors, the Royal and Pontifical University of Mexico in 1553, the University of San Marcos de Lima around 1576. The Viceregal palaces became centers of purely artistic activities, and poetry contests were held on every occasion. The conquest was underway in earnest, for professors, clerics, and artisans were conquerors no less than their companions with crossbow and harquebus who continued to plunge through the tangled jungles and the steaming swamps. Spanish culture, as well as the Spanish conquistador, was marching across the New World.

This vast Spanish conquest, on a truly heroic scale, called forth a literature that is peculiarly heroic in character. Living history had to be written down; it became the chronicle. Mighty deeds had to be sung; they produced the epic. These two genres, chronicle and epic, were thus the beginning of Spanish American literature. Usually they were composed in a Spanish style by Spaniards, who came to participate in the great new adventure. Yet by this token, they may be considered truly American, for they were written by men who were Americans (like so many who came after them) not because they were born in a New World, but because they migrated to one.

THE CHRONICLE

THE conqueror, whether soldier, priest, or navigator, was the representative of the culture he had brought with him to America. His role demanded that he subdue and civilize—and interpret in words. Columbus, naturally, was the first to describe this contact with a new world. While Hernán Cortés (1485-1547), in his famous *Five Letters* * (1519-26), was the first to send his monarch detailed historical accounts of his work, later conquerors and historians continued the record, and their writings form the first great type of colonial literature: the *crónica*—the chronicle, whose subject matter is American. Perhaps the greatest chronicler of them all (from a literary standpoint) was Bernal Díaz de Castillo, of whose book a contemporary American poet has said, expressing the spirit of the whole genre:

> Some twelve years ago in a Paris library I came upon a copy of Bernal Díaz *True History of the Conquest of New Spain*. There, in that still living, still human, still sharply breathing and believable history of Mexico, it seemed to me that I understood for the first time the central American experience—the experience which is American because it can be nothing else—the experience of all those who, of whatever tongue, are truly American—the experience of the journey westward from the sea into the unknown and dangerous country beyond which lies the rich and lovely city for which men hope.[1]

Nowadays, the great mass of chronicles is more interesting to the historian than to the student of literature. But there are some names with which everyone should be familiar: López de Gómara (1510-60), official historian of the crown, set down his not always accurate *General History of the Indies* (1553); and José de Acosta (?-1599) wrote his *Natural and Moral History of the Indies* (1590), a book still cherished by the anthropologist and the man-of-letters. Alvar Núñez Cabeza de

* Cortés, *Cartas Relaciones.*

Vaca (1490?-1564?) recorded his ill-fated adventures in North America in the exciting *Shipwrecks* (1542); Gaspar de Carvajal (1504-84) penned his dramatic tale of one of the most sensational explorations ever made by man, the *Discovery of the River of the Amazons* (Pub. 1894); Cieza de León (1519-60), a soldier of Pizarro's fantastic conquest, compiled his *History of Peru* (1553). Bartolomé de las Casas (1475?-1566) won renown for his *Destruction of the Indies* (1552), with its impassioned but exaggerated descriptions of Spanish mistreatment of natives. Cristóbal de Molina (?-1578), a friar in the retinue of Almagro, recorded in his *Conquest and Settlement of Peru* (1552) the episodes of the hazardous exploration of the Andes; and Alonso de Góngora Marmolejo (?-1576), who came to Chile under the orders of Valdivia and who later was appointed 'witch hunter' (*juez pesquisidor de hechiceros indígenas!*), has given a true picture of men and events in his *History of Chile* (1575).*

There were many others, of course, but one historian is really outstanding among all the *cronistas:* Gonzalo Fernández de Oviedo (1478-1557), who was inspired by the amazing spectacle of a grandiose and virgin continent to write his extraordinary work, *Of the Natural History of the Indies* † (1535-57). A conquistador himself—his stormy career as Royal Officer and Governor took him back and forth from Spain to Castilla del Oro and Cartagena, until he finally became *alcaide de la fortaleza* of Santo Domingo—Oviedo found time to write works on heraldry, court life, and genealogy. His masterpiece, however, is his monumental work on the Indies, the first and the most curious history of Spanish America. To this day,

---

* López de Gomara, *Historia General de las Indias;* Acosta, *Historia Natural y Moral de las Indias;* Núñez Cabeza de Vaca, *Naufragios y Comentarios;* Carvajal, *Descubrimiento del Río de las Amazonas;* Cieza de León, *Historia del Perú;* Las Casas, *Brevísima Relación de la Destruición de las Indias;* Molina, *Relación de la Conquista y Población del Perú;* Góngora Marmolejo, *Historia de Chile.*

† Oviedo, *De la Historia General y Natural de las Indias, Islas y Tierra-firme del Mar Océano.*

the reader can find delight in his descriptions of New World trees and animals and plants, and even minute insects such as the firefly:

> Many flies and beetles there are in all these islands, which flutter about shining at night, like the ones that in Spain are called glow-worms . . . But there is one in particular called the *cocuyo*, that is highly remarkable . . . This insect is . . . as big as the tip of the thumb or a little less. It has two hard wings, beneath which are two thinner ones, which it guards and covers with the top ones whenever it alights; and its eyes shine like candles . . . So that if one be shut in a darkened room, the gleam is sufficient for reading or writing a letter . . . And when there used to be war in this Island of Hispaniola, both Christians and Indians used these lights, so as not to stray from their companions. Especially the Indians, who were more skilled at capturing these creatures, would make collars of them, if they wished to be seen from a league away . . .[2]

But purely as a work of literature, no chronicle ranks with the *True History of the Conquest of New Spain* * (1552) by Bernal Díaz del Castillo (1492-1584). This Bernal Díaz came to the New World as a simple soldier, to seek his fortune. He found it with Cortés in the conquest of Mexico—a fortune that included not only gold, but a number of arrow-wounds (one of which pierced his ribs), a lance-thrust near the windpipe, and a beautiful and noble Indian girl. The story of this conquest, in which a few hundred Spaniards became masters of the Aztec Empire, naturally surpasses any fiction. And Bernal Díaz tells it all, with the flavor of 'I was there!': from the two first attempts to make an expedition into the unknown land; to the armada of Cortés and the burning of the ships; the march inland and the massacre of Cholula; the entry into the great island city of Mexico across the lake-causeway, with

* Bernal Díaz, *Verdadera Historia de la Conquista de la Nueva España.*

cities and towns rising from the land and the water to either side; the capitulation of Montezuma, and his swearing fealty to the King of Spain while weeping like a woman; the sham battle with the other Spaniards who had been sent to punish the rebellion of Cortés; the final bloody march back to Mexico, slaying and branding the aroused inhabitants; and the ultimate surrender of the capital after 85 days of siege. It is hard to imagine a more remarkable story—and no one has ever related it better than Bernal Díaz.

Fully to appreciate the worth of Bernal Díaz, one should judge him not by his own times but by modern standards. Nowadays, criticism esteems the individuality of an author, the democratic criterion in history, and it is precisely in these points that he excels. Compare him, for instance, with Gómara, who was a professor of rhetoric; with Las Casas, who cites Livy and expounds moral consideration; with the later Solís, who writes the conquest of Mexico in the form of lifeless academic history 'as it ought to happen.' Bernal Díaz, luckily, was never a professor of anything; he merely relates events that he saw and in which he himself took part. And he tells them with a freedom from literary formulas, which gives his style its unusual freshness. His descriptions are minute, vivid, concrete; everything comes to life in his pages—an Indian market, for example, and (in this he is almost pathological) even the names and colors of every precious horse on the expedition. Bernal Díaz' pages are crammed with unforgettably lifelike episodes, like this account of a 'squaw man,' one of two captive Spaniards whom Cortés was trying to ransom from the Indians:

> In two days the letters were delivered to a Spaniard named Jerónimo de Aguilar, for that we found to be his name. When he had read the letter and received the ransom of beads which we had sent to him he was delighted, and carried the ransom to the Cacique his master and begged leave to depart, and the Cacique at once gave

him leave to go wherever he pleased. Aguilar set out for the place, five leagues distant, where his companion Gonzalo Guerrero was living, but when he read the letter to him he answered: 'Brother Aguilar, I am married and have three children and the Indians look to me as a Cacique and captain in wartime— You go, and God be with you, but I have my face tattooed and my ears pierced, what would the Spaniards say should they see me in this guise? and look how handsome these boys of mine are, for God's sake give me those green beads you have brought, and I will give the beads to them and say that my brothers have sent them from my own country.' And the Indian wife of Gonzalo spoke to Aguilar in her own tongue very angrily and said to him: 'What is this slave coming here for talking to my husband—go off with you, and don't trouble us with any more words.' [3]

But it is also in his strong personalized point of view that Bernal Díaz' worth stands out. He writes with an undisguised vanity about himself, almost a hatred for the overpraised Cortés, and a passionate conviction· that the conquest was achieved not by the commander, but by the four hundred soldiers of the expedition. His battle scenes, in addition to their color and detail, are alive with the doings of the common soldier. Here, as an example, is an account of the unsuccessful storming of an Indian hill-fortress by the infantry, while Cortés and the horsemen kept watch in the plain:

As we began to climb up hill, the Indians who were posted above rolled down so many huge stones and rocks that it was terrifying to see them hurtling and bounding down, and it was a miracle that we were not all of us killed. One soldier named Martínez fell dead at my feet; he had a helmet on his head but he gave no cry and never spoke another word. Still we kept on, but as the great *Galgas*, as we call these big rocks in this country, came rolling and tearing and bounding down and breaking in pieces, they soon killed two more good soldiers, Gaspar Sánchez, nephew of the Treasurer of Cuba, and a man named Bravo, but still we kept on. Then another

valiant soldier named Alonzo Rodríguez was killed, and
two others were wounded in the head, and nearly all the
rest were wounded in the legs, and still we persevered
and pushed on ahead.

As I was active in those days, I kept on following the
Standard Bearer Corral, and we got beneath some hollows and cavities which there were in the hillside so as to
avoid a chance rock hitting us and I clambered up from
hollow to hollow to escape being killed. The Standard
Bearer Cristóbal del Corral sheltered himself behind some
thick trees covered with thorns which grow in these
hollows, his face was streaming with blood and his banner was broken, and he called out: 'Oh Señor Bernal
Díaz del Castillo, it is impossible to go any further, keep
in the shelter of the hollow and take care that none of
those galgas or boulders strike you, for one can hardly
hold on with one's hands and feet, much less climb any
higher.' [4]

Bernal Díaz has been criticized, particularly in times past,
for these highly original traits. Ticknor (forming his judgments in the last century) concluded illogically that Bernal
Díaz did not know how to write, and that he was vain. Yet
Bernal's very lack of artifice, his strong personal bias, lend
a peculiar value to his book, making it rather a work of
creation than a historical record. In his entire story, told with
artless and amazing realism, he has a perfect flair for the
dramatic, building up more and more strongly to the final
climax. As such it ranks as a masterwork of popular, as distinguished from formal, history—the greatest piece of popular
history in the Spanish language. And in this, Bernal Díaz is
characteristically Spanish, following the anti-classic and popular concept of literature, exemplified by Lope de Vega in
the drama, by San Juan among the mystics, by Cervantes in
the novel. His *True History of the Conquest of New Spain*
may rightly be considered the most Spanish (in this sense)
and at the same time the most American (in his details, his
use of native words) of all the New World chronicles.

Naturally, the second generation of Spanish Americans could not remain long indifferent to this example set by the conquistadors. Native-born chroniclers were soon taking up pens to write about America. Young creoles, mestizos, and even Indians wanted to emulate the success that seemed so attainable; and, since the roads of conquest and exploration were closed to them, they tried for fame in the Church, and in the fields of history and literature. Their efforts were not unproductive, for in the second half of the sixteenth century appeared several writers of note born on American soil. Among them were the Indian historians of Mexico: Hernando de Alvarado Tezozomoc, son of an Aztec emperor, who wrote the *Mexican Chronicle* (c. 1598); and Fernando de Alva Ixtlixochitl (*c.* 1568-*c.* 1648), author of the *History of the Chichimecas.** These writers did not have a perfect command of Spanish, but they used in compiling their narratives such important sources as hieroglyphics, drawings, old songs, and oral traditions.

By far the most important of the native chroniclers is the renowned Inca, Garcilaso de la Vega (1539-1615), son of a conqueror, Captain Garcilaso de la Vega, and a Princess of the Sun, Isabel Chimpa Ocllo. Garcilaso was born and raised in the mysterious and charming city of Cuzco; there he learned Latin grammar from the Spanish priests, and legends of the Inca peoples from his mother's family, men and women of imperial blood. Garcilaso is the first example (among literary figures) of the mixing of two noble bloods, the blending of two cultures. His life is the first experience of the mestizo in a European milieu; for after the death of his father, Garcilaso went to Spain and spent the rest of his days in Seville, Madrid, and Córdoba. There he began his literary work with a translation in 1590 of the *Dialogues of Love* by the Jewish philoso-

* Alvarado Tezozomoc, *Crónica Mexicana;* Alva Ixtlixochitl, *Historia de los Chichimecas.*

pher, León Hebreo. Then, giving up these Neoplatonic studies, he devoted himself to the writing of his *History of the Conquest of Florida by Hernando de Soto* (1605), a work known today by title of *The Florida of the Inca*. This book was in a way the introduction to his masterpiece, *The Royal Commentaries*, the first part of which appeared in 1609.* Here Garcilaso traces in simple and eloquent language the history of the Inca empire. The second part, which appeared in 1617, continues the history, describing the wars of Cuzco, in which Garcilaso's father was one of the principal figures.

In the modern sense of the word, Garcilaso is not strictly a historian, for he introduces into his narrative all sorts of legendary and fantastic episodes more natural to the fiction writer than to the exacting mind of the scholar. Such, for instance, is this account of the omen that terrified Huayna Capac and his people, three years before the coming of the Spaniards:

> While the solemn Festival of the Sun was being celebrated, they saw a royal eagle, which they call *anca*, flying through the air, and pursued by five or six kestrels, and as many small hawks of the kind that is so beautiful that many have been brought to Spain. In Peru they are called *huaman*, and in Spain, *aleto*. They attacked the eagle alternately, and killed him by their blows . . . Besides this there were great earthquakes, for though Peru often suffers from this plague, the earthquakes were worse than usual, and many high hills fell down. The Indians of the coast reported that the sea, in its ebbing and flowing, often extended beyond its usual bounds; and they saw many awful and terrific comets in the air. In the midst of these forebodings, they beheld that, on a very clear night, the moon had three great circles round it. The first was of the colour of blood. The second, which was further outside, was of a black colour turning to green. The third looked like smoke.[5]

* Inca Garcilaso, *Diálogos de Amor, La Florida del Inca, o la Historia del Adelantado Hernando de Soto, Comentarios Reales.*

Such is the charm of Garcilaso's work that Menéndez y Pelayo and Fitzmaurice-Kelly saw in the *Commentaries*—the first work of fiction from the New World—evidence of the taste and imagination of an author who, although working with historical materials, was yet able to produce a work of art.

Quite apart from this imaginative bent, Garcilaso has done posterity a real service by his record of an ancient American empire. In tracing the development of Inca civilization, he was greatly moved by the marvellous achievements of his unfortunate race, some of which were far superior to anything the European had to offer in those days. In view of the fact that there was no written literature in the Quechua language, the modern reader is all the more grateful to Garcilaso for having preserved such a treasure-house of information on the political and social status of his people, their legends and traditions, their customs, cities, villages, countrysides. Even in the second part of his history, Garcilaso has used valuable materials that might otherwise have been lost —the stories related to him by soldiers and conquerors who had been the companions of his father. Indeed, Garcilaso de la Vega, along with Bernal Díaz del Castillo, stands for the earliest manifestation of authentic Americanism in Spanish colonial literature. These two writers typify well the contribution of the chronicle: a genre of primarily historical interest, which sprang from the natural records of the conquest, and yet produced works of enduring literary merit.

THE EPIC

BUT the sixteenth-century conquistador was also a poet. Quite often, he travelled to America to make a name for himself with pen as well as sword. From Spain, great poets like Gutierre de Cetina, Eugenio Salazar de Alarcón, and Juan de la Cueva came to Mexico; Diego Dávalos y Figueroa and Diego Mexía settled in Lima; and minor writers flocked to the new and promising land. Of far greater interest is another type of writer: the simple adventurer and soldier who was so impressed by the beauty he found in scenery and action, in nature and war, that he became a poet. Soldiers, so moved by the epic conquest of a New World, that they had to express themselves in epic poetry! This was what happened to Alonso de Ercilla (1533-94), a twenty-two-year-old Spanish nobleman who, having heard of the great wonders of the Indies, left the retinue of Prince Philip and sailed to Chile. There he fought against the indomitable Araucanian Indians, and was so deeply impressed by their courage and patriotism that he composed his famous poem *The Araucana* (1569-89).

Ercilla's theme might almost be called an epic in reverse. For he relates the sanguinary subjugation of *Chilli*—the Indian name means 'the deepest point of the earth'—in which he participated under García Hurtado de Mendoza. This bloodiest of all the conquests formed a great contrast to the easy taking of the wealthy territory of Peru. It had been attempted previously by Almagro, who was forced to abandon it, and by Valdivia, who lost his life in the undertaking. Hurtado de Mendoza finally achieved a fairly peaceful settlement, defeating the Indian tribes in several battles, reconstructing the destroyed Spanish towns, building new ones with the hope of populating the region with Europeans and thus pushing the Araucanians farther south. But these fierce natives continued to battle the invaders until the beginning of modern times, in that spectacular series of wars known as *las guerras de Arauco*. Theirs was an epic resistance to the Spanish conquest, and it found a true epic poet in the person of the youthful Don Alonso de Ercilla y Zúñiga. At first, Don Alonso was a friend of his young commander, Don García; later, however, he drew his sword to duel in the presence of his superior, who condemned him to death for this act of disrespect and insubordination. The sentence, however, was commuted: Ercilla's adversary joined a monastery in penance;

and he himself was exiled from Chile, and lived to complete
and publish his immortal work, *The Araucana*.

This great epic poem is remarkable, first of all, for its virile
subject matter. In it, we have the spectacle of a nobleman,
who had travelled widely in France, England, and Germany,
expressing no disappointment in the miserable aspect of Chilean
cities. Instead, his mind is engrossed with a military career
of hardships and endurance, with a tale of savage heroism. He
exclaims in the opening stanza:

> Not love I sing, or ladies, or the gay
> whisperings of enamored knight and swain,
> or yet devoted tenderness, display
> of amorous affection, and its pain;
> rather I chant the valor in affray
> of those undaunted warriors of Spain
> who by the sword imposed a cruel yoke
> upon the untamed Araucanian folk.[6]

No, Ercilla is not the courtier poet who praises the beauty of
aristocratic ladies and flatters the ears of his monarch with
sweet words; he is as robust a singer as he is a fighter. In his
first battle with the Indians, his conduct was such that his
fellow soldiers said of him, 'He accomplished with the sword
even more than with the pen.'[7] His literary aim, as he himself says, was to extol the prowess and valor of the Spaniards;
but, being a poet, he could not fail to admire also the greatness
of the Araucanian warriors. So *The Araucana* was dedicated
to them, to their unconquerable spirit, to their love of land
and family, to their hatred of the invader.

To be sure, despite this dominant robustness—which might
almost be called 'Indianism'—Ercilla's work, as a piece of
literature, is related to the classic epic. Thus, the entire atmosphere of *The Araucana* is one of chivalry and honor; it is
as if the eyes of the poet had been closed to ugly reality, to
be opened anew in a higher zone of beauty and imagination.
Sometimes the reader is immersed in the poetry of pure

idealism, as in the following passage, which the poet puts into the mouth of the chieftain Colocolo:

> When the wild boldness of your hearts I see
> I cannot blame you, rather I rejoice;
> only I fear lest this your bravery
> through evil guidance miss the better choice:
> for if among ourselves the quarrel be,
> your very strength our fatherland destroys.
> So, if you still persist in that design,
> strike first of all this aged throat of mine.[8]

Imbued as Ercilla was with classical ideals from his reading of Ariosto, Tasso, Lucian, Virgil, and Homer, he naturally felt at times the desire to write a classical epic. Thus, he introduces the *deus ex machina*, and even stops to tell the story of Dido (attempting, like a true Spanish nobleman, to vindicate her from Virgil's defamation). But these are only concessions to contemporary artistic taste, only occasional outbursts of purely literary ambition in a poet who possessed a very realistic conception of his art.

In general, however, Ercilla has fulfilled his main purpose, to portray a succession of epic and warlike events. He has succeeded well: he is a vigorous poet; he gives a clear picture of the battles; he exhibits descriptive talent; and he usually strikes the heroic note. The entire poem, with its thirty-seven cantos divided into three parts, relates a historical account of the wars. In Part One, which Ticknor calls 'a poetical diary of the expedition,'[9] Ercilla recounts experiences that he did not personally witness. He describes the new land, the customs of the natives, the arrival of the Spaniards, various battles with the Indians, the destruction of cities, and the death of Lautaro. In Parts Two and Three, he continues the historical narrative, relieving the monotony of events by introducing a number of romantic episodes of rather doubtful value. Thus, the second part, while proceeding with the Araucanian wars, offers the reader a description of the battle of San Quintín between

King Philip and the French. Amusingly enough, Ercilla also presents a picture of the victory of Lepanto, before this battle actually took place. Here, too, he introduces fictitious and legendary incidents, like the apparition of Belona and the episode of the magician Fiton. The last part deals, in climactic stanzas, with the imprisonment and death of the great Caupolicán. The closing scenes are written with terrific dramatic intensity and horror: Fresia, wife of the chieftain, arrives in time to see the leader in the hands of the enemy; she accuses him of cowardice for not having killed himself rather than be captured, and angrily throws their child at his feet. Next follows the horrible impalement of Caupolicán, scene of such unbearable realism and brutality that the modern reader can hardly endure it. The poet ends his last canto in a melancholy vein, complaining of his sad fortune and turning his eyes to the Creator:

> And I, who on the world with no restraint
> lavished my life and all its fairest flower,
> and, ever headlong on my folly bent,
> pursued vain hopes up to this very hour,
> seeing now the small fruit for the effort spent
> and great offense I gave to my God's power,
> from this day forth, my error acnowledging,
> I shall do well to weep and not to sing.[10]

For centuries, a battle of critics has raged around *The Araucana*. The discussion centers on the definition of the word 'epic.' Voltaire was the first foreign literary figure to appreciate Ercilla's real worth; in his 'Essay on Epic Poetry' that precedes the *Henriade* (1726), he expresses great enthusiasm for the speech of Chieftain Colocolo. Quite opposite is the verdict of Ticknor, who claims that the first part of *The Araucana* is merely a rhymed story of the wars, with requisite geographical and statistical exactitude, and that the reader must always have a map at hand in order to follow the action. According to him, the work is not 'epic' but 'historic.' The

French critic Alexandre Nicolas, on the other hand, believes that the poem meets the most severe requirements of an epic. He finds it a heroic story of war, exemplifying the courage and magnanimity of the heroes; that it gives a real picture of its century; that it has a perfect unity of action; and that all the incidents derive from a central character whom the reader must admire.

All this controversy seems somewhat academic by modern standards. Nowadays, *The Araucana* is considered easily the most important epic poem of Spanish America—and indeed, the only great classic epic in the Spanish language. Its true poetry lies less in the verses themselves than in Ercilla's lofty conceptions, his noble heart, his chivalrous attitude towards the Indians. For example, the name of the Spanish leader, García Hurtado de Mendoza, does not even appear in the poem; some have thought this to be a result of personal pique, but it seems rather the highest expression of poetic justice. Thus, Ercilla does mention the other captains, but he does not endorse them. He genuinely admired the fortitude of the Indians; he could not tolerate the cruelties of his compatriots and often found himself on hostile terms with his fellow soldiers, for attempting to save the life of some Indian warrior. When one has finished reading *The Araucana*, it is the figures of Caupolicán, Tucapel Lautaro, Galvarino Colocolo, Rengo, that loom in the memory in truly Homeric proportions.

Quite contrary was the purpose of another epic poet, Pedro de Oña (1570-1643), who sung of the same wars in his *Arauco Tamed* * (1596). This native Chilean—he was born in the southern town of Los Infantes de Angol—celebrated the deeds of Hurtado de Mendoza and did not waste any love upon the Indians. As his mother was a distant relative of the Spanish commander, naturally he poured all the exuberance of his muse into an account of Don García's deeds. His composition is a long poem of some sixteen thousand verses (he completed

* Oña, *Arauco Domado.*

only the first part), which describes Don García's arrival in the south of Chile and the battles with the Indians, much as Ercilla had related them. Unfortunately, Oña was not by nature an epic poet, but a soul sensitive to beauty, tenderness, and love; yet, misguided by the literary currents of his time, he devoted all his energies to the composition of a heroic epic.

His *Arauco Tamed* is interesting chiefly in its bucolic passages, its deep feeling for nature. Oña's descriptions, however, are overloaded with poetic formulas, and he seems incapable of expressing directly the emotion that arises from the contemplation of landscape. He sings of the flora of Chile, but, alas, he does not consider the native trees and their Indian names as sufficiently poetic material; so he substitutes others from a European setting:

> Along both of its banks, in thick-set row,
> myrtle, spikenard and willow you may find,
> with fresh and stately trees of varied kind;
> there pine and poplar, elder and alder, grow,
> ash, cypress, towering cedar, lush as though
> they came from Eden; and through their leaves the wind
> in solemn counterpoint intones low words,
> a bass beneath the treble of the birds.[11]

Again, he describes the fauna of his native land; and, although he must have been familiar with the wild animals that roamed the Araucanian forests, his imagination distorts his first impressions:

> Then in the thick and tangled wood you spy
> the bristly snout of an embattled boar;
> now doe and stag invade the forest floor,
> now skips a fallow deer with timid eye;
> now a striped tiger paces boldly by,
> now agile mountain goats appear to soar
> along some precipice's craggy face,
> with other denizens of that wild place.[12]

One must acknowledge Oña's aesthetic sensibility, along with the equally obvious fact that he did not write things as they were. A Chilean critic, E. Solar Correa, blames this on racial escapism and an unbridled imagination. It seems, however, more like a desire to transmute Nature into a poetic motif, as in this description of a river in wintertime:

> From hill to hill the rapid river flows,
> and when the silver dawn is at the full
> the fields seem blanketed with frosty wool.[13]

Oña's vision was clouded with mythological memories and literary figures, and often he saw wonders that no mortal eye could verify. When chief Caupolicán and his beloved Fresia, after resting in an idyllic forest, descend to swim in a clear fountain under the watchful gaze of Apollo, not only is the forest terrified at such beauty (as Oña tells us), but the modern reader is also. Here is the wondrous creature, whom he presents as an ancestress of the stocky, wild-looking, unclean Araucanian females:

> Marvellous soft and wavy is her hair,
> her forehead, neck and hands are all of snow,
> her tiny gracious lips like rubies glow,
> blue are her eyes, her rounded breasts most fair,
> her arms well-turned; and Paros ill could spare
> the veined marble of the waist below.
> Her dainty feet strew silver in the grass;
> the whitest swan is envious when they pass.[14]

And yet, though he certainly lacks the epic grandeur of his master Ercilla, Oña is a distinguished poet in his own right. He ranks as perhaps the greatest epic poet born in the New World; and in his love for his native land, he has given one of the first examples of literary Americanism.

Of course, Ercilla had many lesser imitators in the epic genre. From Mexico to Argentina, pompous versifiers composed countless soporific poems celebrating the military deeds of Spanish captains and the endless adventures of the conquest. One of these works, *Elegies of Illustrious Men of Indies* (1589) by Juan de Castellanos (1522-1606) is actually 150,000 lines long! Other epic writers deserving of mention were Antonio de Saavedra Guzmán, author of *The Wanderer of the Indies* (1599); Bernardo de Balbuena (1568-1627), who in *The Greatness of Mexico* (1604) wrote a lengthy description of that capital; and Martín del Barco Centenera (1535-1605), composer of the prosy *Argentina, and Conquest of the River Plate* (1602).*

This heroic type of verse was sometimes also used to celebrate the achievements of founders of religious orders, saints, or even Christ. The outstanding prototype of these works is *The Christiad* † (1611), by Diego de Hojeda (1570?-1615), a poem of twelve cantos, which possesses sincere religious enthusiasm and a certain elegance of form. In fact, *The Christiad* is generally conceded to be the best sacred epic in Spanish, a minor distinction perhaps, but one that attests the intense literary fervor of the convents and monasteries that formed a spiritual arm of the conquest. Indeed the whole epic genre, like the chronicle that preceded it, was a reflection of the epic conquest of the New World. And, like the chronicle, the Spanish American epic produced, in the writings of Ercilla and Oña, enduring works of literature.

The Baroque Seventeenth Century

When the first heroic flush of the sixteenth century had passed, Spanish America settled down to a life that was at the same time more stultified and more elegant than the rough hardships of the conquest. During the seventeenth century, the great centers of colonial culture were the two Viceregal capi-

---

* Castellanos, *Elegías de Varones Ilustres de Indias;* Saavedra Guzmán, *El Peregrino Indiano;* Balbuena, *La Grandeza Mexicana;* Barco Centenera, *La Argentina y Conquista del Río de la Plata.*
† Hojeda, *La Cristiada.*

tals, Mexico and Lima. World-famous universities, presses, monasteries, literary academies, all these focal points of intellectual activity were already well established and flourishing. Now, the courts of the Viceroys began to vie in refinement with those of the Old World. Spanish was spoken with exquisite perfection in colonial cities; the study of Latin was so universal among cultured people that thousands of poems were written in this tongue. If life was superficial and banal in some sections of these capitals, it was profound and serious in others.

This high level of culture rested upon a rigidly stratified colonial society.

> There was [in Mexico City, for example] an aristocratic ruling class consisting only of European-born Spaniards: The distaste of the wealthy creoles for business or manual work made them a leisure class. From their midst were drawn the students of the colonial universities who crowded the professions, namely law, medicine and the lesser offices of the church. Some became scholars or literati of merit.[15]

This was the upper crust of society, the happy element of pure white blood. Then followed the lower classes.

> The large hybrid population with its complex hierarchy had callings suited to its varying social distinctions . . . The *mestizo* class was conspicuous in the military service, and the term 'Spaniards' used in official documents and reports of campaigns and battles invariably referred to persons of diluted white blood. The trades and industries were also open to this group, though usually the more menial tasks. While the Indians were early taught some of the crafts and might engage in these activities, in the main they, like the Negroes, were condemned to domestic service, hard agricultural pursuits and the heavy work of the mines—slaves in fact if not in theory.[16]

But only a small proportion of the population was thus usefully employed—including the Spanish shopkeepers, and the more technical workers who were organized into *gremios* or guilds like those of medieval Europe.

> A far greater number of ignorant, superstitious, audacious idlers congregated in the cities and towns and became beggars, criminals, gamblers, and frequenters of *pulquerías* [native taverns for the sale of fermented *maguey* —cactus juice]. Indians, Negroes, mulattoes, etc., with a sprinkling of renegade Spaniards called *zaramullos* constituted this unhappy sediment of society and were ever a potential cause of riots and public disturbances.[17]

From top to bottom, this colonial society loved spectacles. The masses were fond of fiestas that lasted for weeks, cock fights, tourneys, and jousts. Negroes and Indians, as well as Spaniards, enjoyed bull fights. Everyone flocked to see *cabalgatas* (parades of gaily caparisoned horses with uniformed riders) and *mascaradas* (processions of costumed masquers, garbed as Moors or Indians, disguised as birds or animals, followed by allegorical floats). The theatre was very popular —both the open-air representation of *autos sacramentales* (popular religious plays) in which Indians took part, and the Spanish *comedias* given in enclosed theatres. The higher classes were fond of ceremonious social functions, like the daily stroll and the *besamanos* (levees) and *saraos* (dancing parties) on the birthdays of the nobility. Then there were pompous processions to the royal palace, receptions, dances, and banquets. The display of luxury was unrestrained on all sides. Along with this festival character, there appeared in colonial society a change of the Spanish spirit due to the new milieu and the mixing of bloods—a tendency towards the rich, the ornate, the overdone.

Americanism began to express itself in a certain baroque style of art and life. Elements of Indian art contributed to the alteration of Spanish architecture in America. Colonial churches were overloaded with jewels and color; saints were overdressed in velvets, silks, and tinsel. Today, this American baroque style marks a definite period in history and is of special interest to art critics; it was not, however, confined to art. There was also a baroque element in fashion and in conversation. Men exaggerated in dress, manners, speech, dancing, praying. They had a florid way about them, a mellow courtesy, a suave approach, that drew comment and satire to the *criollos* (inhabitants of the Indies) whenever they visited the Spanish peninsula. In the artificial and flowery court life of Mexico and Peru, an easy, gallant, or picaresque tongue was always welcomed; court poets tried to surpass each other in ornate phrases, fantastic images, rare comparisons, high-sounding verses, and unusual conceits. People felt a passionate interest in humanistic studies and in theological enterprise. The Neoplatonic writers of Italy exercised a strong influence over South America, so that ideas as well as modes of expression were often elaborate. This tendency has been aptly noted: 'The development of fine-spun concepts and intricate ideas was a natural exercise for the mind of the criollo whose leading mental trait was and is *agudeza*.' Thus, the Creole style in ideas as well as words was overladen, conceptual, and artificial, and it is no wonder that baroque seventeenth-century Spanish America succumbed readily to the literary mode of gongorism.

Gongorism, as students of Spanish literature will recall, is one of the terms applied to that complicated stylistic obscurity that developed in Spain at the close of the Golden Age. Ornate poetry made its appearance, with contradictory effects of color, light, and darkness; obscureness was achieved through abstruse metaphors, mythological references, inversions, pomposity, virtuosity, and conciseness of style with diffusion of thought. Luis de Góngora y Argote, the great 'Prince of Darkness' as he was called, was the outstanding representative of this tendency with his poems *Fable of Poliphemus and Galatea* and *The Solitudes;* and in literary history, the movement bears the name of *gongorismo* or *culteranismo*. Something similar took place in prose, but here the process had to do with ideas rather than words, with a subtle shuffling of concepts, a sharpness of wit. Quevedo and Gracián were the masters of this offshoot of *gongorismo*, usually called *conceptismo*. It is obvious that the Spanish American genius of the seventeenth century was predisposed to these maladies.

Góngora thus became, quite naturally, the dictator of taste in America, the unquestioned master of the new generation of overly receptive writers. In Mexico, for instance, humanism took a stronger hold than in Spain, and continued to dominate thought long after it had spent its force in the Peninsula. And the influence of Góngora was extensive on seventeenth-century Mexican poetry: Don Luis' works were constantly quoted, and imitations of his works appeared in the many literary contests of that time. All these disciples adopted his vocabulary, combinations of words, pompous phrases, and heroic style of composition, as well as his descriptive use of nature for incidental adornment. Because impersonality was characteristic of Góngora's poetry, his imitators betrayed no feeling or emotion in their works; interest was centered in *agudeza* and embellishment, and poetry in general remained superficial. This Mexican gongorism may be studied, for instance, in the poem *Triumph of the Virgin* (1683), by the great Mexican scholar, Carlos de Sigüenza y Góngora (1645-1700), who was himself a relative of the Cordovan 'Angel of Shadows.' Or again, it appears in the *First Dream* (1692?), of Sor Juana Inés de la Cruz, the greatest of colonial poets, and one whose writings are not often gongoristic.* In this composition, the title, verse form, and syntax recall Góngora's *First Solitude*, and the whole work is interesting in this conception. Here, Sor Juana 'goes into the physical processes of sleep and the psychological properties of dreams, in which her soul rises as a cloud of vapor and scales the heights and

* Sigüenza y Góngora, *Triunfo Parténico*; Sor Juana, *Primero Sueño*.

confines of the universe. The poem is characterized by extreme subtlety and obscurity due not to the language but to the abstract nature of the thought.' [18]

A similar situation prevailed in colonial Lima, where Góngora's literary mannerisms gained an easy entrance into centers like the Viceroy's court. In Peru, at the close of the sixteenth century, the influence of Petrarch and Camoens was widely felt; there was an artificial humanism, a good deal of Latin erudition, verse-writing contests, and aristocratic meetings in literary academies. One of the first Viceroys of seventeenth-century Peru, the Prince of Esquilache, was a poet, as was also the last Viceroy of the century, the Marqués de Castell-dos-Rius. And the previous baroque elements of Lima were in harmony with the new technique, which was enthusiastically adopted. One of its most distinguished exponents was Pedro de Peralta y Barnuevo (1633-1743), who, in his epic poem *The Founding of Lima* * (1732), in his short lyrical compositions in Spanish, Italian, Latin, and French, and in his dramatic works, follows the literary caprices of the Spanish master. Peralta was the court poet, and he turned out verses on every conceivable occasion, in a style so deliberately artificial that in one composition to the Viceroy Armendáriz he used throughout only the vowel *a!*

On the other hand, there was a positive side to New World gongorism, in the person of Spanish America's first literary critic, Juan Espinosa Medrano (1632-88?), an ardent exponent of this tendency. For great as was Góngora's sway, he had detractors too. One of these, the Portuguese Manuel de Faría y Soussa, on praising Camoens, bitterly attacked Góngora; at this, gongorists all over the world were incensed by the offense to their master, and rallied to his defense. What is today considered the best essay in praise of *culteranismo* was written in reply by an Indian in the midst of the Peruvian

* Peralta, *Lima Fundada.*

Andes, in a little town called Calcauso. This native, commonly called *El Lunarejo* because of a *lunar* or mole on his face, had an extraordinary career. He was an unknown youth who, when the Bishop of Cuzco visited his native town, recited a poem in praise of His Reverence. The ecclesiastic thereupon took the boy to Cuzco, sent him to school and then to the University. The lad had a precocious mind: 'at twelve he played several musical instruments; at fourteen he wrote comedies; at sixteen he was a professor of art.' [19] In time, he became known as the famous Doctor Espinosa y Medrano, the most brilliant orator of Peru, and an exquisite *conceptista* writer. In his great *Apology in Favor of Góngora* * (1662), he reveals himself as a penetrating critic with a profound understanding of poetry and a clear insight into the realm of art. *El Lunarejo* understood Góngora's message, his brilliant imagination, his mastery of words, and his reasons for enriching Spanish poetry with Latin forms. He was the first to notice the fact that there were close similarities between Don Luis de Góngora and the Cordoba-born writers of the Roman Empire, such as Seneca—an observation that has been used since then by nearly every literary historian.

Despite this almost overpowering influence of gongorism, other tendencies stand out among the greatest writers of the seventeenth century. Colonial society itself, with its types sharply etched in satire, forms the subject matter of the great popular poet of Lima, Juan del Valle y Caviedes (1653?-92). Caviedes, the closest American counterpart of Quevedo, was a peddler and a drunkard who, after dissipating a vast fortune inherited from his father, and having contracted serious diseases, began to compose verses satirizing doctors. He has a good deal in common with Molière, except that the Peruvian was far more vitriolic and direct than the Frenchman. This can be seen, for example, in the title of Caviedes' celebrated

* Espinosa Medrano, *Apología en favor de Góngora*.

book: *Tooth of Parnassus, Physicians' Wars, Medicinal Prowess, Exploits of Ignorance, by Juan Caviedes, a Patient Miraculously Escaped from the Mistakes of Doctors. Thanks to the Protection of Glorious Saint Roque, Guardian Saint against Physicians or against Pestilence, which is about the Same. Its Author Dedicates this Book to Death, Empress of Physicians, to whose Glorious Reign They Present Offerings of Human Lives and Pay Tributes of Health in the Form of Dead Men and Patients!* * Caviedes is completely a picaresque poet. Some of his writings seem to be fragments of *Lazarillo de Tormes,* of Quevedo's *The Knave,* or of *Gil Blas.* His descriptions of Doctor Humpback, Doña Elvira, Doctor Bermejo, and Doctor Roldán are uproariously funny. Everywhere, he is a bold and cruel photographer of colonial Lima. According to Luis Alberto Sánchez:

> He shows in caricature an endless stream of patients, nurses, barbers, doctors, and comic figures of all kinds. Caviedes is a typical creole of the Peruvian coast; he smiles as he makes fun of people; his sense of humor is stronger than his malevolence. He does not have the Andean melancholy of Garcilaso or the high-sierra gravity of 'El Lunarejo' . . . Caviedes' work is the first human document of colonial times.

Combining as he does the two great tendencies of the seventeenth and the eighteenth centuries, learned poetry and an extremely prosaic style, Caviedes stands as one of the most interesting figures of his age. He is admired today, when all the court poetasters—the social parasites who tortured their brains to celebrate the beauty of a lady, the talents of a bishop or a marquis—have fortunately long since been forgotten.

For this seventeenth century which Caviedes satirized, this era of Viceroys and academies and quacks and idlers, contained something more than baroque elegance on a tottering social pyramid. The love of learning was true and sincere, the level

* Caviedes, *Diente de Parnaso* . . .

of culture was high. Had it not been so, New World society could never have produced the two greatest literary figures of those colonial times: Juan Ruiz de Alarcón and Sor Juana Inés de la Cruz. These two Mexicans—the first was a hunchback jurist who went to Spain and became a great playwright, the second an intellectual woman who entered a convent and made her cell a great intellectual center—these two illustrate, in their achievements, the best of the seventeenth century in Spanish America.

ALARCÓN

JUAN RUIZ DE ALARCÓN Y MENDOZA (1581?-1639) ranks as one of the greatest dramatists of the Golden Age, and for this reason most critics include him with Spanish rather than Spanish American literature. As far as is known, he did write all his plays in Spain; most of them were composed for the Spanish stage, and some were even produced at Court; and he published his collected works in Madrid and Barcelona. But all this only serves to highlight the fact that he was the first American, or *criollo* as the colonials were called, to win a place in the literature of the mother country. For the fact that Alarcón was a Mexican (quite as much as Henry James was a North American) is not really open to dispute; nor is it necessary to search for 'Mexicanisms' in his work, as Henríquez Ureña and other recent writers have tried to do. Rather, the essential Mexican quality of Alarcón resides in these things: that he was born in Mexico, that he lived there a great many years including the formative ones of his youth, and that his plays bear the stamp of the classic conception of education typical of the famous University of Mexico.

Of modest if not exactly humble extraction, Alarcón betook himself to Spain around 1613, to struggle for success in law and letters. His Creole birth and his physical appearance were against him from the start. He was a hunchback, extremely short, ugly, and further conspicuous for his red beard. During a dozen years, the Royal Councils refused to recommend him for a juridical appointment—while acknowledging his qualifications of successful studies in Mexico and Salamanca, his experience as judge and lawyer in Spain and Spanish America—because of 'the physical deformity which he has and it is a very great one.' From the important Spanish men-of-letters, his contemporaries, Alarcón received even worse treatment; he was made the target of attacks, crude satire, and ridicule, most of it directed against his unfortunate deformities and the New World elegance of his manners. At long last, he was appointed to a post on the Council of Indies, and he died in Madrid as a relatively obscure jurist.

It is small wonder, then, that one finds no significant traces of Mexicanism or colonial origins in his works. When he began to write for the stage in Madrid, the glory of Lope de Vega was in its zenith. Alarcón had to compete with the greatest literary names that Spain ever possessed; and he had to use their resources and their weapons. All the same, his work is very different from that of other playwrights of the Golden Age: the form of his comedies is more carefully worked out, the psychology of characters more thoughtfully developed. In contrast with Lope and his school, Alarcón pays less attention to theatrical effects than to logical evolution and, above all, to moral principles. His works form a primer of practical philosophy—as Hartzenbusch has remarked—wherein one finds all the elements necessary to master his own life and to obtain the affection and admiration of others. Alarcón's comedies, because of their restraint, their studied construction, their truth of psychology, come closer to modern sensibilities than those of his colleagues; many of his pieces are famous the world over—*Even the Walls have Ears* (a study of the evils of slander), *How to Win Friends* (an exhibition of noble deeds), and *A School for Suitors* * (a truly delightful comedy on how to pick a husband). Indeed, so marked is the unique-

* Ruiz de Alarcón, *Las Paredes Oyen, Ganar Amigos, El Exámen de Maridos.*

ness of Alarcón's work, that Menéndez y Pelayo has defined him—in a phrase that can hardly be improved upon—as 'a classic in the romantic theatre.'

Within his unique type of play, Alarcón has made a still greater contribution to the evolution of the drama: the comedy of character. His immortal masterpiece in this genre is *The Liar*,* which Corneille rewrote in French under the title of *Le Menteur*, and which was the prototype of the *comédie de mœurs* later made famous by Molière. The story of *The Liar* is remarkable even today for its directness and its shrewd observation of human nature. Don García, a young nobleman of otherwise excellent character, has a dreadful habit of lying —telling downright falsehoods, prevaricating, or spinning fantastic 'whoppers' for the sheer delight of it. In a few short days he becomes involved in a duel, a romantic mix-up, an imaginary marriage, and a whole series of embarrassing predicaments brought on by his fault; and he is finally punished by being forced to marry the wrong girl. The play does draw slightly upon the device of coincidence, so commonly used in Alarcón's time. But in the main, the interest, the plot, and the ridiculous situations derive solely from the character of the hero and his lies. One searches in vain for anything similar in the previous history of the drama in all lands.

It is significant in itself that so great a dramatist as Alarcón should have been a Creole. And even more significant that the classic tone of his work should be so directly related to the emphasis placed on humanistic studies in Mexico. For Alarcón, when he was still a youth, received a very thorough training in Greek philosophy and Latin literature at the Royal and Pontifical University in his home town. He became acquainted with Latin comedy in the works of Plautus and Terence, Latin tragedy in the writings of Seneca; he was thoroughly saturated in Aristotelian logistics; and he studied literary style in the works of Cicero and the rhetoricians.

* Ruiz de Alarcón, *La Verdad Sospechosa*.

There is little doubt that Alarcón in Spain—snubbed by the Royal Councils, mocked by his fellow dramatists, ridiculed in society for the hump on his back—took refuge in the literary companionship of classic authors whom he had studied in Mexico. His colonial education thus became a major factor in the interpretation of his plays.

Of almost equal importance is the fact that this gifted Creole sought his fortune on the peninsula rather than in his native capital. Alarcón's writing exclusively in Spain, to the extent of becoming almost identified with Spanish literature, casts further light on the literary evolution of colonial America. By the seventeenth century, all the early fire of conquest was gone. The first glimmers of Americanism, which had appeared in the subject matter of chronicles and epics, were almost entirely snuffed out. Spanish cultural domination over the colonies was complete; the mother country controlled not only the material, but the spiritual commerce of the Indians; the shipping of books was determined in Spain, and novels were strictly forbidden. This 'Hispanization' had reached such an extreme that Alarcón, a Mexican, actually went to Spain and wrote as though he were a Spaniard.

SOR JUANA

SOR JUANA INÉS DE LA CRUZ (1651-95), the greatest literary figure of colonial times, was born, lived, and died in Mexico. Yet she too, like her illustrious compatriot Alarcón (who died twelve years before her birth), wrote as though she were completely Spanish. A woman of rare beauty, intelligence, and charm, she was a leading figure in New Spain during the second half of the seventeenth century—at the very height of the period of refinement and religious intensity and pomposity. Juana de Asbaje y Ramírez, as she was called before she took the veil, was born in a small farmhouse of San Miguel de Nepantla, and baptized in the town of Amecameca, not far from Mexico City. But she came to the Viceregal capital at the age of nine, to live with her grandfather; and in the capital she remained, first as a young girl, then as the darling of the Court, and finally as the most famous nun in Mexico, until she died there at the age of forty-four.

Sor Juana was unmistakably a child prodigy. She learned to read at the age of three—and on her own initiative, as she herself tells the story:

> I was not quite three years old, when my mother sent an older sister of mine to a teacher to learn to read. Mischievousness and affection made me follow her; after hearing a lesson, I was so fired with the desire to learn that, thinking I was fooling the teacher, I told her that my mother wished her to teach me too. She did not believe me . . . but to gratify my caprice she gave me a lesson. I continued to go to the classes and she continued to teach me, but not as a joke now, for experience had convinced her; and I learned in such a short time, that when my mother found out (the teacher had not told her) I could already read and it was too late to stop me.[20]

At that same age, little Juana abstained from eating cheese, because she had heard that 'it made people stupid.' Her love of learning continued to grow:

> When I was six or seven, I could sew and do all the other things that women do, as well as read and write. I heard that in the City of Mexico there were schools . . . where the sciences were taught. I immediately began to torment my mother, begging her to dress me like a boy and send me to the house of some relative in town so that I could attend the University. She refused and she was right, but I gratified my desire by reading all sorts of books . . . and it was useless to scold me or even to punish me.[21]

Juana had only one teacher besides the good lady mentioned above; this was the Bachiller Martín de Olivas, who taught her Latin grammar in twenty lessons. So intense was her interest that she used to cut four or six finger-lengths off her hair (of which she was very proud), and if she had not learned the stint she set herself, when it reached its former length she would cut it again as a punishment for her stupidity: 'It did not seem right that a head so empty of knowledge should be so profusely adorned with hair.' [22]

The young prodigy was equally noted for her charm and beauty, which early prompted the Viceroy, the Marquis of Mancera, and his wife to invite her to court. There she became a favorite lady-in-waiting to the Marchioness. Not a great deal is known of Juana Inés' life at the court, though she was doubtless the intellectual leader among courtiers and ladies, and must have graced many a palace *tertulia* and ball. So outstanding was her genius, that the Viceroy—wishing to ascertain whether Juana had obtained her vast knowledge directly from God or whether she had acquired it—convoked all the outstanding professors, theologians, and humanists of New Spain to meet with her and question her on their particular fields. Forty scholars attended; and Juana answered all questions and satisfied everyone. The Viceroy himself testified to her success, saying that, even as a magnificent galleon would defend itself from a few attacking boats, so Juana Inés freed herself of the interrogations, arguments, and propositions of so many learned doctors. But even with such triumphs, court life was not always easy for the young girl. Her beauty and intelligence attracted many noblemen to her side, probably inspiring one of them with a passion that she reciprocated. At least, this is what one concludes from reading her love lyrics. Apparently, she was soon disappointed and ready to forget; but the experience seems to have left deep scars, for Juana began to think of peace and the cloister where she would have leisure to devote herself to meditation and study among her beloved books.

At the age of sixteen, Juana Inés left the court to enter the order of Carmelites. After three months of religious life, she fell ill; she could not stand the food, the dress, or the rigors of the novitiate. Two years later, however, she entered the convent of San Jerónimo and became a nun irrevocably. Sor Juana was a model sister. She was able to combine her religious duties with her literary and scientific interests, tending the sick, and devoting all her free time to her studies. For weeks on end, she would abstain from seeing the sisters, in order not to waste precious moments in idle gossip, in listening to the disputes of servants, in receiving untimely callers. Books were her abiding passion, and she managed to assemble a library of over four thousand volumes. San Jerónimo became a haven of calm and culture, a literary and social center, where the most distinguished people of Mexico used to visit. The Viceroy Mancera and his wife, celebrated by Sor Juana in famous sonnets, came often to see their friend. After their time, all the succeeding Viceroys, the Count and Countess Paredes, the Count of Monclova, and the Count of Galve paid homage to the poetess. Sor Juana's influence was not restricted to convent life; she was also a civic force.

In spite of her prestige, however, she suffered the criticism of the world and the church. People contended that literature was unsuited to a nun. Clergymen, nuns, and her own confessor tried to dissuade her from writing. One prioress forbade her to use her books because they belonged to the black arts; when she was ill, her physicians advised her not to read. At last, during the final two years of her life, Sor Juana did give up her intellectual pursuits, and dedicated herself to attaining spiritual perfection through prayer and charitable works. She sold her books and gave the money to the poor; she disposed of her astronomical instruments, mortified her flesh, and wrote with her own blood a prayer to Christ. In 1695, when a terrible pestilence lashed the City of Mexico, Sor Juana offered to nurse some of the sisters who had taken ill. Finally, she herself fell a victim to the dread plague, and died on the seventeenth of April of the same year.

During her short life, this intellectual nun wrote poetry, plays, and prose works, not all of which have come down to us. The first volume of her collected poems was published in Madrid in 1689, under the title of *Inundación castálida;* it was followed shortly by a second and a third. Her plays consist of two comedies of intrigue, *Domestic Difficulties,* and *Love is a Labyrinth* (written in collaboration with Juan de Guevara), which rank next to Alarcón's as the best composed by a Spanish American of the seventeenth century; three *autos sacramentales* replete with pure religious fantasy, *The Divine Narcissus, Saint Hermengildus,* and *Joseph's Sceptre;* and two *sainetes* or farces. In addition, she composed several prose works, including her *Critique of a Sermon* (1690), in which she provoked a sensation in the Catholic world by writing a criticism of the celebrated Jesuit Antonio de Vieyra, the 'Portuguese Cicero.' The Bishop of Puebla had this work printed under the title of *Athenagoric Letter,* returning it to the authoress together with a letter signed by the pseudonym 'Sor Filotea de la Cruz.' Sor Juana replied with her now famous *Answer to Sister Philotea* (1691), a work of priceless biographical value, in which she explains her lifelong pursuit of learning in one of the most human and noble literary documents ever written in America.*

But it is chiefly as a poetess that Sor Juana is remembered, and even today her countrymen refer to her under the affectionate name of 'The Tenth Muse.' This great woman's poetry was intuitive. From childhood on she expressed herself in rime, and she was shocked to learn that this was not the case with all people. She had supposed that poetry and beauty were the natural gifts of mankind. Personally, she considered her poetic talent as a divine gift; yet she is not a mystic poetess, but a

---

* Sor Juana, *Los Empeños de una Casa, Amor es más Laberinto; El Divino Narciso, El Mártir del Sacramento, San Heremenegildo, El Cetro de José; Crisis de un Sermon; Respuesta a Sor Filotea de la Cruz.*

very realistic one. Her clear intelligence endows her with great precision even when she is describing her own dreams. Her sonnets of love have all the exquisite Platonism of Petrarch, and in concise and symbolic force they approach Shakespeare:

> My dear, this evening as I spoke to you,
> And saw in all your actions and your face
> That words had lost the power to persuade,
> I wished that you could look into my heart.[23]

Her ballads are comparable to the best in the Spanish language, and they have at times the witty, realistic turn of Góngora's *romances*. Her poems of sorrow, disappointment, and melancholy are heartbreaking. And her satirical stanzas are sometimes worthy of Quevedo. Sometimes, the acidity of her wit is directed at herself—as in these famous lines 'To Her Portrait':

> This that you gaze upon, a painted lie,
> Blazoning forth the niceties of art
> With false syllogisms the hues impart,
> Is a shrewd snare, the sense being ta'en thereby.
>
> This, wherein the flatteries try to cover
> The horrors of the years, and to erase
> The rigors Time has stamped upon the face,
> Age and forgetfulness to triumph over:
>
> Is an artifice most vainly wrought,
> Is a frail flower carried on the wind,
> Is a shield against a sure Fate borne,
>
> Is the idle labor of a vagrant mind,
> Is a solicitude ponderous and out-worn,
> Is corpse—is dust—is shadow—and is nought! [24]

Sor Juana has been branded by some as a gongoristic poet. It is true that she is difficult and abstract in her *First Dream*, and that she uses a few intricate metaphors in her songs of worldly love, which one critic has called 'the most delicate ever written by a woman.' Granted these points, her lyric poetry as a whole is spontaneous and sincere, full of color and light. Although Menéndez y Pelayo did not fully recognize the genius of Sor Juana, he does justice to her when he writes:

The greatest beauty of her . . . poetry is found in lyrics like those interpolated in her sacred play *The Divine Narcissus*, in which she follows the *Song of Songs* and other Biblical models. These lyrics are so beautiful and free of affectation and gongorisms that they seem to belong to the sixteenth rather than the seventeenth century, and to be the work of some disciple of San Juan de la Cruz or Fray Luis de León, rather than of a colonial nun whose poems were called *Inundación castálida*.[25]

One cannot take leave of Sor Juana without mentioning her rare charm as an empirical thinker. Starting from minute concrete observations, she was fond of deducing universal laws of nature. Looking, for instance, at the walls and roof of a room, she inferred that visual lines are straight but not parallel because they finally form a pyramid; and this led her to meditate upon the roundness of the earth. Watching children spin tops, she observed that the toy did not move in circles but in spirals; from this, she went on to theorize about motion. Even while cooking, she would surprise Nature's secrets:

I observe that an egg holds its shape when it is fried in lard or oil, but it goes to pieces in syrup. I observe that in order to keep sugar fluid, one need only pour into it a little bit of water mixed with some citrus fruit. I observe that the yoke and white of an egg are so different that one of them will mix well with sugar as will the other, but together they will not . . . If Aristotle had known how to cook, he would have written much more.[26]

In her *Treatise on Music*,* now unfortunately lost, she is said to have realized the volume of sounds and foreseen the

---

* Sor Juana, *Tratado de la Música*.

chromatic scale, and (according to some overly enthusiastic critics) even to have anticipated the radio. Truth and clarity were the poles of her will. Beauty, she wrote, is nothing but a symmetry that harmonizes all things among themselves. This definition might well be applied to Sor Juana. When she died in 1695, a great light was extinguished. The seventeenth century, the colonial age of baroque elegance, with its cultured Viceroys, its humanistic aspirations, its famous intellectual nun, was all but at an end.

THE HISPANIC PATTERN

COLONIAL life and letters, in the eighteenth century, were little more than aggravated reflections of the mother land. A new century had appeared in the peninsula, a sterile period in which bad taste became flagrant; Spanish literature at home had lost its vigor after Calderón, and French neoclassicism tried in vain to restore it to its pristine glory. In Spanish America the decadence was even greater, and it reflected the Hispanization of the New World.

Three centuries of rule from abroad had given the colonies an almost complete Hispanic pattern. At first, the conquest with all its hardships was something new and different. But the strictly colonial era brought an existence of ease and luxury—which was, as far as possible, a replica of Spanish life on the Peninsula. The gay and glamorous Viceregal courts imitated the Court in Madrid; the army and the clergy were the dominant elements of society, as they were 'back home'; the colonial universities were set up on the model of Salamanca and Alcalá de Henares. There were, too, all the Spanish symptoms of social disintegration and anarchy. The colonial authorities fought ceaselessly among themselves: the clergy demanded religious supremacy in government affairs, while the Viceroys insisted upon their own political sovereignty.

True, there were changes in the purely Spanish pattern of life, because of local environment, climatic conditions, the formation of a new race. But the influence of Creoles and Indians was held to a minimum. Thus, colonial authorities did try to foster education for the native-born, but the type of schooling they imparted was exceedingly impractical and quite out of harmony with the surrounding realities. Whatever influence the aboriginal Indian cultures may have had on Spanish life in general, colonial thought remained thoroughly Spanish, becoming more intensely so in the course of time. The Crown of Spain took elaborate precautions in this regard, by closing Spanish American ports to foreign contacts, by forbidding the introduction of books into the colonies, by suppressing all ideas foreign to the theocratic concept of government.

In the field of colonial literature, this resemblance to Spanish models was even more striking. For in spite of the fact that new and different genres arose, in the beginning no truly dominant Americanism can be discerned in their pages. Although the early chroniclers recounted picturesque native scenes and hitherto-unknown Indian ways of life, these writers were imbued with the spirit of the Spanish codes of chivalry; their minds were so far removed from the realities of life that their works read more like fiction than history. How could it be otherwise? In a world populated by heroes like Cortés, Pizarro, and Balboa; by emperors like Atahualpa and Montezuma; inhabited by unbelievable monsters of land and sea, and enriched by feverish legends of El Dorado and the Fountain of Youth—in such a world, literary realism could not even begin to exist. Even the most matter-of-fact epic poems—such as *The Araucana*, of which Ercilla himself says, 'I wrote at night what I accomplished during the day'—are filled with imaginary episodes.

This flight from reality into the fantastic and the parallel imitation of Spanish forms naturally increased with time. Monks and friars began to create a spiritual world of their own in which they submerged the static consciousness of the Indians. Here was Spain at work: The shadows of Charles V, the Gran Capitán, Saint Teresa, and Don Quixote falling on a new land—the fervent zeal of Spanish mystics conquering Indian souls. Is it any wonder that the great mass of religious poetry, composed by Spaniards, Creoles, and Indians, is lifeless in the extreme? The headlong escape from realism took still another form in the idle refinement of Court life—given over, as it was, to music, dancing, theatrical performances, and other pastimes. Here, the Platonic idea of love hid the violence of primitive passions; religious fears tinged love affairs with a sombre color. This dualism shows in colonial poetry—with, on the one hand, a Petrarchian idealism expressed in complicated gongoristic forms; and on the other, a sensuous but restrained lyricism.

Even the gorgeous baroque flowering of intellectual life marked, in a certain sense, an artificial avoidance of ugly realities. It must be remembered that while the New England Pilgrims were still feeding their souls with Biblical inspiration in the frigid atmosphere of village meeting-houses, Mexico and Peru had splendid universities where scholars vied in fame with the most distinguished names of the old continent. Astronomers, mathematicians, philosophers, and geographers passed from Spanish universities to the colonies, and developed there new schools of thought and new generations of scholars. Is it not significant, for instance, that illustrious figures like Alarcón and Sor Juana were born in New Spain? But all this is only the brighter half of the picture. On the other side was the despotic character of the Spanish conqueror who opened a bloody path through the heart of the continent. After him came the slave-driver and the *encomendero*, who helped to write the 'black legend' of Spain. Some historians have tried to deny the truth of Padre Las Casas' protest against the ill-treatment of the Indians. But the record of cruelty and oppression is clear. Undisputed testimony to it is given by the abiding hatred of the native for the Spaniard; Indian opposition lasted more than three centuries, marked by frequent revolts against the Spanish authorities.

With this state of affairs, the rapid decadence of colonial literature becomes understandable. The sterile eighteenth century—as in the mother country—is best passed over as quickly as possible. Only one new tendency is noteworthy in this society that was crumbling from within: the whisperings of something new and radical from France. Despite the efforts of the colonial Inquisition, the works of the *philosophes* were smuggled into the Spanish colonies. The ideas of Voltaire, Rousseau, Diderot, and Montesquieu were menacing the old established order of things. The impact of their revolutionary theories began to reach a New World that was stirring after three centuries in a rigid colonial pattern. A new star was appearing on the Spanish American horizon; and this star was to be all the brighter for the darkness that had preceded it.

2

The Romantic Upheaval in Spanish America

INDEPENDENCE: THE THRESHOLD OF ROMANTICISM

By the end of the eighteenth century, Spanish America was fully ripe for independence if not for democracy. The Creoles were tired of the unequal conditions that prevailed in the colonies. Taxation weighed heavily on the shoulders of the American born; high governmental offices were the exclusive privilege of the European Spaniard; an absolute monopoly was choking the commerce of the new lands. Criollos and mestizos were the real makers of the Independence movement—which must not be confused with a popular revolution. None of these men had any faith in democratic ideals. They wished to save the colonies of Ferdinand VII, then a prisoner of Napoleon, and to preserve the oligarchical form of government. The great 'liberators'—Bolívar, Belgrano, San Martín, and the others—believed that a liberal monarchy or a perpetual presidency would serve best as a check upon the anarchical tendencies of the masses.

It was only much later that Spanish American leaders came to prefer the republican form of government. The Republics, when they finally came, were on the one hand a negation of the Spanish monarchy, and on the other an imitation of the North American and French democracies. Thus, the two dates 1783 (the end of the American Revolution) and 1789 (the storming of the Bastile) become all-important in Spanish American history. Between 1808 and 1825, Spanish America won independence and sovereignty—a score of nations breaking forth from the old Viceroyalties and Captaincies General, under a splendid democratic formula. The majority of the new governments drew up constitutions on the model of that of the United States, becoming federations or united provinces; the system was not always perfectly suited to the country, and Chile (among others) has corrected the error and is today a unitarian republic. George Washington, naturally, became the ideal of the liberators; and to this day, Spanish Americans consider him the greatest man the United States has produced.

But it was chiefly from revolutionary France that Latin America learned about the new order of things. A few Creoles had the good fortune of living in Europe at the end of the eighteenth century, and familiarizing themselves at first hand with radical thought and action—for example, the Peruvian Pablo de Olavide, a friend of Voltaire, who took part in the tasks of the French Convention. Soon political societies on French models sprang up all over the New World. According to Francisco García Calderón, the Masonic lodges worked secretly against the Spanish and Portuguese rulers. In the Lautaro Lodge, both San Martín and Alvear received their revolutionary initiation. The Lodge of York in Mexico became a Jacobin Club. Unfortunately, not only the liberal ideals of the French encyclopedists, but all the violence of the Revolution took root in Latin America as well: The Terror, the dictatorship of the First Consul, and the Empire, all these exerted an irresistible influence over the new nations. Iturbide, the Mexican Emperor, copied Napoleon; in Buenos Aires they founded a *Directoire* as in Paris; in Paraguay there were Consuls, and Rivadavia was a Girondin lost among the gauchos!

Naturally, then, the intellectual activity of this revolutionary period fed upon French ideas. The famous books of the philosophers had found their way into the New World, to kindle the imagination of future heroes in the Wars of Independence. In 1794 Antonio Nariño, a forerunner of Colombian freedom, translated *The Rights of Man*. Rousseau's *Social Contract* became invaluable to the young South American ideologists, who hastened to deny the divine right of kings and to assert the sovereign rights of the people. Montesquieu's ideas on political and social organization were studied in the universities, as an antidote to the absolute power of the Viceroys. Voltaire, the prototype of free men, was accepted as the professor of skepticism. But France provided generous inspiration in still another direction for young Spanish America, which, having broken politically with the mother country, now sought aesthetic guidance from a new source. It was but a short step from imbibing Rousseau's democratic doctrine, as expressed in his *Social Contract*, to welcoming the refreshing educational theories of his *Émile*, and the novel sensibility and style of *The New Héloíse*. Thus, Spanish Americans opened their minds at the same time to the new notions of human freedom and the new romantic stirrings in literature.

This combined ideological-literary influence of Rousseau constitutes one of the most fascinating chapters in Spanish American cultural history. The current can be traced through many of the leading figures of the Independence movement. Indeed, the most important revolutionists at the end of the eighteenth century and the beginning of the nineteenth—Miranda, Belgrano, Father Camilo Henríquez, Nariño, Simón Rodríguez (Bolívar's teacher)—were ardent disciples of Rousseau. But perhaps the best single illustration of Rousseau's many-sided influence may be seen in the great liberator himself. Simón Bolívar (1783-1830) was nurtured in Rousseau's thought, 'reared according to his precepts, and became a most genuine representative of the romantic school in love, language, and in the quest of liberty.'[1] This influence shows itself in Bolívar's life quite as much as it does in his writings:

From Rousseau's *Discourses* came the basis of Bolívar's vocabulary, to such an extent that in reading Bolívar one is led at times to believe he is reading a translation of Rousseau. When his military successes were to be celebrated with fiestas, Bolívar turned for advice upon the subject to the *Letter to d'Alembert*. The *Social Contract* furnished him with a political code throughout his career; and the *Profession of Faith of the Savoyard Vicar* served him for religion. The style and passion of the *Héloise* are especially marked in his work entitled *Delirios* written after ascending Chimborazo in 1824. Probably his career and accomplishments furnish the best testimonial South America can ever offer to the efficiency of the educational system advocated by Rousseau, for he achieved the independence of three countries and called forth a new spirit in the Spanish American world.[2]

In the field of letters, this new spirit, following the pattern set by Rousseau, produced a dual awakening, which affected both thought and literary expression. Thus, the literary societies became centers of revolutionary thought. And most of the 'patriots' of Independence engaged in feverish literary activity, some of which took the form of the *feuilleton*. Bellicose journalism was the order of the day. Father Henríquez, a liberal priest who had been imprisoned by the Lima Inquisition, set up the first printing-press in Chile and began to publish his newspaper, *Chilean Dawn*, in which he wrote fiery articles against Spanish despotism, and ardent if unpoetical poems to liberty and patriotism. In a similar vein were Monteagudo's and Moreno's writings for the *Buenos Aires Gazette*, Nariño's in *The Bagatelle*, and Lizardi's in *The Mexican Thinker*.[*][3]

Fernández de Lizardi (1774-1827) is an example *par excellence* of this spirit of independence in radical ideas and in the written word. A revolutionary pamphleteer saturated in French philosophy, he resorted to the novel as a vehicle for his theories, achieving fame as the first Spanish American novelist

[*] *Aurora de Chile, Gaceta de Buenos Aires, La Bagatela, El Pensador Mexicano.*

with his work *The Mangy Parrot* (1816), an extraordinary picture of Mexican society on the eve of independence.* This picaresque romance is remarkable for the fact of its appearance in America two centuries after the genre had gone out of vogue in Spain—but only some seventy years after Lesage had published *Gil Blas* in France. It carries the hero, Periquillo (little parrot), through a thousand-and-one adventures as student, wastrel, quack-doctor and all-round rogue, in a racy popular style that is the antithesis of pedantic eighteenth-century Spanish classicism. Here, for instance, is Periquillo's account of a prison in Mexico City:

> There were a million jailbirds in that patio. Some were white, and some were dusky; some half-dressed, others decent; some of them vexed, and some tangled up in their chains; but all pale, showing their sadness and despair in their hollow faces. All the same, you'd have thought they didn't care a whit about their state; for some were playing cards; others were jumping in their gyves; others were singing; others were knitting stockings; others were gossiping, and everyone was managing to entertain himself; all but a few of the nosier ones, who surrounded me to find out why I got thrown into jail.[4]

In still another novel, *Miss Quixote and her Cousin* (1819), Lizardi has written a thinly fictionized commentary on Jean-Jacques Rousseau's theory of education. In yet another, *Sad Nights* (1818), inspired in Cadalso's *Lugubrious Nights*, with some reminiscences of Young's *Night Thoughts*, he recounts his own sufferings during the revolutionary struggle.† Despite the fact that this work is a literary failure, written as it is in a solemn and elegiacal style that Lizardi could not master, it marks the beginning of romantic prose in Spanish America.

Romanticism, from its very first expression in Rousseau, particularly in *The New Héloise*, found enthusiastic disciples in

---

* Lizardi, *El Periquillo Sarniento*.
† Lizardi, *La Quixotita y su Prima, Noches Tristes*.

Spanish America. This novel, in which passion was exalted and the divine essence of human love was sublimated, in which nature was revealed in all her concrete beauty of meadows and lakes and mountains, in which the author felt and expressed the subjective emotions of solitude and bucolic melancholy, struck an instant sympathetic chord. In the Spanish American temperament, exalted passion was a natural inheritance from Spain and had grown unrestrained in a partly primitive society; the Spanish American found himself in the presence of a great magnificence and exuberance of nature, a nature conducive to vague longings and mystic reveries. From Rousseau, Spanish American writers quickly learned the use of the landscape and subjective emotion—their first lesson in modern artistry. The lesson was swiftly improved upon by other French novels of this early pre-romantic period: Bernardin de Saint-Pierre's *Paul and Virginia*, which appealed so deeply to sentimental young souls; Chateaubriand's *Atalá*, with its transports of love and its marvellous pictures of primitive nature; and his *René*, with its disillusion and pessimism. The influence of these works was to last in Spanish America throughout several generations; not until 1867 did Jorge Isaacs, the continent's greatest nineteenth-century novelist, publish his famous *María*, which he could not have written without a knowledge of Chateaubriand and Saint-Pierre. But the first signs of romantic inspiration appeared early, when Spanish American culture and Spanish American political life were still struggling to break free from their Hispanic bonds. In literature, this was indeed a movement of Independence, with a New World quite literally trembling on the threshold of romanticism.

THREE POETS

IT was not easy to snap the chains of a long literary tradition, and Spanish America achieved political independence from the mother country earlier than artistic emancipation. Obviously, eighteenth-century Spain had little to offer the colonies in the way of inspiration; her writers were of the neoclassic school, and the vigor and spontaneity of the Golden Age were absent from their work. When Napoleon invaded the Peninsula in 1808, only one Spanish poet of robust inspiration opposed him. This was Manuel José Quintana. He celebrated the efforts of the Provinces in fighting the foreign invader; he sang of Spain's independence; he wrote fiery odes to progress, to the printing-press, even to vaccination. He was oratorical, verbose, and robust; but to modern ears his poetry sounds like the rolling of an empty drum. As might have been expected, Quintana was imitated in America by writers who took an active part in political struggles, and who confused oratorical tirades in praise of liberty, equality, and fraternity, with real poetry. From this epoch, there have survived a great many patriotic poems, national hymns, songs to army generals, which live today only in the memory of school children (those innocent recipients of this sort of verse the world over) and in the mouths of professional patriots who declaim them to the accompaniment of brass bands at official banquets and military parades.

Such neoclassic expression did not lend itself to praising the glory of the liberators of the continent. Yet the greatest of the liberators was fortunate in finding a singer of great force in the Ecuadorian José Joaquín Olmedo (1780-1847), author of the still-famous *Song to Bolívar* * (1825). Olmedo's was a classic inspiration; he was familiar with Homer, Horace, and Virgil. Indeed, he has been called 'the American Quintana,' and he actually did translate into Spanish some fragments of Pope's *Essay on Man* and a Horatian ode. His neoclassicism is even more specific and unmistakable: The initial stanza of his *Song to Bolívar* (the original Spanish is necessary for the comparison):

* Olmedo, *La Victoria de Junín: Canto a Bolívar.*

> *El trueno horrendo, que en fragor revienta*
> *y sordo retumbando se dilata*
> *por la inflamada esfera,*
> *al Dios anuncia que en el cielo impera . . .*

is a direct imitation of the Fifth Ode of Book III of Horace:

> *Coelo tonantem credidimus joven Regnare . . .*

Nevertheless, Olmedo's *Song to Bolívar* is classical in form only. He drew inspiration for this virile composition from the great Battle of Junín, 1824, in which the best Spanish armies were completely destroyed by the brilliant young generals of Bolívar. And when he wrote about the glorious deeds of the liberation, he threw his classic spirit to the winds. His unrestrained enthusiasm, his wild imagination, fiery metaphors, and burning lines are rather those of a typical romanticist. Bolívar himself satirized Olmedo for this unlimited display of imagination, and wrote to him: 'All the heat of the torrid zone, all the fires of Junín and Ayacucho, all the thunderbolts of the Inca Manco-Capac have never produced a more intense conflagration in mortal mind. You shoot—where not a single shot was fired.' (Here, Bolívar was reproaching Olmedo for describing firearms, when only cold steel was used.) The Liberator continues: 'You set the earth aflame with the burning sparks of Achilles' chariot—which never rolled in Junín. You make a Jupiter of me; a Mars of Sucre; an Agamemnon of Lamar; an Achilles of Córdoba . . .' Thus, the Liberator himself recognized the free inspiration of Olmedo, who, in his *Song to Bolívar*, may be considered a definite forerunner of Spanish romanticism.

Five years before the appearance of this work, a Cuban youth, José María Heredia (1803-39), had composed what is undoubtedly—though few critics have noticed this—the first romantic poem in the Spanish language. This milestone, *The Temple-Pyramid of Cholula* * (1820), was written ten years

* Heredia, *En el Teocalli de Cholula*.

before romanticism appeared in Spain; yet it is unquestionably a romantic work, permeated as it is with the richness and beauty of the Mexican landscape and the poet's ideas on decadence and death. But Heredia was even more than the first romantic poet: He combined in his personality almost all the elements that characterized a Latin American revolutionist of 1820, and in addition all the traits of a great romantic like Byron or Chateaubriand. Emerson would have called him a Representative Man. For in his tormented life and his years of exile, Heredia's life represented the lot of his fellow Cuban intellectuals who underwent persecution at the hands of the deep-rooted Spanish despotism:

> Of the seven leading Cuban poets often spoken of as *The Cuban Pleiad*, Gertrudis Gómez de Avellaneda removed to Spain where she married and spent her life in tranquillity; and Joaquín Luaces avoided trouble by living in retirement and veiling his patriotic songs with mythological names. José Jacinto Milanés lost his mind at the early age of thirty; José María Heredia and Rafael Mendive fled the country and lived in exile; while Gabriel de la Concepción Valdés and Juan Clemente Zenea were shot by order of the Governor-general.[5]

Cuba's struggle for independence was the longest of all the Spanish colonies, since all efforts at liberation failed until 1898; by that time, she had paid a terrific toll of intellectuals, and José Martí, one of the greatest men that the Americas have produced, had lost his life at the hands of the Spaniards. Against such a background of revolutionary struggles, Heredia's romantic existence stands out as all the more typically Spanish American.

Heredia was the son of a liberal Cuban magistrate in the service of the Spanish tyranny. At twenty, he was a conspirator; and, exiled from his country, he wandered through many lands like another Childe Harold, spending two years in Boston and New York and then going on to Mexico. 'Revolution,' he wrote, 'has made me travel a long way in a short time; and I have been, at twenty-five years of age, lawyer, soldier, voyager, language teacher, diplomat, magistrate, historian, and poet.' Heredia's whole life was characteristically romantic, for he was a precocious youth with Byronic ambitions in his heart—ambitions for glory, greatness, love. When a Cuban girl scorned him, disillusion colored his whole life with melancholy, and he exclaimed: 'Only Death can cure my sorrow.' He was unhappy in the United States, where he missed the palm trees, the sun, the ocean breezes of his beloved island; and he could never learn English, to him 'The strange, harsh sounds of a barbarian tongue.' [6] Heredia was more at home in Mexico; he finally became a citizen of that country and attained high public office, becoming a member of Congress and a Judge of the Supreme Court.

A few critics have been deceived by Heredia's use of classical and mythological allusions. But the essence of his poetry —subjectivity and melancholy—is purely romantic. The American landscape appears for the first time in the poems of this disciple of Chateaubriand, Lamartine, and Byron. A vague longing for unuttered beauty tortures him, as it does Shelly. He writes to the evening star, the falling leaves, the pleasures of melancholy, the tempest, the ocean, the sun and the moon. In his poem *The Temple-Pyramid of Cholula*, after observing the beauties of Mexican scenery and Mount Popocatepetl, the poet ponders the mystery of fleeting time. Peoples, kings, cities, have passed; Popocatepetl still remains, but alas not forever:

> All dies by Universal Law.
> Even this world in which we live,
> So beautiful and brilliant,
> Is the shapeless and pallid corpse
> Of a World that is gone. [7]

But it was above all in his famous poem *Niagara* * that Heredia revealed himself as the true singer of American nature. Here, a torrent of words, similes, and metaphors betrays the truly romantic inspiration of the poet who succeeds in conveying to the reader the real impression of a scene terrifying in its greatness and beauty. Heredia gives a perfect description of that natural wonder; then he laments his solitude, far from his beloved land; and finally, he raises his thoughts to the Creator of all earthly things. The unbridled imagination, the frenzy of lyric enthusiasm in this poem are balanced by a perfect unity of form. Listen, for instance, to a fragment from *Niagara*, supposedly translated by William Cullen Bryant:

> Ah, terribly they rage,
> The hoarse and rapid whirlpools there! My brain
>
> Grows wild, my senses wander, as I gaze
> Upon the hurrying waters, and my sight
> Vainly would follow, as toward the verge
> Sweeps the wide torrent. Waves innumerable
> Urge on and overtake the waves before,
> And disappear in thunder and in foam.
> They reach, they leap,—the abyss
> Swallows insatiable the sinking waves.
> A thousand rainbows arch them, and the woods
> Are deafened with the roar. The violent shock
> Shatters to vapor the descending sheets.
> A cloudy whirlwind fills the gulf, and heaves
> The mighty pyramid of circling mist
> To heaven.[8]

Heredia's lines are all the more remarkable in their impassioned sweep when one remembers that chronologically he was not only the first romantic poet of Spanish America, but the first in the Spanish language.

Andrés Bello (1781-1865), a Venezuelan poet and scholar, is the third name always mentioned with Olmedo and Heredia.

* Heredia, *Niágara*.

In his own right, Bello ranks as a great figure in the Era of Independence: just as Bolívar was the liberator, so Bello was the educator of a whole continent. The very existence of so great an intellectual as Bello, in a New World born of despotism and chaos, seems a miracle; it is more understandable when one remembers that, along with its great masses of illiterates, Spanish America has always had a small but very learned elite. Of this class was Bello, who won world fame as educator, philosopher, philologist, internationalist, literary critic, and historian.

Bello was born in Caracas, some twenty-five years before the introduction of the printing press into his native country. He received his education there: lessons in Latin, theology, canon and civil law, Aristotelian philosophy, mathematics, and physics, all of these mainly at the hands of priests. When Bello was not yet twenty, the great German naturalist, Humboldt—who was to spend twenty-five years preparing his monumental *Journey to the Equinoctial Regions of the New Continent*—visited Caracas, exerting on the young Venezuelan a decisive influence that lasted the rest of his life. Humboldt's scientific knowledge, quick imagination, and wide experience must have awakened in Bello a passion for the natural sciences and scholarship. For from 1810 to 1829, Bello lived in England, where he cultivated the friendship of philosophers, writers, and men of science; it was there that he made his fundamental studies of the *Poem of the Cid* and the French medieval epic. A champion of American independence, he came to the new Republic of Chile in 1829, and stayed there till his death, shaping the intellectual life of that nation. Bello founded the National University; he had no equal in America as a scholar of Greek and Latin; he wrote what is still considered the best grammar of the Spanish language. Speaking of his work as a grammarian, a Peninsular critic has declared that Bello 'wished to re-established linguistic unity in America and to check the invasion of new words, without denying the rights of regional and provincial vocabularies. He was the savior of the integrity of the Spanish language in America, and at the same time he taught a good deal to Spaniards of the mother land.' [9]

As a poet, Bello's contribution was only slightly less distinguished. He created a new poetic genre in his *American Silvas* * (1827), stanzas on the tropic regions, which carry the description of fruits, plants, and trees, to the highest levels of artistry. In all his poems there is a strong American note, expressed by local color, references to regional customs, and allusions to the historical background of the continent. But most significant is the way he turns his eyes to the American scene, to find poetic inspiration in those plants that appeal more to the palate than to the artistic sense of the average man: coffee, tobacco, pineapple, avocado, cocoa, and the banana. For him, his native tropics were an earthly paradise, recently devastated by fratricidal wars, but now given over to the idyllic works of peace; here, far from the turmoil of the cities and their vices, was the heart of the American continent—a place where the heroes of the future would arise. In this bucolic mood, Bello has followed a strictly antique classical pattern; he has even been called 'the creator of a new classic form.' Indeed, the very first verse of Bello's *Ode to the Agriculture of the Torrid Zone,* 'Salve, fecunda zona . . .' is a faithful repetition of Vergil's 'Salve magna parens frugum . . . ,' and he ranks for all Spanish Americans as their representative classical poet.

All the same, a few romantic elements are discernible in Bello's work. His two American odes, *Allocution to Poetry* (1823) and *Agriculture of the Torrid Zone,*† were written in London, and they contain that vague melancholy of remembrance that the Portuguese explains so well with the word *saudade*, that intimate feeling of nostalgia found in most ro-

* Bello, *Silvas Americanas*.
† Bello, *Alocución a la Poesía, Silva a la Agricultura de la Zona Tórrida*.

mantic nature poets. The mere fact that Bello focused his attention upon his native soil, disdained by others, shows his classicism to have been tempered by a modern practical sense and a scientific interest in nature. He continued in America, as Menéndez y Pelayo justly observed, that happy wedlock between literature and natural science found in the prose of Buffon, Rousseau, and Bernardin de Saint-Pierre. Furthermore, Bello was well acquainted with the French and English poets of the romantic school. He translated Byron and Hugo, and the latter influenced him considerably. Bello's immortal poem *Prayer for All* * (1843), inspired by Hugo's *La Prière pour tous*, is a perfectly romantic document, just such poetry of twilight as is *Gray's Elegy in a Country Churchyard*, its verses filled with mystery, serenity, and sadness, and floating over all, like a gray mist, the sentiment of death.

Bello, the great classical scholar, with his nostalgic love of tropical nature—Heredia, the Byronic youth, with his torrential verses on Niagara—and Olmedo, the patriot, with his unbridled stanzas to Bolívar—these three poets appeared at the threshold of romanticism in Spanish America. Only one, Heredia, was a true romantic. But all three, in their writings, foreshadowed the great romantic upheaval that lay ahead.

ROMANTICISM RAMPANT

SPANISH America, in the period immediately after the Wars for Independence, was a wonderfully fertile field for romanticism. The new nations, carved out of the old colonial empire, were ruled by their own sons—the Caudillos, who had fought under Bolívar against the Spanish oppressor. In their turn, the Caudillos became dictators, and, paradoxically enough, the founders of democracies; but the democracies existed in name only, because their Presidents, too, soon be-

---

* Bello, *La oración por todos*.

came dictators. Through this chaotic period, a number of factors contributed to the great triumph of the romantic movement: the vastness and primitiveness of the natural setting; the recent revolutionary experience, and the violence caused by the first despotic Caudillos in the body politic; the exaltation of liberty, and the clash between idealistic souls and barbaric social conditions; and the final skepticism and disillusion produced by the shattering of so many noble dreams and purposes. Even the temperament of the Spanish American, more inclined towards lofty sentiment than towards restrained classic reason, pointed the way.

> All was favorable to Romanticism. Political struggles and anarchy produced Byronic heroes, tropical passion was fed with sentimentalism . . . and the fight against tyrants developed the individual. Roles were confused in the uncertain and barbaric life of the newly-born democracies; the poet became the prophet and leader of the masses; he felt himself misunderstood amidst mediocrity, a victim of ignorance and brutality. Melancholy, exasperated individualism, divine inspiration, solitude—these are the romantic elements that appear in Spanish American literature.[10]

Obviously, literature produced by such men and under such conditions was not going to follow blindly the Spanish pattern. Hatred for Spain had not abated. Rather, it had grown more intense; and Sarmiento, that amazing man of the Argentine pampas, advised Americans to forget Spain completely—since it was a barbaric country which had never produced anything in science, education, philosophy, religion, or even poetry! France, England, and the United States were the countries to be imitated. By 1833, Victor Hugo, Lamartine, de Musset, Byron, and Walter Scott were the authors most widely read by young Spanish American intellectuals. Only those writers who could not read French or English would permit themselves to be influenced by the Spanish poets of that time—such as Espronceda and the Duke of Rivas, who, of course, represented romanticism in the Peninsula.

But the triumph of the romantic movement did not come about without a struggle against the old established order in literature. The battle between romanticism and classicism, productive of so many intriguing episodes in Europe, was dramatized in Spanish America by one of the most interesting polemics in literary history. The protagonists in this war of words were truly illustrious figures: on the side of classicism were ranged the famous scholar Andrés Bello and his followers; while the cause of romanticism was defended by the extraordinary Domingo Faustino Sarmiento (1811-88), himself a living symbol of romantic revolt.

A comparison of these two great personalities is illuminating. On the one hand was Bello—'The Hero as Scholar' Carlyle would have called him—a man of vast erudition, yet ruled by social and literary conventions. One of his pupils, José Victorino Lastarria, has left this picture of Bello as a teacher:

In 1834, Bello offered two courses of study in his own home: one in Grammar and Literature, and the other in Roman and Spanish law.

His knowledge of these subjects was broad and profound, but being still under certain cultural influences of that time, he applied to them a narrow concept of methodology. The language study was a complete course of philology covering general and historical grammar, and included the most minute points of grammatical analysis. In these classes, the great teacher continued his method of writing his books as he taught. His treatise on the inflection of the verb and the most interesting chapters in his *Grammar* were discussed in those long and charming conferences with his students. Professor Bello was an exceedingly serious man and very set in his ways of teaching. He never explained in detail; he never allowed refutation of his statements; he talked only, beginning with the exposition of a question, in order to stimulate his students' thoughts. In these conversations he did all the thinking and discussing, usually smoking a big Havana cigar, and speaking with calm and deliberation, without moving one muscle of his face.[11]

Sarmiento, too, was a teacher, but of an almost diametrically opposite type both in pedagogy and in life. In 1829, for instance, Andrés Bello was just arriving in Chile, fresh from his studies in England, to fill a high post in the Ministry of Foreign Affairs, at the invitation of the new Republic. While this same year, Sarmiento was escaping to Chile from the tyranny of Rosas, the Argentine dictator, to work as a laborer in the mines; the legend (perhaps false, but revealing) survives that in those days Sarmiento carried over his shoulder a great sack of encyclopedias on which he used to sleep at night! An autodidact of irregular schooling, Sarmiento began to teach the primary grades when he was only fifteen; later, he was rural schoolmaster and teacher in a secondary school; and the greatest pedagogical achievements of this friend of Horace Mann were in connection with the normal schools and systems of public education in Chile and especially in Argentina.

The famous controversy between these two outstanding figures took place in Chile in 1842. Sarmiento, having crossed the Andes for the third time, was offered a journalistic post on the Valparaiso *Mercury*, from which tribune his voice was heard daily. At the same time, Bello and his disciples were writing for the Santiago *Literary Weekly*.* A battle royal soon broke out between the two periodicals: Sarmiento, the self-taught popular educator, naturally took up the cudgels for a progressive concept of culture, romantic freedom of expression, and the vitalizing effects of French models. Bello and his friends argued quite as naturally for an aristocratic concept of literary standards, the purity of the Castilian tongue, the value of Spanish culture. The opening shot was fired by the *Mercury*, where Sarmiento, in his very first article on literary

* *Mercurio, Semanario Literario.*

matters, commented on a poem by Andrés Bello with the re-
mark that Chilean youth was timid and unimaginative. But the
polemic was really launched on April 27, when Sarmiento, in
review of a recently published language book, wrote these
pointed words:

> Teachers of grammar are useless, for people learn
> by practical example and general discussion; grammar
> has not been developed for the people, because the
> people are the real creators of a language, while
> grammarians are only the maintainers of tradition
> and compilers of dictionaries; orthography must follow
> pronunciation, not etymology.[12]

This was open heterodoxy in a society accustomed to the rigid
canons of Bello's doctrine and the sacred axioms of rhetoric
and grammar. Bello himself seized the gauntlet to put the
offender in the ignominious place he deserved. He advised
Sarmiento not to write upon such topics, and censured him
particularly for his popular appeal and his use of French words
—quoting the well-known verse of Isla:

> Once in Madrid I met a Countess fair
> Who learned to sneeze with a charming French air.[13]

The fight was now on in earnest. Sarmiento had been provoked, and he entered the battle without inhibitions or remorse. He replied with an elaborate defense of French
linguistic influences: First he attacked the purists who 'enslaved in the forms of the language, pay no attention to the
ideas, accidents, and vicissitudes that modify them.' Then he
explained that Spanish Americans had to turn to the French
language for new expressions, since they could not find them
in Spanish, a tongue which could not interpret criticism, history, drama, legislation, and so on. The mystic writers of Spain
could not satisfy modern needs; and the Spanish language
itself had ceased to be the master, taking instead the post of
humble apprentice. Here, for instance, was a catalogue of

current books, with 500 publications listed in Spanish, and only
50 of them by Spanish authors. All this was the fault of cleri-
cal and political despotism, which had produced Spanish and
Spanish American isolation; 'and now,' he exclaims, 'modern
liberty finds these countries in utter misery and igorance.' Is
it any wonder then, that all Spanish-speaking nations must
borrow ideas from other countries? and with these ideas, the
foreign expressions are introduced. Some day, there will be a
renaissance of Spanish thought, and then nobody will fear
gallicisms, neologisms, and the other kinds of new words.

Bello retorted like the grammarian that he was, with a praise
of purism and the standards of academicians. He quoted from
Tocqueville:

> A country in which *belles lettres* are cultivated is an
> aristocratic country; all the products of intelligence, as
> well as the affairs of government, must be directed by an
> aristocratic class. Literary life and political activity re-
> main almost entirely in the hands of this class.[14]

And Bello even went so far as to say that a country must have
in language as in politics a group of learned men to legislate,
for it would be just as ridiculous to entrust the people with
the making of their laws as to entrust them with the making
of their language.

This was too much for Sarmiento, who replied in a vitriolic
tone, discussing his favorite theme of continuous democratic
progress. He ridicules Bello and his followers, who 'study the
origin of words and the niceties of form in order to understand society and democracy.' Then he takes up Academies:
an Academy must be an institution like Congress, obeying the
will of the people and their poets; in France, the Académie is
devoted to the study of serious problems, not only to the com-
pilation of words; and in England, where there is no Academy,
the language borrows words freely from all sources and yet
there has never been any linguistic anarchy! Grammarians to

the contrary notwithstanding, there are reciprocal influences among tongues; as the world changes, so does language. France is right to allow Hugo and Dumas to alter the modes of expression if by so doing they delight millions of readers. Aristocracies value perfection in style as much as ideas; while in democracies, style is careless and vehement and daring, inspired by the urgency of the thought it conveys.

Sarmiento then turns his attention to Spanish America, to prove that a romantic freedom of style under French influences is natural and productive. How ridiculous, he cries, to develop a classic style in a society without culture! The France-inspired Argentines, even while at war with Rosas, had written more verses than the Chileans at peace. And why? Because Chile is deadened into inertia by admirable classic models and the influence of grammarians. Exile these pedants, he cries; send them off to Spain where they belong; throw the works of Cervantes, Fray Luis de León, and Garcilaso into the fire. Give youth the cult of true knowledge and not of externals—and style will follow, as the result of ideas passionately expressed!

In the face of this violent personal attack, Bello laid down his arms. But his disciples continued the argument, and to them Sarmiento addressed a few more articles in which he upholds a full romantic creed. He demands a new literature, an authentic expression of modern society; a literature based upon truth, whose only master shall be nature itself. The norm of the age was and ought to be liberty. Enthusiasm should be the first prerequisite of the writer, and the sole fountainhead of beauty; only the thought can be sublime; not the word, but the idea that strikes directly to the heart! Romanticism as a term had now been dragged out into the open; and the controversy became a veritable free-for-all. In the *Mercury*, Sarmiento and V. F. López, another Argentine refugee, argued loudly for literary liberty and romanticism. In the *Literary Weekly*, the editor Lastarria and the contributors Sanfuentes,

Tocornal, and Vallejo, all of them disciples of Bello, upheld classical principles. The struggle between the two periodicals grew bitter, even brutal at times. But with the withdrawal of Bello from the discussion, the advantage had shifted to Sarmiento's side, and the *Weekly* was on the defensive. The young Chileans, goaded by this upstart foreigner, were publishing original literature—to show that they could produce it!

Sarmiento, bitter and unrelenting, was hammering home his point. Vallejo had written an article on the negative aspects of romanticism, and Sarmiento came out with a brilliant defense of the movement. Of course romanticism had its shortcomings, he declared; but so did all the great movements of civilization, the French Revolution, the struggle for American Independence, Christianity itself! Anyhow, romanticism was already dead and buried in Europe; and it deserved to be studied philosophically, as a serious literary revolution, a genre that was cultivated by the most famous men of the time. And here Sarmiento let fly his most telling shaft, advising American writers to recognize their insignificance before the great European romanticists whom they were presuming to criticize:

> Let us ask a question, just one question, to shame these frogs, who insult with their scornful croakings the sun of civilization, a sun so remote from them, that it does not even stop to listen. What are we in our small corner compared with the poorest of the romantics? [15]

After all, when Victor Hugo publishes a book, declared Sarmiento, the whole world listens in reverence. Hugo's mistakes are of more value than the phraseological niceties of the Chileans. Hugo is of more value as a living writer than are Horace, Virgil, Racine, and Moratín as dead ones. So the *Weekly* thought that Hugo's *Ruy Blas* was a monstrosity because it made a minister-of-state out of a lackey? And why could not one of the lowly born be a better man than a

Spanish grandee in a rotten aristocracy? Did not all the Spanish American Republics have generals and plenipotentiaries who once were lackeys?

There was no answer possible. The controversy came to an end with Lastarria, the rival editor, becoming converted to the principles of Sarmiento. The *Literary Weekly* survived approximately six months and then disappeared, leaving in its place a great modern newspaper aptly entitled *Progress.** Romanticism rampant had become romanticism triumphant. The struggle in Chile had been more vocal than in other lands, but it typified what was going on all over Spanish America. The romantic movement had conquered, or was to conquer, in all the Spanish American countries—and it was to hold intermittent sway, amid countless conflicting tendencies, for the rest of the nineteenth century. Sarmiento had been right in his analysis of cultural anarchy; because of the differing conditions in the young republics, with their varying stages of development and accessibility to European modes, romanticism appeared earlier or thrived later in some countries than in others. But in the main its development was governed by the two poles that Sarmiento had recognized: on the one hand, the chaos of new nations born between civilization and barbarism; on the other hand, the overpowering influence of France.

CIVILIZATION AND BARBARISM

In his famous polemic, Sarmiento had praised the young Argentine poets who wrote verses while fighting a tyrant. The example was significant. For one of the most important single blocks of Spanish American romantic literature was that produced by the 'writers of the tyranny of Rosas.' The regime of Juan Manuel Rosas, dictator of the La Plata provinces, stands out as perhaps the most brutal episode of the whole 'legend of blood' that darkens Spanish American history. Dur-

* *El Progreso.*

ing this period of absolute despotism, Argentine intellectuals were naturally among the chief victims of spies, secret police, and strong-arm squads. And these young writers not only fought the tyrant in revolutionary societies, but they also recorded his infamies in a whole series of novels, short stories, and prose works, which still live today by the very passion of their hatred.

Important among these young 'Unitarians'—as the anti-Rosas party was called—was Esteban Echeverría (1805-51), who introduced romanticism into Argentina. Echeverría had visited France, where he became an ardent follower of the romantic movement, reading authors such as Shakespeare and Schiller. His poetical volumes, *Elvira, or the Bride of the Plata* (1832), *Consolations* (1834), and *Rhymes* (1837), were little more than imitations of Byron. But after founding a secret revolutionary group, 'The Brotherhood of May,' he composed his real masterpiece, *The Slaughter-house*,[16] a prose story, or (to be more exact) the unfinished draft of a novel denouncing the tyranny.* Even nowadays, when blood-curdling realism is commonplace, it is hard to find the equal of this sketch, scrawled off at top speed by an author under peril of his life.

The action of *The Slaughter-house*, as the name implies, takes place in an actual *matadero* where fifty head of cattle are being butchered. The savage scene is minutely described: the red banners of the Rosas faction, the slaughtering and the distribution of meat, the escape of one of the bulls who gores a child to death, leaving the headless trunk to spout blood! For this is more than an ordinary slaughterhouse; it is the rendezvous of the *mashorca* (the 'gallows-plus') or band of assassins who keep the despot in power. And just at the height of the bloody spectacle, a passing Unitarian is sighted by the butchers, a youth of twenty-five with his beard cut in the shape of a U. The leader of the hangmen, 'Killer of Seven,'

* Echeverría, *Elvira o La Novia de la Plata, Los Consuelos, Rimas; El Matadero.*

falls upon him, pulling him from his horse; the youth is bound hand and foot and his beard is clipped into the Federalist pattern. The thugs then prepare to beat him—but at this moment, the young Unitarian, struggling to free himself, breaks bleeding from his bonds and dies before the eyes of his astonished executioners. The whole story is a sombre and terrible vignette, against a background of howling curs, bedraggled Negresses, circling vultures—a slaughterhouse that represents the real *matadero* tyranny of Rosas.

A work of still greater power is the mighty indictment of the terror written by Domingo Faustino Sarmiento [17] himself, in his immortal *Civilization and Barbarism: The Life of Juan Facundo Quiroga* * (1845). It is difficult to appraise this famous book, a biographical study of Facundo, Rosas' gaucho lieutenant, which ranks nowadays as perhaps the most representative volume ever produced in the southern continent. *Facundo* is written in an irregular and faulty style; the author seems unaware of the most elementary notions of grammar; and yet the style, especially in those passages where Sarmiento excoriates the tyrant, becomes majestic, romantic, lyrically tragic. It is definitely not a 'literary' book. Rather, it is a work that has grown and grown in magnitude, since it was composed nearly a century ago, until today it stands at the very forefront of Spanish American letters.

Facundo is a book without a proper plan; it aims to give a historical and sociological explanation of the causes which have produced the tyranny. The introductory section describes the Argentine countryside, and the types and customs it engenders. The gaucho is shown as a product of this environment, be he 'guide' or 'bad gaucho' or 'singing gaucho' or 'follower of footprints':

> The print-follower is a grave, circumspect personage, whose assertions are accepted as gospel in the lower

* Sarmiento, *Facundo, o La Civilización y la Barbarie.*

courts. His own consciousness of knowledge gives him a certain reserved and mysterious dignity. Everyone treats him with consideration; the poor man, who fears the harm of his calumny or denunciation; the landholder, who may be in need of his testimony. A robbery, for instance, has been committed at night; no sooner is the crime discovered than they run to a footprint of the thief, and when it's found, they cover it with something lest the wind blow it away. Thereupon the print-follower is called; he looks at the print, and proceeds to follow the trail, glancing only now and then at the ground, as though his eyes could see in bold relief this footstep which is imperceptible to others. He follows it through streets, across gardens, and finally steps into a house, pointing out his quarry with the cold words: 'This is the man.' The crime is proved, and rare is the criminal who resists the accusation.[18]

These gauchos, Sarmiento explains, hold their gatherings in the *pulpería* or country store, where they drink and gamble, and organize their bands, and win reputations by their skill with the knife.

Young Facundo, the future tyrant, is shown growing up against this background of *pampa* and *pulpería*, and acquiring the nickname 'tiger of the plains' for his bravado and cruelty. As a boy, he knocks down the schoolmaster who tries vainly to discipline him; as a youth, he works as a peon, enrolls in the army and deserts, and finally sets fire to the house where his parents are sleeping. He turns common thief, and, upon being released from the San Luis prison in a jailbreak, he proceeds to kill the official who gives him his freedom. From that day on, he becomes the perfect type of barbarian, the man without God or law:

> Dominated by rage, he used to kill with his bare fists, dashing out the brains of a friend over a card game . . . splitting open the head of his son Juan with a hatchet-blow, because he couldn't find any other way to make the youngster shut up . . .[19]

Facundo becomes a gaucho *caudillo*, and gradually through treachery he rises to be a commandant and the boss of several provinces, over which flies his black flag with a skull and crossbones. At length, only Rosas and Facundo remain on the political horizon, and Rosas has the gaucho chieftain ambushed and shot. Now that Facundo is dead, the tyrant can rule from Buenos Aires—and the third and concluding section of *Civilization and Barbarism* is devoted to the atrocities of the Rosas regime.

As a book, *Facundo* can best be appreciated by the way it has remained fresh and compelling through nearly a century.[20] Despite its careless style, its often-pedestrian phrases, its schoolteacher-like explanations and lessons in history, this unique volume remains today one of the most extraordinary books ever written. Its specific merits are the many, priceless anecdotes, episodes of a naturalism worthy of Gorki. Blanco Fombona, a critic not always inclined to do justice to Argentine writers, has said of it:

> As a work of literature, there is nothing more living . . . more fortuitous than Facundo's pictures of the pampas and its characteristic types. These are classic pages in their way. Years will pass; the form of civilization or the aspect of barbarism which they outline shall have disappeared, but these pages will remain . . .[21]

And *Civilization and Barbarism* has something more to recommend it than even this durability. Sarmiento, the great apostle of romanticism, was able to practice what he had preached. In his masterpiece, with all its intensity, its power of evocation, its disregard of style and emphasis upon vehement ideas, he carried out all the principles that he had upheld. His great work is considered today the acknowledged *chef d'œuvre* of the Argentine romantic school—and indeed, as perhaps the most important single book of any sort ever produced in Spanish America.

Equally famous in its time, though a modern critical revaluation is rapidly relegating it to a secondary position, was the novel *Amalia* (1851-5), one of the most widely read of all the denunciations of the tyrant. This vast two-volume book was the chief accomplishment of José Mármol (1817-71), who won the title of the 'poetic hangman of Rosas.' As a young intellectual, Mármol was once imprisoned by the dictator, and twice forced to flee abroad for his life; after the fall of Rosas, he returned to Buenos Aires, received several public offices, and held the post of Director of the National Library until his death. As a writer, he was completely a romanticist, composing two poetical tragedies, *The Poet* (1842) and *The Crusader* (1851), and an imitation of Byron's *Childe Harold*, *The Pilgrim* (1847). His most famous work, *Amalia*, is a long 700-page novel in the Walter Scott style—though written without Scott's genius—which unfortunately bores and amuses the modern reader with its countless melodramatic episodes, its dull dialogue, its artificial characters who symbolize loyalty, love, primitive bestiality, or spotless purity.*

Amalia's chief interest nowadays is a historical one. In point of time, it is the first novel written in Argentina. And for the modern reader, it preserves an incredible and passionately written picture of the horrors of the tyranny. Mármol's stilted pages come to life when he is describing the minute ins-and-outs of the dictatorship, real events and historical personages who appear under their own names, atrocities that are recorded with the crudest realism. From its opening pages, a nightmare of blood hangs over the novel, and the plot is still a 'spell-binder': Six Unitarians try to escape from Buenos Aires to Montevideo, on the tragic night of May 4, 1840, but they are betrayed by their guide. Only one—Eduardo, the hero—gets off alive, thanks to the help of Daniel Bello, a Unitarian disguised as a Federalist. Amalia, Daniel's cousin, cares for the wounded liberal, and the two young people fall deeply in love.

---

* Mármol, *El Poeta, El Cruzado, El Peregrino; Amalia*.

Meanwhile, Rosas is enraged that one Unitarian should have escaped, and he commissions Doña Josefa Escurra, sister-in-law of the tyrant, and directress of the dread secret police, to find the rebel, who can only be identified by an enormous wound in his thigh. Aided by the Negro servants, who act as spies in every house, Doña Josefa grows suspicious of Amalia and pays her a visit; there the female tyrant meets Eduardo, and upon leaving leans her hand against his thigh, causing the youth to faint. From then on, Eduardo is a hunted man, fleeing from house to house. In the midst of the 'terror,' in October 1840, when the bandits of the *mashorca* are roaming the streets of Buenos Aires, Amalia and Eduardo are secretly married—but the Federal police break into the house immediately and assassinate the bridegroom. Obviously, the situations and the setting are powerful in the extreme, and in more gifted hands *Amalia* might have become a great novel. As it is, with its false literary style and antiquated technique, the book is one that a modern reader can only wade through with the greatest difficulty.

As one of the more celebrated works produced under the tyranny of Rosas, Mármol's *Amalia* deserves a place beside Echeverría's *The Slaughter-house* and Sarmiento's *Civilization and Barbarism*. Of the three, only Sarmiento's book is an enduring masterwork. But the whole body of Argentine romanticism, including even the poetry composed in imitation of Lord Byron, has a particular value in the history of Spanish American literature. It illustrated the close connection between romantic writing and chaotic life under the tyrants. And it released a new current, which was to have its flowering in the later genre of gaucho literature.

The struggle between 'civilization and barbarism' produced yet another literary colossus who loomed large in the romantic era: Juan Montalvo (1832-89), the implacable enemy of the Ecuadorian dictator García Moreno. Montalvo truly lived the existence of a romantic hero, passing his days in suc-

cessive periods of exile and active struggle against the forces
of oppression. He began his attack on the tyrant as an unknown youth writing from an invalid bed; he founded his
great journal *The Cosmopolitan* in 1866 to carry on the fight;
even while he was out of the country, he published vigorous
diatribes against the 'perpetual dictatorship'; and when at
length García Moreno was assassinated, Montalvo remarked
from abroad: 'It was my pen that killed him.' Later, when
Veintemilla seized the government, Montalvo attacked this
petty tyrant, and tyrants in general, in his terrible and savage
Catiline Pamphlets (1880).*

In literature, too, Montalvo was a confirmed romantic, a
disciple of Byron, Hugo, and Lamartine. When he visited
France as a young man, he tried to persuade the poverty-
stricken and ailing Lamartine to accept the hospitality of
Ecuador: 'I have flowers there to offer my great guest; I
would take you to my father's house; we should plunge together into the woods of Ficoa, and proceeding along our
forest path, you would feel yourself suddenly inspired by the
divine fire at sight of the poetic lakes of Imbabura.' Of Montalvo it was said that he used to tremble at the very sound of
Byron's name!

But Montalvo's unique distinction as a writer does not rest
upon his works attacking tyranny. Unlike Sarmiento, whose
battle against Rosas bore such a similarity to the Ecuadorian's
fight against García Moreno, Montalvo was a great stylist. His
greatest productions were written in exile—like his amazing
continuation of *Don Quixote*, the *Chapters that Cervantes
Forgot*, begun in 1866 and completed during his first seven
years in Panama. Here, as in his essays, Montalvo shows himself to be one of the great masters of Spanish prose, possessor
of a vigorous, effervescing, and compelling style. His skill in
manipulating words was further enriched by his acquaintance

* Montalvo, *El Cosmopolita; Catilinarias.*

with classic authors; 'until his time,' writes Isaac Barrera, 'no comparable effort had been made to renovate the adipose and mentally stagnated Castilian language.' But it is in his *Seven Treatises*, written in Paris in 1873 and published in 1882, that Montalvo reaches his greatest heights as a disciple of the French essayist Montaigne.* These discourses on literary and moral matters, richly adorned with episodes and descriptions and learned allusions, rank with the best essays ever composed in Spanish.

Montalvo, like Montaigne, had an incredible talent for spinning anecdotes to such an extent that they obscured the main thread of his essay. Here, for instance, is an illustrative disquisition of his in the midst of a passage on literary plagiarism as practiced by Crisipus and Corneille:

> In a certain institution of higher learning there was once a student extremely noted for his wit, and the gifts of fortune, and the social position of his parents. Furthermore, he was rich, and his wardrobe was so well-stocked that it contained enough clothes to dress all his fellow-students. But this gentleman-scholar had the habit of doing like the writer Crisipus, namely, taking what he wanted wherever he found it; and his pantaloons, coat and hat were always whatever ones he could lay hands on . . . Now this was a regular daily occurrence with him; and often as not he would seize up and put on an outlandish 'French tower' of a hat belonging to a certain elderly professor . . . I remember bumping into him once in the doorway of the Archbishop of Quito, all rigged out in a fine black mantle and the aforesaid turret on his head, its brim broken and flapping so that it looked for all the world like an antique *tricorne* . . . He was charging along at top speed, like he always did, and sailed past me without even stopping . . . And just as I was going on into the school-building, up comes an old cleric, hobbling along clopety-clop, and calling to me: 'Have you seen that crazy Vincent anywhere? He's gone

* Montalvo, *Capítulos que se le Olvidaron a Cervantes, Siete Tratados.*

off in my mantle, mistaking it for his own cape.' 'Your mantle, Sir,' I cried, 'and Doctor Angulo's hat—there he goes!' [22]

And along with his ability to delight and entertain the reader, Montalvo's ideas are penetrating and memorable—as in this celebrated comparison of Washington and Bolívar:

> The renown of Washington rests not so much upon his military prowess, as upon the success of the enterprise which he brought to completion with happiness and good judgment. The fame of Bolívar carries with it the noise of arms . . . : trumpets sound, horses neigh, all is a warlike roar about the Spanish American hero . . .
> Washington was surrounded by figures as noted as himself . . . : Jefferson and Madison, men of high noble counsel; Franklin, earthy and celestial genius, who snatched the sceptre from the tyrants, and the lightning from the clouds . . . Bolívar had to hold his lieutenants in check, and fight his own compatriots and the thousand-and-one elements conspiring against him and against Independence, at the same time that he battled the Spanish hosts . . . Washington founded a Republic, which grew into one of the greatest nations of the earth; Bolívar likewise founded a great nation, but, less fortunate . . . he saw it fall apart, and his work disfigured if not destroyed . . . [23]

Montalvo's *Seven Treatises*, it is clear, do not rank as romantic writings, but rather as highly personal literature in the manner of Montaigne. Yet Montalvo himself, in his life and his admiration for the European romanticists, stands out as a striking figure of the romantic era in Spanish America. He was, with Sarmiento, one of the greatest names connected with the literary struggle against tyrants, a movement which included the famous group of Argentine *proscriptos*, Juan Cruz Varela, J. Rivera Indarte, Vicente Fidel López, Juan María Gutiérrez, and Juan Bautista Alberdi, all of whom were exiled from Buenos Aires and continued their fight against Rosas from Chile and Uruguay. A literary struggle, in short, of civilization against barbarism, which was one of the chief features of the romantic movement.

MARÍA

WHILE the Argentine writers represented the virile native roots of romanticism, the more sentimental foreign-inspired aspects of the movement were being cultivated in other quarters of Spanish America. Any number of 'Indianist' novels were turned out, most of them stimulated by Chateaubriand's *Atala*, though Walter Scott and Fenimore Cooper did not lack disciples. These novels have been studied seriously,[24] though the genre as a whole appears artificial and lacking in literary merit by twentieth-century standards; in general, the Indians of such books have a purely European psychology and a lofty chivalrous manner of speaking and acting. Representative of the whole group is *Cumandá, or A Drama among Savages* (1871) by the Ecuadorian Juan León Mera (1832-94), a novel notable for its idealized natives and its feeling for nature. Also deserving of mention are *Caramurú* (1848), by the Uruguayan Alejandro Magariños Cervantes (1825-93), in which only the name of the hero is authentically indigenous; *The Martyrs of Anáhuac* (1870), by the Mexican Eligio Ancona (1836-93), interesting for its folklore and serious attempt at historical reconstruction; and *Little Henry* (1879), by Manuel de Jesús Galván (1834-1910) of the Dominican Republic, who based his novel on Father Las Casas' chronicle.*

But the real masterpiece of the sentimental romantic school is *Maria* † (1867) by Jorge Isaacs (1837-95), a novel that has been more read than any other written in Spanish America. Apart from furnishing autobiographical material for this romance, Isaac's life is almost entirely devoid of interest. His

* Mera, *Cumandá, o un Drama entre Salvajes;* Magariños Cervantes, *Caramurú;* Ancona, *Los Mártires del Anáhuac;* Galván, *El Enriquillo.*
† Isaacs, *María.*

education in boarding school, the financial ruin of his parents, his diplomatic appointments and unsuccessful business ventures—these events are of much less significance than the simple fact that his youth was passed on an estate in the Cordillera Central, an estate which he has made immortal in his one novel. For in literature, too, Isaacs did nothing noteworthy outside of composing *Maria;* he had previously published a volume of *Poems* (1864) in which he imitated Lamartine; he subsequently gave up literature altogether.

Maria alone, however, is sufficient to secure Isaacs' fame. The story is pure idyll—so much so that it seems almost an American adaptation of *Atala* or *Paul and Virginia:* Ephraim, the hero, comes home from his Bogotá school to the Valley of Cauca, where he finds his orphan cousin Maria grown into womanhood. The two young people fall in love, and live brief enchanted hours in a magic circle of fond parents and faithful servants. But alas, Maria suffers from epilepsy; and, lest the emotions of love aggravate her illness, Ephraim's father sends the young man to Europe to complete his medical studies. During his absence, Maria grows worse; Ephraim is called home, but too late. He arrives to find Maria dead. This is indeed idyllic elegy: the idyll of two young souls that find one another at the springtime of life; the elegy of love cut short, and the death of youth and beauty. The characters themselves are all of one piece; and Isaacs, with a rare sense of harmony, has placed them in a limited environment to form a synthesis of the patriarchal country home of Colombia.

Even the style of *Maria* is elegiacal. Isaacs had the gift of sentimentality; his pages are full of sad presentiments and fatal augurs; his sentences have the cadence of autumn leaves and twilight whisperings. No small part of the novel's charm derives from the masterful romantic interpretation of the landscape:

> The herons were leaving their nests, skimming upward into undulating lines silvered by the sun, like ribbons

fluttering freely in the wind. Swarms of parrots were rising from the reeds to fly towards the near-by cornfields; and the 'diostedé' was saluting the new day with his sad and monotonous chant from the heart of the mountain-side.[25]

This is no landscape invented according to a literary formula, but real countryside thinly veiled by the writer's sensibility. At times, the emotion becomes so strong that natural scenes are transmuted into subjective pictures, rather than the mere vision of the eyes:

> Already I could hear the roaring current of the Zabaletas; I could just make out the branches of the willows. I paused at the sight of the hill. Two years before, on such an afternoon, which then harmonized with my happiness and now was indifferent to my grief, I had seen from this spot the lights of a house where I was awaited with loving solicitude. Maria was there . . . Now the house was closed and silent . . . A few steps from the path that the creeping weeds were starting to blot out, I saw the broad stone where we had sat reading on those happy afternoons. It marked the boundary of the confident garden of my hopes: then were the doves and thrushes fluttering about chirping and cooing in the leaves of the orange trees, while the wind scattered dry leaves on the cold terraced stepping-stones.[26]

It is this very sensibility that gives Isaacs' work its permanent value. There is abundant Americanism in his pages, to be sure, not only in the scenery but in episodes of local color, as the servants' wedding or the country dance. But the greatness of the novel rests upon its handling of a universal human theme: love and death. Sophisticated critics can easily find in *Maria* the defects of exaggerated sentimentalism and all the other shortcomings of the romantic school. Yet the modern reader, weary of complicated techniques and surfeited with brutal realism, can still find solace in the simple and ingenuous pages of this great Colombian novel. And long after the criticism has been forgotten, *Maria* will continue to delight and touch succeeding generations.

Such a novel could not fail to provoke many imitations, all of them naturally much inferior to the original. South America has produced many spiritual sisters of *Maria, Josephine, Carmen, Lucy, Angelina,* and so on.[27] But the idealistic romantic novel had already given its best with Isaacs' matchless idyll. Romanticism had shot its bolt; Rousseau, Chateaubriand, Saint-Pierre, Hugo, Byron, had done their work in Spanish America. The reaction was setting in, just as it had after the romantic movement in France; only the Spanish American reaction—like the appearance of Spanish American romantic literature—was bound to be irregular and unchronological. Crude realism had already appeared in Argentina, some thirty years before the publication of *Maria.* Realism was soon to show itself in the Indianist novel *Birds without Nest* * (1889), by the Peruvian author Clorinda Matto de Turner (1854-1909), who saw the natives as social rather than literary characters, and who felt compassion for their injustices and oppression at the hands of the whites. But in playing itself out, the romantic novel had fulfilled its purpose: it had paved the way for the realistic novel that was to reach full development in twentieth-century Spanish America.

The End of Romanticism

ROMANTICISM in Spanish America—it cannot be repeated too many times—was not a formal movement as it was elsewhere. The romantic tendency, of definitely European inspiration, was generally connected with the turbulent period of emerging national life in countries which had thrown off their Spanish shackles and sought new inspiration from other lands. But even in this respect, there was no chronological regularity. Romanticism appeared earlier or lasted later in some countries

* Matto de Turner, *Aves sin Nido.*

than in others, largely according to their accessibility to foreign influences. Thus, the first Spanish American romantic was Heredia, a Cuban who travelled in the United States at a time when romantic writers were popular. The first Argentine romantic was Echeverría, who visited France when romanticism was in full sway. Sarmiento made his great defense of the romantic style in Chile, when—according to his own words—romanticism was 'already dead and buried in Europe.' And *Maria*, unquestionably the greatest Spanish American romantic novel, appeared after Blest Gana, the Chilean realist, had published three novels imitating the technique and literary theories of Balzac.

Yet despite these anachronisms, it is possible to look over the whole course of the romantic movement in Spanish America, and indicate with some degree of accuracy the main divisions of precursors of romanticism, out-and-out romantics, and post-romantics. These distinctions can be observed especially in Spanish American poetry, which went through a long evolution, and the final phases of the trend stand forth clearly. New and more refined influences acted upon the later post-romantic poets. Heine, Edgar Allan Poe, and Bécquer brought a novel musical charm into verse. They also brought more intimate themes and a new order of emotions, a new vocabulary, and a new technique. Byron and Hugo were too loud for the tender ears of the generation of 1870; romanticism had then reached its greatest development, and, like a tree that has given its fruit, it was ready to die.

In country after country, it is possible to trace this evolution of romanticism towards its final more exquisite period. Spanish America as a whole produced scores of romantic poets,[28] and these writers, throughout the middle part of the century, well illustrate the chief features of the movement: its tragic intensity, patriotic fervor, love of nature, exaltation of amorous passion. Thus, among the typical romantics, one can name Manuel Acuña (1849-73), a profound and skeptical

Mexican love-poet, who committed suicide at the age of twenty-three; Olegario Andrade (1839-82), an Argentine civic poet of merit, greatly influenced by Hugo and Longfellow; Gregorio Gutiérrez González (1826-72), a Colombian who, in his verses *On the Cultivation of Corn in Antioquia* * (1869), continued the descriptive type of poetry introduced by Bello; and Juan Clemente Zenea (1832-71), a Cuban whose melancholy stanzas are full of references to cemeteries and lost youth. But romantic poetry seemed to gain in lyrical expression as it approached the final over-refined phase of the movement.

Perhaps this can best be seen in the works of the three greatest romantic poets of Spanish America, Zorrilla de San Martín, Pérez Bonalde, and González Prada. The title of 'greatest romantic poet of the continent' has been assigned to the Uruguayan Juan Zorrilla de San Martín (1855-1931), who achieved fame throughout the Spanish-speaking world for his *Tabaré* † (1888), an indigenous legend of great beauty. This poem of six cantos, variously classified as epic or verse-novel, relates the tragic love story of Tabaré and Blanca, a part-Indian youth and a Spanish maiden, in lines which give life to the symbolic ideal of a whole continent. No less illustrious is the name of Antonio Pérez Bonalde (1846-92), the greatest Venezuelan poet of modern times and the translator of Heine and Poe. Under the influence of these two masters, he created that intimate type of elegant romanticism that was later to lead to the modernist movement. Finally, it was the Peruvian Manuel González Prada (1844-1919), who composed the most perfect verses of this post-romantic school. This remarkably talented writer was, in his life and in his works, a paragon of bitterness; for a good many years he was, from his solitary retirement, an almost single-handed 'opposition party.' And at the same time, he was a writer of pessimistic and polished

---

* Gutiérrez González, *Sobre el Cultivo del Maíz en Antioquia.*
† Zorrilla de San Martín. *Tabaré: Novela en Verso.*

poetry, the sort of stanzas that opened the way for the coming expression of modernism.

Thus, apart from its irregular spread, one sees that romanticism did run a full course in Spanish America. During the better part of sixty years, this foreign mode held sway across continents which had formerly been rigidly dominated by the mother country. It would be false to suppose, however, that the influence of Spain did not continue to be felt even during the romantic era. For one thing, there was the example of the Spanish romanticists. Even deeper were the age-old patterns of Hispanic culture. The early despotisms had done much to shatter the outward forms of this cultural development; in Paraguay, to take one example, under the fanatical isolation of the dictator Francia, old schools were closed and libraries assembled during colonial times were turned into playing-card factories! But there were thinkers still interested in what went on in Spain, and writers who followed the literary fashions of the Peninsula. The Spanish school of *costumbrismo* had disciples in the New World; though, ironically, those who described customs in American nations soon found themselves producing literary Americanism even while following Spanish models. Popular among the *costumbristas* was the Mexican Ignacio Manuel Altamirano (1834-93), a pure-blooded Indian and a soldier of Benito Juárez in the battles against Maximilian. As a poet, Altamirano had been an interpreter of the Mexican landscape; as a novelist, he wrote sketches of life in his native land—such as his *Christmas in the Mountains* (1870)—which are still read by his countrymen today. His example was followed by other Mexicans: José López Portillo y Rojas (1850-1923), whose *A Plot of Ground* (1898) shows the influence of the Spanish novelists Galdós and Pereda; and Rafael Delgado (1853-1914), another disciple of Pereda, and author of *The Lark* (1891).*

* Altamirano, *La Navidad en las Montañas;* Portillo y Rojas, *La Parcela;* Delgado, *La Calandria.*

But possibly the strongest example of the continuing Spanish current may be found in the works of the great Peruvian Ricardo Palma (1833-1919), a writer so original that he belongs to no school, save possibly the one founded by himself. To find any parallel for his satirical pen, and indeed any marked literary influence upon his works, one must go clear back to the Spanish seventeenth century and the mordant wit of Quevedo. It is no coincidence that Palma's subject matter should be drawn chiefly from the days of Spanish colonial domination, a period which he has interpreted uniquely in his delightful work, a world masterpiece of its type, the ten volumes of *Peruvian Traditions* (1872-1906).*

Palma's whole life was more or less bound up with his literary labors. Until he was nearly forty, he was chiefly known as a verse writer in a generation of romanticists. Like many another young enthusiast, he visited Europe and paid his respects personally to his favorite authors; characteristically, he was not impressed with Lamartine, but felt affectionate admiration for Zorrilla, the Spanish romantic poet who was 'then quite an old man.' Subsequently Palma, starting in his thirty-ninth year and continuing till he was past seventy, the recognized dean of Peruvian letters, published his celebrated *Traditions*—some of the volumes under titles that revealed the acidity of his pen: *Old Clothes, Motheaten Clothes, Broken Crockery.* During the latter part of his life, he was the Director of the National Library, rebuilding the great collections which had been partly destroyed by the Chileans during the War of the Pacific—a labor that would have won him renown even if he had not been the famous author of the *Traditions.*

These *Peruvian Traditions* have proved nearly as hard for critics to classify as for lesser writers to imitate. This new genre—a short sketch that was not history, anecdote, or satire, but a distillation of all three—naturally had imitators all over

* Palma, *Tradiciones Peruanas.*

Spanish America. None of them ever succeeded in coming anywhere near the work of Ricardo Palma, or in filling the recipe that he himself wrote for the concocting of a 'tradition':

> The *tradition* is a popular tale, and it's not a popular tale; it's history, and it's not history. The form must be light and merry, the telling swift and humorous. I conceived the notion of sugar-coating pills and dispensing them to the public, without worrying myself over scruples . . . A little bit, and quite a little bit of lying, a dose of the truth be it ever so infinitesimal, and a great deal of nicety and gloss in the style, and there you have the recipe for writing *traditions*.[29]

Following his own formula, Palma embroidered 'traditions' around all sorts of colonial episodes: the indiscretions of a high-born lady, the amorous adventures of a viceroy, an obscure stabbing on a cobbled street, an out-of-the-way and half-forgotten miracle come to life in his pungent, richly wrought, and almost always ironical style.

In his traditions, Palma has an almost magical power of evoking the past, often starting quite simply with some modern item that has survived from colonial times, such as a refrain or an old building:

> Across the street from the Chapel of the Miraculous Virgin, there is a house of a special architecture, a house *sui generis* which doesn't look like any other house in Lima. In spite of the breadth of its patio, the building is damp and exhales a humid vapor.[30]

But he is really at his best when writing wittily of the more talked-about women of past centuries, such as the famous actress *La Perricholi:*

> Mica Villegas was an actress of the Lima theatre, the turner of the head of the most excellent Lord Viceroy of these Kingdoms by the grace of His Majesty Charles the Third; and her illustrious lover, who never would have got a seat in the Academy for his pronunciation of

the Castilian tongue, used to apostrophize her whenever he got mad, which happens frequently among those who are fond of each other, calling her Perichóli. *The Perichóli*, whose life has been written by a better-trimmed pen than that of your humble servant, was a wench of scant beauty. It seems that his Excellency the Viceroy did not have a very delicate palate. On the other hand, Maria Castellanos, as I have had the pleasure of saying, was the prettiest little Lima brunette who ever wore four-and-a-half inch heels.[31]

Quite obviously, Palma cannot be classed with any modern school of writers; he belongs rather with the immortal wits like Rabelais, or 'poor Yorick' himself—Laurence Sterne. Surely, this Creole inheritor of Quevedo, with his racy reconstruction of Spanish colonial times, is a far cry indeed from his romantic contemporaries who were busy reproducing the stanzas of Lamartine and Victor Hugo and the sentimental grandiloquence of Chateaubriand.

But cases of Spanish influence, as on Ricardo Palma, were only the exception that proves the rule. Basically, the romantic movement in the new nations meant a liberation from Peninsular models. It was the first step towards the discovery of the native artistic genius. But Spanish America was too young, too inexperienced; her writers only substituted one source of inspiration for another. They had discovered French and English literature, but they followed them too closely. All the same, through the imitation of European tendencies, Spanish Americans had laid the groundwork for much that lay ahead. The romantic upheaval had released new forces that were to grow into the outstanding contributions of Spanish American literature. Native themes had been uncovered, if not exploited; the once-scorned American landscape had become a subject for some. Sarmiento, the apostle of romanticism, had unwittingly, in his pages attacking gaucho caudillos, laid the foundations of literary interest in the gaucho. The novel, so long forbidden in colonial times, had produced its first masterpieces, and had already recoiled from romantic idealism to the ugliness of a real world.

Even in the imitation of foreign masters, something genuinely Spanish American was about to take place. By 1888, South America had become probably the most cosmopolitan continent on earth. Her Europeanized writers had acquired a great variety in expression and a certain facility in selecting the best from many cultures. They began to rework and elaborate all the materials they had borrowed from the Old World; and the poets, in particular, soon discovered they had a new voice, a voice that was neither Spanish nor French, that sounded different from all other voices. At last Spanish America had her own poetry: a lyrical expression which was true to the many sided nature of her culture, a combination of elements only a few of which were authentically of the New World. As this novel poetry was neither classic nor romantic, neither European nor American, it was difficult to know what to call it. Spanish Americans were sure it was something new, something very modern, and for lack of a more definite name they labelled it *Modernismo*.

3

Modernism and Spanish American Poetry

THE MODERNIST MOVEMENT

TOWARDS the close of the nineteenth century, a new and extraordinary literary phenomenon appeared in Spanish America—a movement developed in the New World, but one that was to revive and revolutionize expression in the entire Spanish language. This movement of modernism was Spanish America's first original contribution to world literature, and as with most world movements a specific date can be assigned to its birth. Following the usual practice, this date must be marked not by the beginnings of the new trend, but by the appearance of the first epoch-making book of the new school.[1] The year in question was 1888; the book was *Azure*, a volume of verse and short stories; and the author was Rubén Darío, then a poor and unknown Nicaraguan poet, who was destined to become the most illustrious name in Spanish American letters.*

Without Darío, modernism might never have become a world force. It was his amazing genius that carried the new expression to its greatest heights; it was Darío personally, rather than the trend as a whole, who won followers in the Peninsula, and whose influence is still strongly felt today.

* Darío, *Azul*.

But modernism was emphatically not a 'one-man show.' Before the publication of *Azure*, modernist tendencies had appeared in other poets—Martí and Casal in Cuba, Gutiérrez Nájera in Mexico, Silva in Colombia, and still others. The modernist movement proper, given formal impetus by Darío, boasted a dozen or more distinguished poets from different parts of Spanish America—such as the Mexican Nervo, the Colombian Valencia, the Peruvian Santos Chocano, the Bolivian Jaimes Freyre, the Uruguayan Herrera y Reissig, the Argentine Lugones. There were also significant prose writers, like Díaz Rodríguez in Venezuela, who won fame with his stories, and Rodó in Uruguay, one of the most important figures in Spanish American literary history. In addition, there were modernist journals galore—the famous *Azure Review* and *Modern Review* in Mexico, the *American Review* and the *Latin Review* in Buenos Aires, *Pen and Pencil* in Chile, to name only a few.* Thus, in its continental sweep, in the number and distinction of its adherents, in the publication of organs upholding its principles, modernism ranks as a literary movement on the grand scale.

It was, too, a movement representative of the cultural life of Spanish America. Whereas the *symbolistes* represented only Parisian decadence and poetic refinement, the Spanish American modernists, some of them equally decadent in their lives and equally refined in their artistic creations, reflected the culture of an entire New World. The point must be stressed, again and again, that this culture was definitely not indigenous in its origins or its expressions; it was a European culture, shaped very largely under the tutelage of France. The cosmopolitan and predominantly French pattern of Spanish American culture had reached its zenith in the last third of the nineteenth century. Starting with the days of the liberation from Spain, French influence had spread into nearly

* *Revista Azul, Revista Moderna, Revista de América, Revista Latina, Pluma y Lápiz.*

every phase of cultured life: The homes of the well-to-do were cluttered with French furniture, statuary, and curio cabinets. All those who could afford to made a journey to Paris, many families of South Americans even remaining permanently in that capital—a tragic situation studied by the novelist Blest Gana in his book, *The Transplanted*. Young intellectuals, of course, had long made it a custom to go on a pilgrimage to France; and the example of French literature had been paramount all through the romantic movement.

Obviously, such a cultural development took little from native Spanish America. It was exotic, in that it drew elements from distant sources. It was artificial—a mode of life and thought based on the imitation of alien ways, and the ignoring of realistic problems like poverty, illiteracy, and the oppression of Indian masses. Above all, it was *afrancesado*—Frenchified. And modernism, in literature, was all of these things: exotic, artificial, and inspired upon French models.

This use of French sources was not, however, any mere imitation on the part of the modernists. Spanish America was quite independently undergoing a reaction against Romanticism, and her poets were naturally attracted by the nuances and techniques that had appeared in French poetry after the romantic movement. They welcomed the ideas of 'art for art's sake' and plastic beauty exemplified by Gautier; they plunged into Parnassianism, that search after impersonal perfection in form, of which Leconte de Lisle was the leading exponent; they adopted many of the principles of symbolism, as practiced by the followers of Verlaine—the musicality and vagueness and shade which the French master called for in his famous *Art of Poetry:*

> Music first and foremost of all!
> Choose your measure of odd not even,
> Let it melt in the air of heaven,
> Pose not, poise not, but rise and fall . . .

Let every shape of its shade be born;
Color, away! come to me, shade!
Only of shade can the marriage be made
Of dream with dream and of flute with horn.[2]

But the modernists were not concerned with imitating these French writers so much as with appropriating their innovations. And the Spanish American poets went still farther into foreign literatures in their search for new poetic methods and themes. They learned literary freedom from Walt Whitman, musicality from Poe; they imitated the Spanish poets of their own time, and they turned to Spain's Middle Ages, the ballads, and the Golden Age; they paraphrased Victor Hugo. Perhaps no one illustrated this literary cosmopolitanism better than Darío himself, for—in addition to all these—he was at one time fond of Shakespearean images, and at another he made a study of Portuguese poetry; from Carducci and Longfellow, he learned the use of pentameters and hexameters; he was dazzled by the fiery inspiration of D'Annunzio, and he once attempted bucolic poetry after the manner of Virgil.

From all these multifarious elements, modernism created a poetry of its own, one which was entirely new, new in form and vocabulary and subject matter and feeling. The renovation spread to prose as well, introducing an entirely new type of expression. Not since the seventeenth century had anything comparable happened to Spanish as a literary language. Only now the situation was reversed: the mode of this new ornate modernism spread from Spanish America to the Peninsula as a great revivifying force. It must be emphasized, of course, that this influence on the mother country was effected in large part by Darío's genius, rather than by the Spanish American modernists as a group. But it was none the less overwhelming. Upon Darío's death in 1916, the critic Henríquez Ureña wrote:

With the death of Rubén Darío, the Spanish language loses its greatest poet of today,—the greatest because of the aesthetic value and the historical significance of his work. No one, since the times of Góngora and Quevedo, has wielded an influence comparable, in renewing power, to Darío's.[3]

The force of this renovation has extended to contemporary times: virtually all the great modern Spanish stylists—Valle-Inclán, Azorín, Benavente, even Ortega in lesser degree—owe a debt to modernism; and of course all modern Spanish poetry is related to it.

So it is doubly significant that modernism as a movement should have developed the way it did in the New World. Darío wrote of it himself, pointing out its relation to the Spanish American genius:

> We had this movement of modernism in America before it appeared in Castilian Spain, and for very clear reasons: Partly, it was because of our close material and spiritual commerce with the different nations of the world; but chiefly, because there exists in the new generation of American writers an immense thirst for progress and a lively enthusiasm, which constitutes their greatest potentiality, and through which, bit by bit, they triumph over the obstacles of tradition, the walls of indifference, the oceans of mediocrity.[4]

Here, in the words of its greatest exponent, is the secret of modernism in Spanish America. If in its sources the movement was cosmopolitan and *afrancesado*, in its creation it expressed the artistic originality of a new people.

By temperament, the Spanish American has always been artistic rather than practical. The new race, produced by the association of Spaniard and Indian, had by its very origin the right to a rich artistic and spiritual life. For all the lust of the conquest, Spaniards of the sixteenth and seventeenth centuries belonged to a splendidly gifted nation. Spain's painters were Velásquez, Murillo, El Greco; her philosophers, Vives, Fox Morcillo, Juan de Valdés; her mystics, Saint Teresa, Saint

John of the Cross, and Fray Luis de Leon; her writers, Cervantes, Lope de Vega, Calderón, Góngora. At the same time, the new lands had known marvellous civilizations, of which the Mayan, Aztec, and Inca cultures were only the last examples. Astronomy, architecture, engineering, agriculture, and government had all attained a highly specialized development; and the artistic genius of these native peoples, as expressed in poetry, music, sculpture, basketry, pottery, and metal and bone work, was nothing short of astounding. With such an inheritance, it is not surprising to find the Spanish American temperamentally lost in a world of industrial and material achievements, but eagerly inclined to express himself in music and painting and poetry.

It was this creative spirit which, as Darío himself recognized, gave rise to modernism. By 1882, there appeared in almost every country of Spanish America young poets with a new understanding of their art, a new spirit of adventure, a desire to discover new worlds of imagination and beauty. Their chief aim was to be original, and to make of poetry an art in itself without any dogmatic purpose. Naturally then, they embraced the art-for-art's sake theories from France. It is not known if the Latin Americans were acquainted with Edgar Allan Poe's *Poetic Principle*, but every line of his literary manifesto can be applied to their verses, every word of his insistence that the purpose of poetry has nothing to do with didacticism, morals, or religion, his definition (which antedates that of contemporary critics by a hundred years) of pure poetry. This then was the goal of the 'new generation,' as Darío called them.

And it is significant in this connection that the young poets were impelled towards these tendencies by two of the greatest moulders of American youth: Sierra and Martí. Justo Sierra (1848-1912), the noted Mexican pedagogue, was among the first to urge his disciples to undertake the study of French poetry; and José Martí (1853-95), the great Cuban patriot, is

generally accounted a precursor of the modernist movement.
Martí, Cuba's national hero, ranks as one of South America's
titanic figures; he achieved renown as an educator, an orator,
a man of action, a journalist, and a martyr to the cause of
liberty. In his poetry, Martí was distinguished for his clarity
and simplicity, a trait he himself recognized in the title of his
Simple Songs * (1891). In some of these, like *The Girl from
Guatemala*, he fulfils all the canons of musicality, and the mixture of clearness and vagueness, laid down by Verlaine; in his
Spanish Dancer, he is as plastic as the best modernist; while in
others, he exhibits that nostalgia for the eighteenth century
and that Byzantine sensuousness, which are so noticeable in
Darío. But Martí is a precursor of modernism primarily for
his break with the 'obstacles of tradition . . . and oceans of
mediocrity,' and his pointing the way towards literary liberation.

Of course, there were other precursors too—notably the
many exquisite post-romantics who paved the way for the advent of modernism, just as post-romanticism had preceded
Parnassianism and symbolism in France. Some of these writers
had a direct influence on figures who were outstanding in the
modernist movement; thus, the Mexican Salvador Díaz Mirón
(1853-1928) influenced such noted poets as Darío and Santos
Chocano. Strictly speaking, Díaz Mirón, the author of *Chips
from a Stone* † (1901)—like Martí and Justo Sierra—belongs
on the borderline of modernism. At first a romantic, both in
his imitation of Byron and Hugo and in his romantic principles
of conduct which led him to fight duels, he was later a per-
fectionist in form. Basically, however, modernism did not
spring from the example of any single forerunner, but from
the operation of two deep-rooted and widely separated tendencies: On the one hand, the desire of a young generation of
Americans for new artistic expression; on the other hand the

* Martí, *Versos Sencillos.*
† Díaz Mirón, *Lascas.*

inspiration of certain European techniques. So it is hardly surprising to find two distinct tendencies within modernism itself. There was an earlier movement of escapism, in which poets wrote of exotic and imaginary themes, and took refuge in an ivory tower of poesy. Later, there was a wave of New-Worldism in which modernists turned their attention to Spanish America's own history and landscape and people. In all of this, however, there was a certain continental unity, a common aesthetic sensibility, a similarity of artistic forms; even the 'New Worldists' were escapists in their lives and the handling of native subjects. And both of the trends appeared in turn in the works of that incredibly fertile genius, Rubén Darío.

THE ESCAPISTS

MANY modernist poets—and their work was most typical of the movement—sought to escape from reality into a fanciful imaginary world. They searched for inspiration in far-away climes and foreign writers: Casal was greatly attracted by Japanese patterns; Gutiérrez Nájera followed the Spanish Bécquer and the French Gautier; Silva was fond of the English pre-Raphaelites, and imitated some of the musical schemes of Poe; Jaimes Freyre was attracted by Scandinavian mythology; Nervo found a haven in Buddhist philosophy. As a result, they wrote of oriental splendor, Greek goddesses, Versailles, Salome's dance, and the like; their verses were peopled by satyrs, nymphs, centaurs, peacocks, and swans. Because of this, the modernists have often been charged with artificiality. They were nevertheless quite sincere, as all escapists are, and their exoticism was only a protest against hard bitter realities.

This is very evident in the three acknowledged precursors of modernism—Casal, who suffered with a painful form of tuberculosis; Gutiérrez Nájera, whom fate had made hideously ugly; and Silva, an almost neurotically sensitive spirit who committed suicide at thirty-one. All of them hated the real world in which they found themselves imprisoned, and Casal, for example, had but one ambition: 'to behold another sky, another mountain, another shore, another horizon, another sea. Other people, other races, with different habits of thought.' This escapist attitude was typical of the sensitive temperament of the early modernist poets.

> The young idealist of those days felt himself a spirit thrown . . . into an environment to which he did not belong. He had a soul above the sordid aims of his fellow-men, and his art and his ideals were things beyond their comprehension . . . Finding little sympathy in the world of men, and having none of the missionary zeal that would have converted them to his way of thinking, he naturally turned away and found solace in the world of the imagination.[5]

One of the earliest, and one of the most completely malad-justed, of these escapist poets was Julian del Casal (1863-98). A tubercular invalid who spent all his life in his native Havana, he yet wrote, in perhaps his most representative poem, *In the Country*, 'the atmosphere of a sick-chamber attracts my languid senses more than the fragrance of a mahogany forest'! Decadence and a fondness for macabre details permeate his verse; in his filigreed love poems he expresses little passion, but rather the sentiments of what one might call a worldly an-chorite. Even his total despair is marked by a certain tone of indifference, reminiscent of Baudelaire:

> My heart was a vase of alabaster, where there grew in fragrant solitude, beneath the purest gleam of a star, a single white lily—prayer. Withered is this flower of deli-cate perfume, like a virgin consumed by anemia. Today in my heart grows a purple rosebush—blasphemy.[6]

Darío found him a tormented visionary with 'something of the other world in his strange pupils,' but in his verses Casal seems rather the cold and perfect Parnassian, the virtuoso of the rhymed measure. Something of this dualism may be seen even in the titles of his volumes of verse—*Leaves in the Wind*

(1890) and *Busts and Rimes* (1893)—with their implications of desolation and refuge in art.*

Equally tormented in his life, but of greater depth as an artist, was the Mexican Manuel Gutiérrez Nájera (1859-95), as exquisite in verse as he was hideous in body. Gutiérrez Nájera played a significant role in the formation of modernism, in his direction of the *Azure Review* which he founded in 1894; for the kindly reception it accorded to all efforts at literary novelty, his journal was as important as Darío's book of the same name. Had he lived longer, and been less burdened by his journalistic activities, Gutiérrez Nájera might have become a much greater poet. As it was, his life was a minor edition of Darío's own tragedy: alcoholism, physical ugliness, eroticism—and the escape into song. In his poetry, he was a romantic as concerns the emotions he expressed, the mystical longings of the spirit, the sad elegy of love. Thus, in his *Saddest Night* † he evokes a weird atmosphere of tragedy and mystery, in which the cries of unhappy women, the trotting of invisible horses, and the screams of cats mingle with the eerie wails of lost souls. This is pure romanticism, but in many other respects Gutiérrez Nájera was a modernist. His verses, with their clarity and perfection of form, their incomparable polish and subjectivity, exhibited a mastery of French Parnassianism and symbolism. His prose was plastic like Gautier's; his poetry musical like Verlaine's. But all this was tempered by his native Mexican candor in contrast with French intellectualism. Thus he was a typical precursor of modernism—a member of that sensitive, inwardly tortured group, pretending to accept his destiny with tragic calm:

> To remember, to forgive, to have loved, to have been for a moment happy, to have believed . . . and then, to recline wearily upon the snowy shoulder of oblivion.[7]

* Casal, *Hojas al Viento, Bustos y Rimas.*
† Gutiérrez Nájera, *Tristissima Nox.*

But the most sensitive of the three precursors, and the one who had the greatest influence upon later modernist poets, was the ill-starred Colombian José Asunción Silva (1865-96). Silva was a morbidly sensitive and frustrated soul who had nothing in common with the rigid centuries-old atmosphere of his native city. Bogotá in those days had a completely colonial aspect: massive buildings, quiet patios, monotonous plazas, the cathedral with its odor of flowers and incense and melted wax. Social and intellectual life was colonial, too: señoras said their prayers in the evenings and gossiped in the afternoons; old gentlemen played cards and discussed politics; the Bishop was the arbiter of literary taste, with his elegant and empty sermons; poets composed gallant and perfect sonnets in eleven-syllable lines with conventional rhymes and required accents; and grammarians and cautious stylists prided themselves on their pure Castilian style and classic forms. In such a milieu, Silva was a rebellious spirit, tormented by the hidden demon of acute sensibility. He did not write sonnets, but free verse; he lived his own life, with tragic intensity; he was a free thinker, and he believed in free love. His literary friends were not the ancient writers of Spain, but the decadent moderns— Poe, D'Annunzio, Baudelaire. He was misunderstood, maligned, persecuted; and his whole existence was a series of hammer blows from fate: crushing economic burdens, the death of a beloved sister, the shipwreck of the *Amérique* with some of his finest manuscripts on board. Finally, he felt the approach of insanity:

> I am thine; thou art mine. I am madness. Mad? And why not? Thus died Baudelaire; thus died Maupassant. Then why should you not die thus, poor debauché who abused everything, who dreamed of ruling over art, of mastering all science, all knowledge, and of draining all the glasses into which Life pours its supreme intoxication?[8]

In his thirty-first year, Silva put a bullet through his heart.

But this unhappy youth had given something new to Spanish poetry—a music, a pessimism, a lyric quality never heard before. In his writings one can trace the effects of Mallarmé, Verlaine, and Baudelaire; some passages suggest Bécquer, and others are clearly reminiscent of Poe's *Annabel Lee* and *The Bells*. Yet Silva's muse was a very personal one. His poems of childhood have a strange mixture of ingenuousness and shadowy melancholy. And his love poems rank among the finest ever written in the Spanish language, particularly his celebrated *Third Nocturne:* *

One night,
One night filled with murmurs and perfumes and the
    music of wings,
One night
When fantastic fireflies blazed in the moist nuptial
    shadows,
By my side slowly, clasped to me, pale and silent,
As if a presentiment of infinite bitterness
Agitated the most secret depths of your heart,
Over the blossomy path through the meadow
You wandered;
And the full moon
Scattered white light over bluish skies, boundless and
    deep.
And your shadow
Frail and languid,
And my shadow
By the rays of the moon projected
Over the gloomy sand,
Joined together
And were one,
And were one,
And were one,
And were one long shadow,
And were one long shadow,
And were one long shadow . . .[9]

* Silva, *Nocturno III.*

No less an escapist was the Colombian Guillermo Valencia (1872-   ), a poetic disciple of his unhappy countryman Silva. But Valencia's escapism was more a matter of artistic preference than inward torment. Of aristocratic family and solid classical training, and one-time candidate for the presidency, he yet possessed the same refinement and acute sensibility that characterized the author of the *Nocturnes*. His cosmopolitan temperament led him to make studies of French, Italian, and Portuguese poets, whose works he translated admirably in *Rites* (1898); and he even published a volume, *Catay* (1928), containing translations from the Chinese.* Of all the modernist poets, he was the most purely Parnassian, in his cult of form, the perfection of his rhymes, the metallic sonorousness of his stanzas. Some of his poems, like *Reading Silva* and *The Camels*, have achieved continental renown, and place him in the very forefront of modernism.

Both of these celebrated works well illustrate Valencia's fondness for the exotic imagery of which he was such a master—as, for instance, this picture of the languid lady fingering a volume of poems:

> She wore a flowing garment, embroidered, translucent,
> In voluptuous folds of changing color uncertain,
>
> And, as she reclined on a divan of crimson velvet,
> Her hands, like parasites clinging, ice-cold yet living,
>
> Sustained a volume long-shaped and daintily fashioned,
> A book of poems of mingled sweet and bitter.
>
> The soft, warm tips of those pale and delicate fingers
> Toyed lightly with the pages of fine Dutch paper . . .

Or again, this picture of the two camels, doubtless symbolizing two poets:

> With supple necks and clear green eyes, with hair
> Tawny and smooth like silk, with heads held back

* Valencia, *Ritos, Catay*.

And nostrils wide, two camels with an air
Of languor pace the Nubian desert's track.

They raise their heads to find their course, then halt
The dreamy progress of their hairy limbs—
Beneath the red dome of that fiery vault—
Mute, at the cisterns' base, as daylight dims . . .

This poem, indeed, expresses the very height of Valencia's escapism—his idea that the poet must needs escape from the prosaic world. 'In *Los Camellos*,' writes Dundas Craig, 'the camels represent the poet himself and a sympathetic friend, in all probability José Asunción Silva. Both are men of deep culture, with an intense love of beauty, and the same scorn for the vulgar who care for none of these things. They have therefore abandoned their fellows and are sojourning in the desert.'

But the escapist trend in modernist poetry was by no means confined to these unfortunate precursors and their immediate disciples. The love of the exotic was a natural one to the poetic temperament, and it appeared quite as strongly in well-rounded personalities, as the distinguished Nervo and the intellectual Jaimes Freyre. The Bolivian Ricardo Jaimes Freyre (1870-1933) was an exotic poet by choice. A diplomat who served as Secretary of Foreign Affairs and Minister to Río and to Washington, an educator who was co-founder of the University of Tucumán, he was much more of a balanced intellect than a Bohemian. Yet he was a poet, too. He looked the 'artist,' with his smooth Moorish complexion, his fierce mustachios, his mane of wild hair. And he was a pioneer modernist, founding in 1896 (together with Darío and Lugones) the short-lived *American Review*. In fact, he was the only member of the modernist movement to write a volume on poetical theory, his anti-classical and highly original *Laws of Spanish Versification* (1912).

Jaimes Freyre was, then, an escapist by intent, and in his

one significant volume of poems, *Barbaric Fountain* (1899),* he wrote on subjects from Norse mythology—Lot, the elves, Valhalla, Ultima Thule. His verses have a remarkable power of evoking the magic of the North, as in his *Mournful Voices:*

> Over the snowy steppe
> The sledge glides on;
> The distant howling of the wolves
> Mingles with the panting breath of the dogs.
>
> It snows.
> The wide expanse seems shrouded in a veil
> Sprinkled with lilies
> By the wings of the north wind . . .
>
> Between the sepulchral shrouds
> Of earth and sky,
> Advances in the East
> The freezing twilight of the winter dawn . . .[10]

But despite his 'barbaric' songs, Jaimes Freyre paints in the end the triumph of Christianity over paganism; a strange new deity appears in the Northern forests, and despite the thunderings of Thor:

> In the sacred wood the old psalms sound no longer,
> Nor the soft voice of Freya as she sings in the distance.
> On Orga's tongue the divine song is extinguished.
>   Tall, alone in the shade,
> Stands a silent god with wide arms extended.[11]

This is exoticism indeed, but of a very special variety. Jaimes Freyre closes his eyes to the realities of daily life; but his verses on distant themes have about them a vague universal melancholy and a trenchant meaning.

Similarly profound in his escapism was the greatest Mexican modernist, Amado Nervo (1870-1919). Like Jaimes Freyre, he helped establish one of the leading organs of the new movement, the *Modern Review*, which he founded in 1898 with

* Jaimes Freyre, *Leyes de la versificación castellana, Castalia Bárbara.*

Valenzuela. And Nervo, too, was a diplomat, serving for thirteen years as secretary to the Mexican legation in Madrid, and at his death being the Mexican Minister to Uruguay. But Nervo was a man-of-letters above all—his complete works fill twenty-eight volumes—and his story was that of the inward life, reflected in his verse. As a young man he had studied for the priesthood, but stopped short before the final step. His early poems reflected a certain pantheistic sentiment; later, he wrote almost like a mystic.

> Nervo, however, did not attain to this power of mystic absorption without struggle. Like Darío, like Verlaine, he experienced the seductions of the flesh and the torments of a stylite; but the combat between the soul and the body, the spiritual and the material, Christ and Pan, which in Darío ceased only with death, had in the Mexican poet an earlier and happier ending.[12]

In consequence, it is not surprising to find Nervo's poetry characterized by an ascetic melancholy and an ultimate serenity, which in his last years took on an oriental tone as he became absorbed in the principles of Buddhism. Most of his verses are devoted to this inward road, but perhaps Nervo best summarized himself in *Translucency*:

> I am a pensive soul.
> Do you know what a pensive soul is?
> Sad, but with that cool
> Melancholy
> Of all soft
> Translucencies. All that exists,
> Turning diaphanous is serene and sad.[13]

This translucent spirit was also a consummate craftsman. Nervo's poetry is marked by musical effects, innovations of metre, transparent imagery. But often he uses this outward perfection of form to convey some sense of inner mystery, as he does in *As in a Dream*:

Yesterday came Blanca;
Silent she looked at me,
And more mysterious seemed than e'er before:
As are the things that in our dreams we see . . .

Slowly, very slowly
She deigned to smile on me,
But with expression rare, like that of those
Whose lips enwreathed with smiles in dreams we see . . .

What melancholy gazed
From her dark eyes on me!
The melancholy that no words can tell
Saddening the faces that in dreams we see . . .

She looked on me, and went
Away with step so free,
So light—none lighter ever was—a step
Like that of phantoms which in dreams we see . . .[14]

Federico de Onís has called attention to the resignation which
marks Nervo's religious thought—an emotion typical of the
Mexican, with his attitude of submission and uncomplaining
acceptance of destiny. This unworldly 'turning of the other
cheek' is expressed by Nervo in perfectly worked cameos, like
Revenge:

Somebody at my roof throws stones, and then
Hides his hands quickly, and as guiltless poses.
I have no stones, for only rosebushes
With sweet fresh flowers my garden ground encloses;
But still it is my fancy and my way
To hide my hand, too, after throwing roses! [15]

For Nervo's escape tended towards sublimation, as may be
noted in the titles of some of his books—*Serenity* (1914), *Elevation* (1916), *Plenitude* (1918).* He was one of those rare
souls who manage to escape from the torments of the outer
world to the peace of the world within.

* Nervo, *Serenidad, Elevación, Plenitud.*

RUBÉN DARÍO

BUT of course, the greatest of the escapist poets was Rubén Darío (1867-1916). Darío's whole life and entire poetic creation can be understood only by the psychology of escape. He exhibited always an incredible contrast between the sordidness of his existence and the exquisite beauty of his poetry, almost a dualism of his nature, as he himself recognized in commenting on the difference between his wide dark-skinned Chorotega Indian face and his slender transparent hands of an aristocrat. In real life, Darío, at his most prosperous, lived in cheaply furnished tasteless apartments with advertising handbills on the walls; in his verses, he inhabited the court of Heliogabalus, with its gold and silk and marble. His real mistresses were women of the type of Francisca Sánchez, humble and devoted but little more than a servant; his poetical loves were pallid Princesses or Marquises from Versailles. His entire worldly career was one of economic failure and complete moral disintegration; his poetical career was an unparalleled example of achievement and artistic integrity!

Darío started life on January 18, 1867, in Metapa, Nicaragua, under the more prosaic name of Félix Rubén García—later assuming the surname of 'Darío' from a relative.[16] Raised by his aunts and an uncle, the child was nervous and sickly, afflicted with nasal hemorrhages and night-terrors. He was precocious, too: he wrote his first poems when he was eleven, for a Holy Week procession a little shower of verses designed to fall from a paper pomegranate that hung near his house. The first books he laid hands on were *Don Quixote*, the works of Moratín, the *Thousand-and-one Nights*, the Bible, Cicero's *Epistles*, Mme de Stael's *Corinne*, and a spine-chiller entitled *The Cavern of Strozzi*—strange fare for an adolescent genius! Until he was twenty-one, Darío lived now in Nicaragua, now in the neighboring Republic of San Salvador—distinguished only for his romantic-style long hair, his youthful amorous entanglements, his early journalistic efforts which landed him in prison, and his extensive reading of Spanish classics while occupying a subordinate post in the National Library at Managua.

In 1886, Darío, on the advice of friends, left Central America for Chile, where he was to pass some of his most formative years. His life in Santiago was one of abject poverty and bitter struggle; to earn a living, he wrote for the *Epoch*, receiving wages that never quite paid for his food and lodging. But he did become a close friend of Pedro Balmaceda, the son of the President; and in the well-stocked library of this wealthy youth, Darío became familiar with the latest French authors, the Parnassians and the symbolists. From Santiago, Darío went to Valparaíso, where he was a customs employee and also wrote for the *Herald*. It was here that he finally brought out *Azure* (1888), which instantly aroused attention in the critical world, but did little to improve the author's economic situation. In the end, Darío became a foreign correspondent for the great Argentine newspaper *The Nation*,* a publication with which he was connected for the rest of his life. He formed other lasting patterns, too, about this time: Before leaving for Europe on his new assignment, he revisited Central America, where he married a childhood sweetheart, Rafaela Contreras; two years later a son was born—and Darío promptly abandoned his wife and child! He never saw Rafaela again, for when he returned to Nicaragua a few years later, she had already died; shortly thereafter, he was forced into a marriage with Rosario Murillo, from whom he became estranged almost immediately. Darío evidently was not cut out for wedded bliss.

Journalism was not a congenial life for the poet, either, though it was his one gainful occupation. Still, his connections with *The Nation* enabled him to travel abroad, and to live for many years in Buenos Aires, Madrid, and Paris. Darío was a

* *La Época, El Heraldo, La Nación.*

vagabond by nature—he describes himself in *The Singer Travels across the Earth*—and he never took roots in any of these capitals. Paris was perhaps his spiritual home. On his first visit there, he met Verlaine, pouring out all his youthful admiration to *pauvre Lelian* who was then in the last stages of alcoholism. The Nicaraguan, unfortunately, was not long in following his poetic master on the paths of dipsomania. Young Darío perfected his habits of dissipation in the 'artificial paradises' of Buenos Aires, and soon he was back in Paris once more, to live in Montmartre. Darío was now a complete Bohemian: he wore a beard; he became a confirmed gourmet, regaling himself with delicacies like golden pheasant; he used to shut himself up in his garret room to drink rum for weeks on end. When he went to Madrid to represent Nicaragua at the third centenary of *Don Quixote*, he became 'incapacitated,' and his friend Martínez Sierra had to read his verses for him.

But the incredible books of poems continued to appear, *Profane Prose* in 1896, and *Songs of Life and Hope* in 1905.* Darío was a master now, his glory recognized by the most important critics of Spain; the leading Spanish writers—Valle-Inclán, Unamuno, Castelar, Campoamor, Benavente, Baroja, Jiménez, the Machados—were all his friends and admirers. Only one thing was lacking to make the apotheosis complete: honor in his own country. Darío went home to Nicaragua in 1907, where he was acclaimed like a conquering hero: In León, he was carried on the shoulders of the crowd, and fêted with champagne; in Managua, he was greeted by cheering throngs, brass bands, electric-light displays, church-bells, and a symbolic crown from the Young Ladies' Normal School! Still further distinctions were in store for him: Darío had long cherished diplomatic ambitions—he had already held several posts as Consul and Boundary-Commissioner and Envoy—and now he was appointed Minister to Spain. It was one of the hap-

---

* Darío, *Prosas Profanas, Cantos de Vida y Esperanza.*

piest moments of his life when, in the gold braid of a borrowed ambassador's suit, he kissed the hand of the beautiful Spanish Queen. But the Nicaraguan Government soon stopped sending his salary, and he had to give up the Legation and return to Paris.

Decadence set in rapidly. At the beginning of 1911, his will power quite gone, he was a helpless tool in the hands of the Messrs. Guido, a pair of unscrupulous impresarios. They used his name as director of a commercial magazine; they took him on tour through Spain and Spanish America; they exhibited him in Paris at a daily 'subscription banquet.' Darío was now gravely ill with cerebral anemia, and he escaped at last—trying in vain to recuperate in Mallorca, and in a domestic ménage with poor Francisca Sánchez in Barcelona. But his meager means were gone. A Nicaraguan adventurer persuaded him to come to America on a lecture-tour; in New York, Darío fell ill with pneumonia; penniless, he accepted the hospitality of the Guatemalan dictator, Estrada Cabrera, who installed the dying poet in a hotel where wine ran free and parasites crowded the sick-chamber. At last, his wife Rosario swooped down upon him and removed him to Nicaragua, where he was operated on for acute cirrhosis—the result of extreme alcoholism—and died under the surgeon's knife on February 6, 1916.

But this unstable and childlike human being was endowed with the 'sorrowful gift of genius.' Darío's three most important books—*Azure, Profane Prose, Songs of Life and Hope*—were landmarks in the development of the new modernist movement. *Azure,* which gave official direction to modernism, was definitely Parnassian, with its emphasis on form and imagery. *Profane Prose,* Darío's second great book, marked the high point of modernism; it continued the Parnassian tendency in plastic pieces like 'Frieze,' but in poems like 'The Kingdom Within,' it revealed the influence of symbolism as well. *Songs of Life and Hope,* Darío's greatest collection, showed in addition the effect of his study of old Spanish ballads; of all his works, it was the richest in technical mastery, and the strongest in lyric beauty. Darío later published still other volumes of poetry, *Ode to Mitre* (1906), *The Errant Song* (1907), *Song to Argentina* (1910), *Autumn Poem* (1910), which contain some of his finest work,* but his outstanding achievement lay in his first three great books. No other Spanish poet had contributed so much in the way of innovations in versification and the releasing of new types of artistic expression.

> Darío . . . gave vogue, and finally permanence, to a large number of metrical forms: either verses rarely used, like the ennea-syllabic and the dodecasyllabic (of which there are three types), or verses, like the alexandrine, to which . . . [he] gave greater musical virtue by freeing the accent and the caesura. Even the hendecasyllable acquired new flexibility when Darío brought back two new forms of accentuation that had been used by Spanish poets during three centuries but had been forgotten since about 1800. He also attacked the problem of the classic hexameter, which has tempted many great modern poets . . . He introduced, finally, the modern *vers libre* . . .[17]

But Darío's exotic images and delicate nuances of shading were as much an innovation as were his new techniques. In his verses, he was able to escape almost entirely from the murk of his real existence into an imaginary world of ideal beauty. True, traces of his life do find their way into his poems—the pleasures of the flesh particularly, and the agonies of doubt and remorse. But he spends much of his time singing of that poetic universe which he created, and which he peopled with swans and pagan deities and eighteenth-century Pompadours:

> I am the singer who of late put by
> The verse azulean and the chant profane,

* Darío, *Oda a Mitre, El Canto Errante, Canto a la Argentina, Poema del Otoño y Otros Poemas.*

> Across whose nights a rossingnol would cry
> And prove himself a lark at morn again.
>
> Lord was I of my garden-place of dreams,
> Of heaping roses and swan-haunted brakes;
> Lord of the doves; lord of the silver streams,
> Of gondolas and lilies on the lakes.
>
> And very eighteenth century; both old
> And very modern; bold, cosmopolite;
> Like Hugo daring, like Verlaine half-told,
> And thirsting for illusions infinite.[18]

The swan, indeed, was Darío's sign and symbol. It was the perfect example of beauty serving no useful purpose, and he praised the Wagnerian bird again and again, as in these lines from *Blazon:*

> Olympian-proud and white as snow,
> With rosy agate beak, the swan
> Makes his short stainless wings to glow
> That open sunward a chaste fan . . .
>
> Give love then, Countess, to the swans,
> Gods of a land with charm that teems;
> Of perfume made, with ermine fans,
> Of dawning light, of silk and dreams.[19]

Equally characteristic was Darío's paganism, as expressed in poems like *Colloquy of the Centaurs* and *Palimpsest*—not the genuine feeling of classic antiquity, but the artificial and decadent Hellenism of France. He seemed to have a special gift of evoking music and exuberance from quasi-pagan themes, as he does in *Spring Song:*

> Now is come the month of roses!
> To the woods my verse has flown
> Gathering fragrance and honey
> From the blossoms newly blown.
> Beloved, come to the forest,
> The woodland shall be our shrine
> Scented with holy perfume
> Of the laurel and the vine . . .

> Sweetest, of that glorious hymnal
> I shall choose the fairest phrase
> To enrich with ancient music
> The full cadence of my lays.
> Sweet as sweetest Grecian honey
> Will my song be when I sing,
> O Beloved, in the season
> Of the Spring! [20]

Yet, for all his escapism, Darío's works contain still another note, which made him not only 'the poet of the swans' but also 'the poet of America.' Starting especially with *Songs of Life and Hope*, themes of pan-Hispanism and Americanism appear strongly in his works. His famous 'Optimist's Salutation,' expressing his faith in the Hispanic spirit after the mother land had lost her last colonial possessions:

> Famous and fruitful races, blood of Spain the prolific,
> Spirits fraternal, souls all luminous, greeting! [21]

his *Cyrano in Spain*, *Goya*, and other poems attest to his profound penetration of the Spanish heritage. Possibly his most celebrated work of this sort is the magnificent 'Litany for Our Lord Don Quixote,' of which these brief extracts will serve as a sample:

> Pray for us, generous, pious, and most proud one;
> Pray for us, chaste, pure, heavenly, unbowed one,
> Pray for the worthless, intercede for our sod!
> Since we are now without vigor or glory,
> Without soul, without life, without your grand story,
> Without foot or wing, without Sancho or God!
>
> From so many sorrows, from griefs heart-wringing,
> From supermen of Nietzsche, from Aphonic singing,
> From the prescriptions that doctors give to us,
> From the epidemics of horrible blasphemies
> Of the academies,
> Good Lord, deliver us! . . . [22]

And, incredible as it seems, this escapist Darío won renown not only as an interpreter of Spain, but as a poet of the New

World as well. His 'Columbus,' 'Tutecotzimí,' and 'Song to Argentina' all strike a note of firm and profound Americanism. In 'To Theodore Roosevelt,' he sounded a protest against 'Yankee imperialism' that gained him the applause of a continent; while in 'Salutation to the Eagle,' he foreshadowed a Pan-Americanism which was then little more than a feeble hope. For Darío was the complete master of modernism in all its many ramifications. His was the greatest technical skill, the greatest success with metrical innovations. He was the escapist *par excellence*—and at the same time the poet of that New Worldism which was to mark the end of the modernist movement.

New Worldism

EVEN before Darío broke with his earlier formalism to write verses on Spanish and American themes, other writers had discovered poetic material in the New World. Indeed, the evolution from a period of escape to one of thoughtful realism was characteristic of the entire modernist movement, which went through three phases, not always clearly differentiated from one another: First appeared a basic native sensibility that expressed itself in the evasion of reality and the taste for things cosmopolitan. Second came a similarity of artistic forms, due to the assimilating genius of the school and the prevailing influence of French literary models. And third, a growing consciousness of racial values and Spanish American social and political responsibilities. This final tendency appeared in some of the most confirmed escapists—like Darío himself, in spite of his avowed detestation for his own times; in the mystic and sensitive Nervo, whose *Epithalamium* sings of the beauty of the Castilian tongue and the future spiritual unity between Spain and her former colonies; in Valencia, who, for all his Parnassianism, frequently used his pen with vigor on social questions. With certain poets the new stirrings took more open forms: now a revolt against swans and *fêtes galantes;* now a choice of subject matter drawn from the Conquest, or

the South American landscape, or some simple scene of daily
life. This later phase of the modernist movement is generally
referred to under the term of *mundonovismo* or 'New Worldism'—though it should be remembered that the earlier type of
modernism, for all its artificiality of themes, represented none
the less the poetic aspirations of a New World.

An important figure in the reaction against the exotic type
of modernism was the Mexican Enrique González Martínez
(1871–1952). A physician for seventeen years in the towns of
Mazatlán and Mocorito, he was later a professor in Mexico
City, and finally a diplomat to Argentina, Chile, and Spain—a
career which aptly symbolizes the broadening horizons of his
poetry. At first he was a disciple of Gutiérrez Nájera, and like
most modernists was much influenced by Baudelaire and Verlaine, of whose poems he published 'versions' in his *Gardens
of France*. But in his later books he expressed a new concept
of the function of poetry: art for art's sake is not enough, for
art must lead to truth and goodness; the poet must seek to
penetrate externals and discover the hidden mysteries of human existence. These ideas found expression in his *Silenter*
(1909), *The Hidden Paths* (1911), and *The Death of the Swan*
(1915).* For it was against Darío's 'Olympian birds' that
González Martínez vented his disdain—in the famous sonnet,
'Wring the Neck of the Swan,' which put an end to the her-
aldic pomp of modernism:

> Wring the neck of the lying feathered swan
> That gives a white note to the azure fountain!
> It glides in grace, but never thinks upon
> The soul of things, the voice from out the mountain.
>
> Flee from every form and every fashion
> Through which life's latent rhythm does not roll;
> Only life itself adore with passion,
> And let life know this homage of your soul.

* González Martínez, *Jardines de Francia, Silenter, Los Senderos
Ocultos, La Muerte del Cisne.*

> Observe that sober owl which takes his flight
> From Olympus and the refuge Pallas made
> To rest himself in silence on his tree.
> Although he has no swan's grace, you can see
> His sober profile sharp against the shade
> Interpreting the mystery of night.[23]

Yet, for all his advice to discover 'the soul of things,' González Martínez remained very much of an aloof artist—Isaac Goldberg calls him an 'intellectual pantheist.' He was able to discard the swan, but only for another symbol: the owl; it was for other modernist poets to come closer to reality.

One of these, surprisingly, was the Uruguayan Julio Herrera y Reissig (1875-1910), whose life was the very essence of escapism. Although his family had been prominent in public affairs, he deliberately turned away from the world and withdrew to an attic in the Calle Ituzaingó of Montevideo, a retreat that he named the 'Tower of the Panoramas' after a set of engravings on its walls. Here a Bohemian group gathered and issued extravagantly novel verse which provoked a storm of controversy. Herrera's own poems were characterized by exuberance of vocabulary, extraordinary figures, obscurity, rapid impressionism—in short, by every manner of out-of-the-way effect. But his subject matter, oddly enough, was often drawn from ordinary daily life, and he excelled in painting humble rustic scenes in which his love of nature and the landscape of his native country—Uruguay—is revealed. Perhaps this contrast between novelty of form and simplicity of subject can be best seen by comparing some of the *précieux* titles of his volumes—*The Matins of the Night* (1902), *Violet Poems* (1906), *Twilight Pianos* (1910),*—with his realistic sketch of a workingman's 'Supper':

> A clatter of tin proclaims the evening meal . . .
> The laborer sets his fat bulk down, and takes

* Herrera y Reissig, *Los Maitines de la Noche, Poemas Violetas, Pianos Crepusculares.*

The lion's share, like monks with the Pope's own seal;
Left hand relieving right, good speed he makes . . .

And as his hungry brood the victuals praise,
Sniffing the savory mess, he works his jaw,
And while his merit more than appetite he weighs,
Crams double soup and cabbage down his maw . . .

Then as he hiccoughs by the embers' glow,
And, sunk in pipe-smoke, nothing more can want,
The winter's lulling tales make murmur low,
Of Riding Hood and the Wolf, Snow White, and the
    Ant . . .
The children, chicken-like, their mother near,
Shudder with ecstasy and simple fear.[24]

Equally interesting is the case of the Argentine modernist
Leopoldo Lugones (1874-1938), a poet who, like Darío, exhibited many different phases in his verse, including one period
of frank Americanism. He too exhibited conflicting trends in
his life and works. An avowed socialist and ardent nationalist,
he was long active in public life, serving as Director of the
National Council of Education, representing his country on
the Committee of Intellectual Co-operation of the League of
Nations, and publishing a number of books on Argentine history. Yet as a poet, his first three volumes were chiefly concerned with novelty of form and expression: *Mountains of
Gold* (1897), with its unrhymed free verse in the style of Walt
Whitman; *Twilights in the Garden* (1905), with its ironical
use of all the devices of Parnassianism; and *Sentimental Lunar
Almanack* (1909), with its frequent terms from medicine and
chemistry and physics.* But the main contribution of Lugones
was his realism, which first appeared in *The Bachelor:*

> . . . By an evil-looking trunk
> A bed stands white and cold,
> And on its rusty nail

* Lugones, *Las Montañas del Oro, Los Crepúsculos del Jardín, Lunario
Sentimental.*

> A water color, in a blue
> Plush frame, hangs, growing old.
>
>   The dress coat in the closet
> Crucified on its rack
> Smells heavy with carbolic;
> And over the bulky inkstand
> Is a pensive bust, Balzac . . .[25]

Lugones' realism reached a climax in his *Century Odes* of 1910, written on the occasion of the hundredth anniversary of Argentine Independence, and containing songs to different cities and a hymn 'To the Cattle and the Harvest Fields.' In later works, *The Book of Landscapes* (1917) and *Manor-house Poems* (1928), he continued his realistic pictures of native scenes,* writing brilliantly concrete verse, at times narrative and discursive, and again shrewdly evocatory. Thus, in 'Journey,' with its tone of desert-like desolation, he suggests the emotions of the Argentinian lost in the pampas-like expanses of his own soul:

> I met upon the road
> A woman and a man,
> And a tree that genuflected
> Before the wind;
> Farther on, a browsing burro;
> And farther still, a heap of stone.
> And in three thousand leagues of my spirit
> There was no more than these:
> A tree, a stone, a burro,
> A woman, and a man.[26]

But of all the modernist poets, perhaps the most completely American was the Peruvian José Santos Chocano (1875-1934). In the Preface to Chocano's first book, Darío thus addressed him: 'Yours is the muse representative of our culture, our modern Spanish American soul.' Chocano lived his Americanism as passionately as he wrote it. He was a revolutionist in politics,

* Lugones, *Odas Seculares, El Libro de los Paisajes, Poemas Solariegos.*

a champion of the Indian, a vigorous protester against 'Yankee imperialism'; his life was one of intrigues, arrests, crusades; he was assassinated while riding on a streetcar. Yet, although he wrote that 'The United States holds fast with an iron ring one foot of Latin America [Panama],' he felt a great admiration for his Anglo-Saxon neighbors, and was fond of remarking: 'Walt Whitman has the North, but I have the South.' And in his very Americanism, he was grandiloquent almost to the point of megalomania, rather than realistic—as may be seen in the titles of his books: *The Soul of America* (1906), *Let There Be Light* (1908), *First Fruits of Gold from the Indies* (1934).* He was tropical, bombastic, Hugoesque, enlarging everything he touched. Typically, he used to call himself the grandson of a fierce captain of the Conquest and an Inca princess. His vision of America did indeed resemble the immense panorama of the first discoverers, whether his verses dealt with colonial times or more recent American themes. Naturally, he was at his best when his exuberant racial lyricism had free play in a poem like 'Horses of the Conquistadors':

> The horses were strong!
> The horses were eager!
> Their necks finely-arched; and shining
> Their flanks; and musical their hoof-beats.
>> The horses were strong!
>> The horses were ready!
>
> No, not the warriors only,
> With plumes and cuirasses and fire-brands and banners,
> Conquered the primitive forests and the Andes:
> The horses of Andalusia, whose sinews
> Had sparks of the flying race of the Arabs,
> Stamped their glorious hoof-prints
>> Upon the dry lava-fields,
>> Upon the wet marsh-lands,
>> Upon shores of loud rivers
>> And upon silent snows;

* Santos Chocano, *Alma América, Fiat Lux, Primicias de Oro de Indias*.

Upon the pampas, the mountains, the woods and the
  valleys.
The horses were strong!
The horses were eager! . . .[27]

This final Americanist phase reached perhaps its highest expression in the work of the greatest modernist prose writer,
and indeed the *modernista* who ranks second only to Darío:
José Enrique Rodó (1871–1917), the Uruguayan essayist. His
masterpiece, *Ariel* * (1900), a slender volume of some hun-
dred-odd pages, has had possibly more effect on the emergence of genuine Americanism than any other book ever written in Spanish America. Rodó once remarked that 'the children of today, the men of the future, asked what is the name
of their country, should not reply Brazil or Chile or Mexico,
but America'; [28] and he, more than anyone else, helped cement
this spiritual unity of which Bolívar had dreamed in vain.
Ariel has none of the Americanism of local color or picturesque description; its Americanism is one of prophecy, of
direct appeal to the ideals of an entire continent. Rodó's *Ariel*,
indeed, ranks as the ethical gospel of the Spanish-speaking
New World, much as Emerson's *Self Reliance* was the gospel
of the Anglo-Saxon nation to the North.

Rodó's entire existence was made up of his studies, his ex-
cursions into politics, and above all his literary labors. He
was one of those rare souls so devoted to his work, that he
seems to have had little if any time for a private life. As
he himself said of Montalvo, he pursued 'the vocation of literature, with the same fervor and perseverance and respect and
application which one would give to religious vows.' [29] In
his physical appearance, Rodó was striking, to say the least:
extremely tall (close to six feet, four inches), with an aquiline
nose, waving his arms energetically as he walked—so that he
used to remind observers of a condor of the Andes, that bird
which is the symbol *par excellence* of Spanish America. Despite

* Rodó, *Ariel.*

ll his symbolic Americanism, Rodó passed almost his whole life in his native Montevideo, where in 1895 he helped found the *National Review of Literature and Social Sciences;* from then on, his house on the Calle Cerrito became one of the great intellectual and literary centers of the continent. Here he wrote his beautifully polished essays, *The Motives of Proteus* (1909), *The Gallery of Próspero* (1914), *Men of America* (1920), in a classically perfect prose that has been the despair of all imitators.*

But it is mainly for *Ariel* that Rodó is remembered and revered. In this masterful essay, he analyzes the nature of democracy, and the dangers attendant upon its development, the twin perils of mediocrity and materialism which can give it the aspect of Caliban:

> Upon democracy weighs the accusation of guiding humanity, by making it mediocre, to a Holy Empire of Utilitarianism . . . According to . . . [Renan] democracy is the enthronement of Caliban. Ariel can but be vanquished by its triumph . . . These judgments have a lively interest for us Americans who love the cause and consequence of that Revolution which in our America is entwined with the glory of its origin . . . To confront the problem one must first recognize that if democracy does not uplift its spirit by a strong ideal interest which it shares with its preoccupation by material interests, it does lead, and fatally, to the favouring of mediocrity . . .[30]

Rodó sees a solution to this fatal 'levelling down' in the processes of selection, by which, after offering equal opportunities to all, a democracy should give rewards to those who exhibit merit. In the United States, Rodó finds the very incarnation of utilitarianism, in spite of certain outstanding virtues: the translation of liberty from an idea to a reality, the glorification of labor, the preservation of individualism and re-

* Rodó, *Los Motivos de Proteo, El Mirador de Próspero, Hombres de América.*

ligious liberty, the great diffusion of public education. But besides these good points, he discerns a Titanic materialism, an ineptness for choosing leaders, a colossal bad taste, a creeping venality in politics, and the growing influence of a plutocracy composed of trusts and monopolies.

It is this Caliban-phase of democracy that Rodó warns Spanish America not to copy—but even while describing it, he looks forward to the triumph of the spirit:

> But please remember that when I . . . deny to their utilitarianism the right to impose itself as typical of the future on the world as mould or model, I do not in the least assert that its labours are wasted even in relation to those things which we may call soul-interests . . . The work of North American positivism will also at the end serve the cause of Ariel. That which this people of Cyclops have achieved for the direct purpose of material advantage, with all their sense for what is useful and their admirable faculty of mechanical invention, will be converted by other peoples, or later, even by themselves, to a wealth of material for the higher selection.[31]

Ariel, then, is a trumpet-call to the higher life, an appeal to young Spanish Americans to keep their eyes firmly fixed on that vision: 'Ariel triumphant signifies ideality and order in life, noble inspiration in thought, unselfishness in conduct, high taste in art, heroism of action, delicacy and refinement in manners and usages.' [32] In Darío, modernism had given Spanish America a new literary expression, and laid a groundwork of stylistic excellence for future writers; in Rodó, modernism produced a philosophy of equal magnitude, ideals of Americanism that were to inspire the intellectuals of a continent for generations yet to come.

Post-War Poetry

THE end of modernism as a movement is roughly marked by the First World War. True, some of the leading *mod-*

ernistas continued to write for many years, and the after-effects of the renovation are still important today. But starting with the second decade of the twentieth century, a new generation of poets has come to the fore. According to these latter-day schools, modernism must give way and a new poetry must be created in its place. Within this literary anarchy, every poet is the founder of his own school; manifestoes and bizarre theories have appeared in every country, and there are imagists, creationists, cubists, surrealists. Some idea of this incredible diversity of tendencies may be seen from even the briefest glance at the work of post-war poets. Here, for instance, are a few representative names: Enrique Banchs (1888-), an Argentine poet of markedly archaic tendencies, who composes ballads in the style of the ancient Spanish *romances;* the Colombian Luis Carlos López (1880–1950), remarkable for his sense of humor and his skill at dramatizing unpoetic themes like a post-card or a barber; Ramón López Velarde (1888-1921), the initiator of a whole current of Mexican nationalistic poetry; and Jorge Luis Borges (1900-), one of Argentina's leading young intellectuals, and an exponent of Spanish ultraism.

Post-war poetry does, however, possess a certain unity. The varying schools exhibit certain common traits, notably a demand for 'pure' poetry. They all hate accent, rhyme, emotionalism, romanticism, and they choose *outré* models. Góngora, the great revolutionary seventeenth-century poet, has been revived by them; Mallarmé, the French symbolist, is considered a precursor; Valéry, Cocteau, T. S. Eliot, are in fashion. Under this new rule, poetry loses all social contact, and becomes an art solely for the initiated reader. For the new poet, there must be a complete separation between art and life; poetry should be uncontaminated by human sentiment, ideas, or even concrete reality; nothing is so much to be shunned as the example of the romantic poet, a plebeian writer in that he sang of his own human sufferings and joys, which appealed to everybody; the post-war artist, on the contrary, must not only cease to imitate life, but he must distort it, so as to produce art.

One of the most interesting single events in this contemporary period is the emergence of women in the realm of Spanish American letters. Formerly relegated to a role of unimportance in intellectual life, women are today coming to the fore in journalism, lecturing, editing, teaching, writing, and more particularly in the field of poetry. Some of this change is due to the growing material prosperity of countries like Argentina, Brazil, and Chile, where men are too busy with practical tasks in the pampas, the mines, the rubber plantations, the factories, to pay much attention to poetry—which is thus permitted to become a feminine art. Be this as it may, Spanish America boasts a good number of distinguished twentieth-century poetesses, the first of whom was the Uruguayan Delmira Agustini (1890-1914), generally considered a postmodernist. The daughter of wealthy parents, she gave early indications of musical and poetical talent. Love and death were the favorite themes of her verses, and she loved and died tragically: after a brief unhappy marriage, she was killed by her estranged husband. She left behind, however, a number of volumes—*The White Book* (1907), *Morning Songs* (1910), *Empty Chalices* (1913)—which exhibit a violent and sensuous lyricism, expressed in an irregular form of much novelty.* Following her example, three women have attained positions of the highest rank among contemporary Spanish American poets: Gabriela Mistral, from Chile; Juana de Ibarbourou, from Uruguay; and Alfonsina Storni, from Argentina.

Although 'Gabriela Mistral' (Lucila Godoy Alcayaga), (1889-1957) is a Chilean by birth, she may be said to belong to the entire Spanish-speaking world. Her life has been intense and tragic, and her poetry is indeed a mirror of her sorrows.

---

* Agustini, *El Libro Blanco, Cantos de la Mañana, Los Cálices Vacíos.*

In her youth she was a rural schoolteacher, and after a decade of distinguished pedagogical work in Chile, she was invited by the Mexican Government to aid in reorganizing the school system of that country. Subsequently, she has occupied high positions in the consular service of her country and in the League of Nations, and her name is today symbolic of feminine accomplishment in Spanish America. Early in life, she lost a loved one, and to him she devoted many of her best poems. Later, she turned from the barrenness of her own existence towards a passionate humanitarianism, which finds intense echo in her verse; her soul is wrenched when she pleads with Christ to save a corrupted humanity, when she bemoans the fate of the Jewish race, when she pities the unmarried mother or the forlorn child. Even the names of her two books of poems—*Desolation* (1922) and *Tala, or A Thorny Tree* (1938)—evoke visions of burning sands, barren horizons, and death.* At times, indeed, her emotional power is so strong that her poetry ceases to be artistic expression, and becomes instead the cry of an evangelist lashing out against injustice and cowardice. Her dominant trait of all-embracing compassion may be seen in poems like 'Hymn to the Tree':

> O Brother tree, fast fixed in earth
> By brown hooks 'neath the soil that lie,
> Yet raising thy clean brow aloft
> With fervent yearning for the sky!
>
> Pitiful make me towards the dross
> Whose dark mire feeds me, low and dumb,
> Yet never let the memory sleep
> Of that blue land from which I come! . . .
>
> O, may my soul, in each estate—
> Youth, age, joy, grief, whate'er befall—
> Still hold the self-same attitude
> Of love unchanging, love to all! [33]

* Mistral, *Desolación, Tala.*

Juana de Ibarbourou (1895-   ), though a native of Uruguay, is no less continental in her appeal, and she has even been formally consecrated as poet laureate of Spanish America, with the title of 'Juana of América.' From a feminist standpoint, her career represents just the opposite of Mistral's: happily married at eighteen, she has lived an existence of satisfied domesticity and maternity, and later of retired meditation. In her verses, she was at first the pagan singer of the flesh and of riotous blossoms, but hers is a healthy paganism. She excels, above all, in transmuting the sensuous forms of nature into subjective moods and aesthetic expressions—as in 'Bond':

> I grew
> Only for you.
> Cut the acacia boughs that demand
> Only destruction at your hand!
>
> My blossom blew
> Only for you.
> Uproot me—in its natal hour
> My lily doubted were it candle or flower.
>
> My waters blue
> Flow for you.
> Drink me—never crystal knows
> So pure a tide as in this channel flows.
>
> Wings I knew
> Only for you.
> Pursue me! (Quivering firefly,
> Veil your flame from every eye!) . . .[34]

Apart from praising the joys of life and love, she has also a deep feeling for her native landscape, which she describes in verses full of color and fragrance. During the past ten years she has given herself up entirely to meditation, finding inspiration in mystical reading and Biblical topics, a change of interest which is reflected in her different volumes of poetry: *Diamond Tongues* (1918), *Wildroot* (1922), *Rose in the Storm*

(1930), *Holy Pictures from the Bible: poems in prose* (1936).*

Quite different from the other two great modern poetesses was Alfonsina Storni (1892-1938), a typical product of twentieth-century Buenos Aires. Born in Switzerland, brought up in the Argentine provinces, she came to the 'big city' by the River Plate while still very young—and struggled there as a teacher and a journalist, feeling herself lost in 'the spiritual poverty of the century,' and finally ending her life by leaping into the sea. In her verse, she has left remarkable pictures of city life, with its downtown streets and skyscrapers and traffic; and, most of all, she has expressed in poetry all the longings of her frustrated existence. A person of wide culture and penetrating intellect, she was not gifted with the spontaneity of Juana de Ibarbourou, or the intense feeling of Gabriela Mistral; yet she surpassed them both in her concept of the purpose of poetry. In her numerous books—*The Restless Rosebush* (1916), *Sweet Pain* (1918), *Irrevocably* (1919), *Languor* (1920), and *Ochre* (1925)—her style evolves from romanticism to symbolism, and finally to a perfect synthesis.†
This pure simplicity of her verse gives her work at times a classic perfection, such as one sees in her brief poem 'Running Water':

> Yes, I move, I live, I wander astray—
>   Water running, intermingling, over the sands.
> I know the passionate pleasure of motion;
>   I taste the forests; I touch strange lands.
>
> Yes, I move—perhaps I am seeking
>   Storms, suns, dawns, a place to hide.
> What are you doing here, pale and polished—
>   You, the stone in the path of the tide? [35]

---

* Ibarbourou, *Las Lenguas de Diamante, Raíz Salvaje, La Rosa de los Vientos, Estampas de la Biblia (Poemas en Prosa)*.

† Storni, *La Inquietud del Rosal, El Dulce Daño, Irremediablemente, Languidez, Ocre*.

In speaking of contemporary Spanish American poetry, one cannot avoid mentioning Vicente Huidobro (1893–1948) poetically a third-rate talent, but at the same time a writer who has achieved wide notoriety for his literary manifestoes. This Chilean lived for many years in Paris, and speaks and writes French as well as his native language; he is thoroughly a product of French poetry, imitating every known Gallic writer from Rimbaud to Reverdy, Cocteau, and Cendrars. It was in France that he founded his revolutionary school of 'creationism,' declaring that 'the first duty of the poet is to create; the second, to create; and the third, to create.' Obviously, Huidobro is here treading the familiar vanguardist path where 'a rose is a rose is a rose.' In his *Art of Poetry*, and the famous *Manifesto* of 1917, he gave expression to poetical theories which attracted wide attention, but his creative work was not able to maintain his reputation. The reader may judge for himself why, from this sample poem:

LANDSCAPE
AFTERNOON PROMENADE TO BE CONDUCTED IN PARALLEL
ROWS
THE TREE
WAS
TALLER
THAN THE MOUNTAIN
BUT THE
MOUNTAIN
WAS SO WIDE   THE
THAT IT CROSSED   RIVER
THE BOUNDARY-LINE   WHICH
FLOWS
OVER
THE
FISH

WARNING! DON'T
PLAY ON THE GRASS!
FRESH PAINT
A SONG LEADS THE LAMBS TO THE STABLE [36]

Quite opposite is the case of the extremely gifted 'Pablo Neruda' (Neftalí Reyes, 1904-   ), perhaps the leading young poet of Spanish America. A Chilean by birth, he has been in his country's consular service for the past dozen years, in the Orient, Argentina, and Mexico. He has won wide acclaim for his poetry, and many of his volumes—*Twilight Book* (1919), *Twenty Love Poems and One Song of Despair* (1924), *Residence on Earth* * (1925-1931)—have already been through several editions. By technique, Neruda is a surrealist, as his poetry exhibits all the formal devices of that school; but temperamentally, he is a romantic. From this antinomy are derived the salient aspects of his expression: violent symbols, antipoetic metaphors, and a rich vocabulary—employed to sing the anguish of his soul, eternally overladen with grief and despair. Sensuous and rebellious, Neruda has poured into his poetry all his desires, dreams, and experiences, with such a complete surrender of self as to be disconcerting or occasionally childlike. But all this self-revelation is expressed by novel and concrete images. Neruda creates an atmosphere of intense reality with a succession of word-ideas, particularly adjectives denoting temperature, colors, noises, smells, and tastes; prominent among his recurring symbols are doves, swallows, bees, butterflies, roses, poppies, grapes, salt, fishes, and humidity.[37] In form he frequently uses free verse much in the manner of Walt Whitman, while in content he might be called a poet of the sense, were it not for the fact that he is tortured by untold revelations and spiritual doubts. Here, for instance, are some typical passages, from his poem 'Only Death':

> Alone, I sometimes see
> Coffins with veils unfurled,
> Starting with pale deadmen,
> With women and their dead tresses,

* Neruda, *Crepusculario, Veinte Poemas de Amor y una Canción Desesperada, Residencia en la Tierra.*

With bakers white as angels,
With pensive girls married to notaries,
Coffins going up the vertical river of Death,
On its course
That purple river
On its course upward, with its sails swollen,
Swollen by the silent sound of death . . .

I don't know, I know little, I hardly see,
But I believe her song has the color of wet violets,
Of violets accustomed to the humidity of earth,
Because Death's face is green,
And Death's glance is green,
With that sharp humidity of a violet's leaf
And its grave color of exasperated winter . . .

There are countless other excellent contemporary poets, too numerous for one to do much more than mention: The Peruvian César Vallejo (1892–1938), an intensely mystical and revolutionary poet, who sought—in Black Heralds (1918) and Trilce (1922)—to capture the soul of his people in verse, and who died as a result of his activities in the Spanish Civil War; the Mexican Xavier Villaurrutia (1903–1950), author of Reflections (1926), Nocturnes (1933), and particularly Longing for Death (1938), a volume of exquisite poems on love death; the Ecuadorian Jorge Carrera Andrade (1903-   ), a very 'advanced' poet as can be seen by the titles of some of his books, Latitudes (1934), Biography for the Use of Birds (1937), Micrograms (1940), and World Almanac (1940); and the Cuban Eugenio Florit (1903-   ), born in Madrid but now considered an American, who shows himself—in Kingdom (1938) and Four Poems (1940) *—to be an accomplished disciple of the great Spanish poet Juan Ramón Jiménez. Indeed, the very fact that there are today so many noted writers

* Vallejo, Los Heraldos Negros, Trilce; Villaurrutia, Reflejos, Nocturnos, Nostalgia de la Muerte; Carrera Andrade, Latitudes, Biografía para Uso de los Pájaros, Microgramas, Registro del Mundo; Florit, Reino, Cuatro Poemas.

of verse—not to mention the numerous promising young poets who will undoubtedly develop into first-rate figures in the near future—is in itself highly significant. It indicates that poetry is still ardently cultivated in Spanish America in this century of prose, and that the nations to the south are producing distinguished and original poets in the very midst of the machine age.

NEGRO VERSE

WITHOUT assuming the role of an augur, it is permissible to point out a new movement which is encouraging for the future of Spanish American poetry. This is the emergence in the last few years of a highly original genre: Negro verse. That is to say, poetry on Negro themes, using Negro rhythms, and composed by members of both the African and the European races. One critic has divided this rich field into poems of evocation, satires, cradle songs, vendor's cries, dances, elegies, and social poems, all of which have one uniting link—a 'beat' which makes them suitable to the dance. Technically, Negro poetry abandons the syllabic principle of Spanish versification; musical effects are based entirely on rhythm, and enhanced by alliteration, parallelism, onomatopoeia, internal rhyme, endless repetition of vowel sounds, and even instrumental devices reminiscent of Vachel Lindsay's 'Congo.'

This poetry takes on a different tone according to its varied subject matter. Now it is profoundly sensuous in its description of Negroid dances, congas, candombes, sones—as may be seen from this stanza of 'Rumba':

> Swing it, baby, the rumba and the drum blow,
> mabimba, mabomba, sugarspoon and jellyroll.
>
> Swing it, baby, the rumba and the drum blow,
> mabimba, mabomba, sugarspoon and jellyroll.
>
> See black Tomasa dance the rumba,
> José beside her out the rumba.
> She shakes a hip, and she shakes the other,

he stretches, he shrinks, he flings his haunches
and his paunch, and crawls, and struts,
first on one heel, then the other.

Hotcha, hotcha, hotchachee.
Hotcha, hotcha, hotchachee.[38]

Again, it becomes uncanny and mysterious when dealing with
liturgical themes, weirdly mournful funeral ceremonies, or
magical incantations as in the special songs to kill snakes.
Here, for instance, the mood of a strange African ritual is con-
veyed by exotic words:

> The Council broke out,
> Blessed be God!
> The tombs resound
> in the house of the Lord.
>
> The members signed,
> Blessed be God!
> with yellow chalk
> at the door.
>
> The rooster died,
> Blessed be God!
> on the red altar
> of the great Obatalá.
>
> Aé, Aé,
> the devil departed
> —crab of Regla!—
> jumping sideways.
> In his hood appear
> pasteboard eyes:
> wizard of Senegal!
> Taboo and Carnival! . . .[39]

On the other hand, Negro verse is sentimental and touching in
the cradle songs or *nanas*, which retain the tenderness of
motherly words even when transposed into aesthetic forms.

Already, two figures have become well known throughout
Spanish America as the highest exponents of this new Negro

poetry: Guillén and Ballagas, the first a mulatto, and the second a member of the white race. The Cuban Nicolás Guillén (1904-   ) has shown himself particularly adept in this type of Hispano-African interpretation. With his extensive knowledge of Spanish literature, he has been able to give elegance and precision to Negro motifs, notably in his masterly treatment of dramatic scenes and humorous workaday episodes. In his first two books, *Motives of 'Son'* (1930) and *Sóngoro Cosongo* (1931), he gave lyric dignity to popular songs, dances, and street-cries.* But Guillén was not content with mere poetic externals, or even with profound interpretations of the Negro soul. He carried his art still farther in his *Songs for Soldiers and 'Sones' for Tourists* † (1937), in which he expresses a profound feeling of human solidarity that goes beyond racial differences and national boundaries. Here Guillén becomes a classic poet, in the sense that he now has a clear understanding of his art and an absolute control of his technique, as well as something to say. Here, for instance, is an extract from a poem that combines the spontaneity of the old Spanish ballads with a modern intensity of tone:

> A ruddy-white soldier
> and a soldier dusky black
> go, drenched in sun,
> trudging the same road.
> Shouldering Mausers they go,
> knives fixed in their belts;
> wearing yellow uniforms they go,
> with a song on their lips.
> Their star-wheeled spurs
> glitter with fierce brilliance,
> as they go scattering in the dust
> their five points of sound . . .
>
> The two soldiers halted,
> and on the dark road

* Guillén, *Motivos de Son, Sóngoro-Cosongo.*
† Guillén, *Cantos para Soldados y Sones para Turistas.*

there was now no Mauser at the shoulder,
no knife now in the belt,
now no hard spurs,
no yellow uniform now.
To the people again
the little soldiers returned,
when the two of them knew,
the ruddy-white, the dusky black,
on the sunbaked road
where the road ended! . . .[40]

In his latest work, *Spain* * (1937), Guillén feels the remote call of his Spanish forefathers; here, he becomes the poet of democracy, expressing the anguish of a nation dying from internal struggles, yet ending with a note of hope, like a cloud on a blood-red horizon.

Another Cuban, Emilio Ballagas (1908–1954), has distinguished himself in the field of Negro poetry. Although Ballagas is a member of the white race, few poets have such an intimate knowledge of Negro psychology and folklore. Many of his poems—in *Joy and Flight* (1931), *Notebook of Negro Poetry* (1934), *Eternal Flavor* (1939)—exhibit mannerisms of recent 'pure poetry,' but the undertone of most of his work is authentically native.† More dramatic than Guillén, Ballagas succeeds in giving his compositions a dynamic movement, and a sensuous tropical beauty like that with which he endows his 'Peddler':

'Housewife!'

Through the street the peddler goes,
like a kerchief of foam,
like a wave of pleasures.

'Housewife!'

On wheels of breeze and sun
the peddler passes, singing.

---

* Guillén, *España.*
† Ballagas, *Júbilo y Fuga, Cuaderno de Poesía Negra, Sabor Eterno.*

The peddler pulls a big lip,
and the big lip drags a Negro.
The Negro, gleaming with sweat,
pushes the cart . . .

The ear goes swimming
in rivers of star-apple and mango,
and the senses breathe
music in the cry of pineapples . . .[41]

Also outstanding in Negro poetry is the name of the Puertorican Luis Palés Matos (1899–   ), who has introduced into his verse a rich African vocabulary and daring symbols. Palés Matos has no equal in the use of onomatopoeic devices and syncopated rhythms, as may be seen in his 'Black Dance':

Calabó and bambú.
Bambú and calabó.
The great Corocoro says: tu-cu-tú.
The She-Corocora says: to-co-tó.
The sun of iron burns in Timbuctoo.
The black dance beats in Fernando Po.
The pig in the mud grunts: pru-pru-prú.
The toad in the pool croaks: cro-cro-cró.
Calabó and bambú.
Bambú and calabó . . .[42]

Likewise deserving of mention in this genre are the Cubans José Zacarías Tallet (1893–   ), author of several dance compositions; Alejo Carpentier (1904–   ), musician and poet; Marcelino Arozarena (1912–   ), who has written a few songs of intense Negroid inspiration; and Ramón Guirao (1908–49), author of *Bongó* (1934) and of a very comprehensive anthology of Negro poetry.[43]

The orbit of this Negroid poetry is naturally of small diameter. Popular in its conception and technique, it is destined primarily to serve as a basis for future experiments in a more intellectual form of art. In musical combination, for instance, it has already produced a few operas of some merit. But it must soon exhaust its vein, and the repetition of motifs is bound to become monotonous—a fact foreseen by Guillén when he broke with his self-imposed patterns and enlarged his philosophical horizons. But Negro poetry is chiefly interesting as a 'straw in the wind,' indicating some of the future currents of Spanish American verse. Like the work of the three noted modern women poets, this Negroid verse is a genuine product of the American soil. This turning to native motifs, to the races and prairies and cities of a New World, is another aspect of the same tendency that has shown itself in the postwar revolt against modernism. First, Spanish America achieved her literary independence from Spain; she is only now foregoing her French models, which were so dominant in the swans-and-Versailles era of poetry. The new schools, for all their anarchy, perceive that there is poetical beauty in the elemental forces of life and death, beauty in the concepts of the human brain and in all created things, and above all that there is beauty in the native American scene. In modern poetry, this coming Americanism is still on the horizon—but it is already a well-established fact in another genre which embraces both prose and poetry: the typically Spanish American field of gaucho literature.

Gaucho Literature

THE GAUCHO: ORIGINS OF FOLK LITERATURE

SPANISH America's literary history, like her history in general, may be viewed as a continuous struggle for independence. That is to say, for 'literary Americanism.' This concept does not imply any chauvinistic notions of originality at all costs; it does not suggest that to treat of new topics, Spanish American writers must necessarily abandon the achievements of literary technique and tradition. Rather, it describes the growing effort of a New World to express that which is closest to its soil and truest to its racial temperament. This literary independence has not been achieved either quickly or completely; even today it remains partly a goal. Yet there has been a steady movement towards this end—a development in which folk literature, like that of the gaucho, has played a significant role.

Generally speaking, the trend towards literary Americanism has roughly kept pace with Spanish America's politico-social evolution. The process received its first impulse in the romantic era following the wars of liberation, a period which may be characterized as one of incomplete independence. Writers used American themes and described regional landscapes, but the influences of Hugo, Byron, Scott, and Espronceda were only too obvious in their works. A strange impulse seemed to keep Spanish America constantly turned towards Europe; so, while petty tyrants disguised their despotisms under the name of democracy, poets sang the wonders of American nature in a Byronic tone. Still, the first stage—emancipation from Spain—had been achieved, and the new trend was under way. At first, an 'aristocracy' remained dominant in cultural activities, an elite of army men and members of the higher clergy and rich landowners, who could probably boast of a strictly European cultural background. But gradually the levelling force of a pseudo-democracy created a middle class of Creoles and mestizos, which rose to considerable dominance. From this group began to emerge some of the continent's most distinguished writers, bringing with them a more mixed culture and point of view, in which European and American elements were mingled. Finally, there were also lower classes in the cities, and a picturesque rural population, which came in time to occupy more important roles. It then became necessary to democratize literature and to include in its scope the life of men long unnoticed, but who were in many ways the very backbone of the South American nations.

This meant, of course, a descent from pure intellectual art into the more popular regions of poetic folklore. That is precisely what happened in Argentina, a country with a rich and typical rural life, and the first nation of Spanish America to take this literary step. Indeed, the development of the gaucho genre in the Argentine will serve as an excellent example of the origins of Spanish American folk literature. To understand how this new type of American man gave rise to a new form of literary expression, it is necessary first of all to study the gaucho himself.

The gaucho is, above everything else, a product of the pampas. Few people outside the Argentine Republic realize the enormous extent of the territory which composes the pampas region. This vast land stretches from the Atlantic Ocean itself on the east, to the Chilean Andes on the west; and from Bolivia, Paraguay, and the Gran Chaco on the north, to the most southerly point of the continent. The central part of this zone, which extends some six hundred miles from Chile to Buenos Aires, is an immense desert of thorny bushes, broken at times, in the proximity of villages and cities, by woods and verdant pastures. At some future date, irrigation may transform these plains into cultivated fields like those that already delight the eye around Mendoza and San Luis. But today the pampas is still a region of desert-like immensity, much as it has appeared in the descriptions of hundreds of awe-stricken writers since colonial times. Few have surpassed the pages of the modern travellers Robert Cunninghame Graham and W. H. Hudson, two Englishmen whom Argentina claims as her own; or the evocatory passages of Sarmiento, who wrote of the pampas a hundred years ago:

> Its own extent is the evil from which Argentina suffers; the desert encompasses it on every side and penetrates its very heart; wastes containing no human dwelling are, generally speaking, the unmistakable boundaries between its several provinces. Immensity is the universal characteristic of the country: the plains, the woods, the rivers, are all immense; and the horizon is always undefined, always lost in haze and delicate vapors which forbid the eye to mark the point in the distant perspective where the land ends and the sky begins . . . it is the image of the sea upon the land; the earth as it appears upon the map, the earth yet waiting for the command to bring forth every herb yielding seed after its kind.[1]

Across these pampas, in pre-Spanish times, roamed the savages who bore the very name *Pampas*. The Pampa Indians early became an equestrian race, due to the fact that the horses brought by the first conquerors into Buenos Aires, Tucumán, and Chile soon wandered into the central plains and there multiplied abundantly. These mounted Indians attacked the Spanish settlements and wagon-caravans in bloody assaults called *malones*, killing the men and kidnapping the women. The mixed population of the pampas increased substantially in still other ways.[2] Many city mestizos and even Creoles voluntarily sought refuge among the plains people:

> The mestizos, not so well fitted for being servants in the cities as the Negroes, were replaced by them; and, not finding anything to do because of the lack of industrial activity, they left for the Indian frontier which thus became their natural abode. In this way we have the beginning of that sub-race of transitional people typified by the *Gaucho*.[3]

Not a great deal has been discovered about the first appearance of the gaucho type on the pampas. His existence is known about 1775, but the time of change from the Spanish *vaquero* (cowboy) into the mestizo gaucho is still somewhat vague. For lack of historical knowledge, scholars have offered a philological explanation—which has only served to complicate the problem by giving several dozen etymological derivations for the word *gaucho*.[4] Perhaps the most reasonable derivation is from the Araucanian word *Guacho* which today means 'motherless,' 'illegitimate,' and 'orphan.' [5]

These orphans of the pampas formed a new type of society on the Argentine plains, a very primitive society in direct contrast to the refined and easy life of the cities. The gauchos— thriving on the abundance of wild horses and cows, wandering from place to place according to the shifting of the river channels and the migrations of the cattle, leading a semi-savage nomadic existence—had many similarities to the Bedouins. Sir Walter Scott characterized them trenchantly:

> The vast plains of Buenos Aires are inhabited only by Christian savages known as *Gauchos*, whose furniture is chiefly composed of horses' skulls, whose food is raw beef and water, and whose favorite pastime is running horses to death. Unfortunately, they prefer their national independence to our cottons and muslins.[6]

In fact the gauchos not only disdained imported cottons and muslins, but they depended almost exclusively for their necessities upon the horse and the cow. Their means of transportation, their food, part of their dwellings, their beds, their furniture, their boots, their fuel, their lassos, their water buckets, their boats to cross the rivers, and even the strings of their guitars were derived from these two animals. Whenever the gaucho needed 'luxuries,' such as adornments for his horse, perfumes for his girl, or liquor, he obtained them by exchanging rawhides or ostrich feathers with the *pulpero* or storekeeper. More than a cattleman, the gaucho was a hunter and horsebreaker in a primitive happy world that did not know property laws, merchants, industry, formal education, or organized religion.

It is small wonder, then, that the gaucho developed into an extraordinary semi-savage figure, dressed in his characteristic costume: A long *poncho* served him as cloak, blanket, or even shield in a duel; beneath it he wore a richly embroidered undergarment, and over this a *chiripá*, a single oblong cloak very much like a Roman skirt; he covered his head with a hat, and wore high horsehide boots with spurs.[7] And the gaucho was as much of a romantic type as he was a picturesque character. Jealous of his reputation as a brave man, he would fight only with his *facón*, a double-edged blade that was a cross between a sword and a dagger. He carried this *facón* in a leather belt, decorated with silver coins, and it was his sole weapon apart from his indispensable saddle equipment. The gaucho, of course, never rode without his lasso or his *boleadoras*—a primitive hunting device, consisting of three round stones or metal balls covered with hide and attached to leather thongs, and designed to be thrown at the legs of a running animal.

Even the gaucho's sports were closely connected with his pampas environment. Hunting, for ostriches or deer or partridges, was a favorite pastime; so was gaming, whether at cards or at the *taba*, which was played with the knucklebones of sheep. But the favorite gaucho diversion was horse racing and its related equestrian exercises. One of these was the so-called 'ring game,' in which a horseman running at full speed had to pass the point of a lance or long stick through an iron ring hanging from a cord. Another was the epic game called the Duck (*El Pato*):

> For this game hundreds of gauchos would ride several leagues to take part. They divided themselves into lines facing each other; then an old man threw into the air a leather ball equipped with two handles. Inside this ball there was a dead fowl. The horsemen then rushed to seize the ball and the one who arrived first took possession of it and had to hold it outstretched in the air by one handle, offering the other to his enemies. His teammates surrounded him in a protective circle while the enemy force tried to break through to seize the prize, using their horses as battering rams . . . The winner, or the one who was the final possessor of the trophy, took it to a ranch and cooked it for his lady love.[8]

The very best synthesis of this wild gaucho type, his character and his appearance, is to be found in the impassioned pages of Sarmiento:

> These men, Spaniards only in their language and in the confused religious notions preserved among them, must be seen before a correct estimate can be made of the indomitable and haughty character which grows out of this struggle of isolated man with untamed nature, of the rational being with the brute. It is necessary to see their visages bristling with beards, their countenances as grave and serious as those of the Arabs of Asia, to appreciate the pitying scorn with which they look upon the sedentary denizen of the city, who may have read many books, but who cannot overthrow and slay a fierce bull, who cannot provide himself with a horse from the pampas, who has never met a tiger alone, and received him with a dagger in one hand and the poncho rolled up in the other, to be thrust into the animal's mouth while he pierces his heart with his dagger.[9]

Yet for all his semi-savagery, the gaucho was also to produce much poetry. Even Sarmiento, the great enemy of gaucho primitiveness and lethargy, did not fail to see the poetic aspects of gaucho life, and the great possibilities of an original folk literature springing from this rural atmosphere. Indeed, the very setting of the gaucho's existence moved him to express himself in song. The superb natural phenomena, the profound beauty and mystery of the endless plains, were in themselves strong evokers of poetic emotions:

> How can such feelings fail to exist, when a black storm-cloud rises, no one knows from whence, in the midst of a calm, pleasant afternoon, and spreads over the sky before a word can be uttered? The traveler shudders as the crushing thunder announces the tempest, and he holds his breath in the fear of bringing upon himself one of the thousand bolts which flash around him. The light is followed by thick darkness; death is on every side; a fearful and irresistible power has instantaneously driven the soul back upon itself, and made it feel its nothingness in the midst of angry nature; made it feel God himself in the terrible magnificence of His works. What other coloring could the brush of fancy need? [10]

So it is quite understandable how—from such a natural background, and especially from the human isolation in the presence of such forces—there should have arisen the rich body of gaucho folk literature. This indigenous poetry was of two sorts: the songs and improvisations of the gauchos themselves; and the popular epic poetry composed about them, which, from its acceptance by the gauchos, merits to be classed as folk literature. Later, to be sure, the gaucho found his way into formal literary productions, in the drama, and particularly in the novel. But the beginnings of the gaucho genre are to be seen in the unwritten works of the gauchos themselves—in the song of the troubadour, or *gaucho cantor*, raising his voice on the limitless prairies.

THE PAYADOR

GAUCHO poetry began quite naturally and simply. The man of the pampas was impressed by the incredible natural environment all around him; at the same time, he was moved to express in song the lonesomeness of his own life, his melancholy, the tender side of his nature, his dreams of love. Every good gaucho thus became a singer, and it was a disgrace in the pampas not to play the guitar. Some gauchos of course excelled at this art; and soon there sprang up a veritable class of singing gauchos, modern guitar-playing *trovadores*, whose verses were heard through the evenings in the solitude of the pampas, under the low-hanging stars. At first the minstrel, or *payador* as he was also called, sang his own love-laments or improvised lines for the popular dances of his time, the *cielito*, the *vidalita*, the *triste*. He never memorized these songs, but extemporized them according to his own moods, and most of them have unfortunately been lost. Here is one, however, that has been preserved—a *vidalita* or lyric song sung to the accompaniment of the guitar, while the refrain is repeated by the chorus of bystanders:

> The palm-tree is over the grass,
>   The sky is over the tree;
> I am over my horse,
>   My sombrero is over me!
>
> I wish that I had been born
>   Wild grass out on the plain;
> And never had seen you passing,
>   And never had suffered this pain.
>
> Little white dove, *Vidalita*,
>   With a breast of blue,
> Say that I suffer, *Vidalita*,
>   Because my love is untrue.
>
> Little white dove, *Vidalita*,
>   With a breast of gold,

Carry my love, *Vidalita*,
  As much as can be told.

Little white dove, *Vidalita*,
  With a breast of red,
Say that I weep, *Vidalita*,
  Because my love is dead.[11]

The gaucho minstrel gradually evolved into something of an institution, not merely a solitary singer but the center of social activity. The *payador* rode from country store to country store, and he was welcomed in all festivals and gatherings. An eyewitness thus described him:

> The Cantor has no fixed abode, he lodges where night surprises him; his fortune is in his verses and his voice. Wherever the wild mazes of the *cielito* are threaded, wherever there is a glass of wine to drink, the Cantor has his place and his particular part in the festival. The Argentine gaucho only drinks when excited by music and verse, and every country store has its guitar ready for the hands of the Cantor who perceives from afar where the aid of his art is needed by the group of horses about the door.[12]

As was to be expected, the *payador* was popular with the young ladies and hated by those of his brothers who did not have the gift of song. Since the singer was fond of satire, sometimes the aftermath of a party was a bloody battle with the *facón!*

Some idea of the life of a *payador*—with its component elements: the audience, the amorous adventure, and the fight—may be had from this anecdote:

> In 1840 a Cantor was sitting on the ground, crosslegged, on the banks of the majestic Paraná, in the midst of a group of gauchos whom he was keeping in eager suspense by the long and animated tale of his labors and adventures. He had already related the abduction of his love, with the difficulties overcome on the occasion; also

his misfortune (that is to say, the killing of a man), and the dispute that led it; and was relating his encounter with the soldiery, and the stabs with which he defended himself, when the noisy advance and the shouts of a body of troops made him aware that this time he was surrounded. The troops had in fact closed up in the form of a horseshoe, open toward the Paraná river, the steep banks of which rose twenty yards above the water. The Cantor, undismayed by the outcry, was mounted in an instant, and after casting a searching look at the ring of soldiers and their ready weapons, he wheeled his horse toward the river's bank, covered the animal's eyes with his poncho, and drove his spurs into him. A few moments after, the horse, freed from his bit so that he could swim more easily, emerged from the depths of the Paraná, the minstrel holding him by the tail, and looking back at the scene on the shore which he had quitted, as composedly as if he had been in an eight-oared boat. Some shots fired by the troops did not hinder him from arriving safe and sound at the first island in sight.[18]

This then was the gaucho cantor, the *payador* of the pampas —a transplantation of the Andalusian popular singer into the New World environment. In his songs or *payadas,* he used a very picturesque style full of objective images and metaphors, and he sang his verses in a voice warm with pathos and emotion. He employed eight-syllable quatrains, the old ballad form, and his language was the sixteenth-century Spanish spoken by the conquerors and kept intact in certain isolated regions. Possibly the most interesting form of the payada was the one called the *Contrapunto,* which was performed in the following manner: Two gauchos would sit on the skulls of oxen, tuning their guitars, while bystanders stood around them in a circle and urged them with yells and applause into a singing match. Then one singer would challenge the other to explain, for instance, the origin of time and space; the second singer would improvise half a dozen stanzas and end by asking a question in his turn. In this way they often passed hours, sometimes days, in a sport that was a real tournament of wit, to the great delight of the spectators.

This noble art of the *Contrapunto* has not yet vanished from the Argentine scene:

> Upon rare occasions, if one is lucky, one may hear a *payada* in the traditional style, with challenge and acceptance, according to rule and canon, and then the song flashing back and forth, criss-cross of question and answer, lunge, parry and riposte, guitar answering guitar, and then the circle of listeners with their bravos and bursts of applause. In the days before the radio, before the opera in Buenos Aires was broadcast on the pampa winds, and Lily Pons was on tap in the *pulperia*, the *contrapunto* was an institution in the land. Every country-store had its champion; and travelling singers, often coupling their profession as ranch hands with their noble art of song, roamed here and there, their guitars slung across their shoulders, their ponchos often tattered, but their hearts and lips touched with the fire of poesy, ever ready to make a match with the best, and assured everywhere of a welcome and an audience.[14]

The *gaucho cantor*, however, and the art of *contrapunto* are already largely things of the past. In general, the *payadas* have disappeared almost completely, for they were transmitted by word of mouth, and the gaucho was not fond of memorizing. But gaucho poetry developed in still another direction, by means of the written word. From its original lyric chant and dance accompaniment, this folk verse evolved ultimately into more elaborate poetical forms. Indeed, it was as epic poetry that gaucho verse was to acquire its greatest significance and survive permanently.

THE GAUCHO EPIC

GAUCHO literature finally reached its maturity in that type of poetry which critics have called 'epic.' The transition from sung to written verse came about by degrees. At first, written gaucho poetry remained anonymous, as in the *romances* or ballads which have survived; later, as in the work of Bartolomé Hidalgo (1788-1823), it crossed the border-line between popular verse and established authorship. In form, too, the change was a gradual one: the *payadas* evolved into the gaucho narrative, and later into the gaucho epic. These narratives at first oral, then written, told of the achievements of gaucho heroes, fights between Indians and Spaniards, episodes of the Rosas regime, the death of Facundo Quiroga, and daily happenings in the life of the plains. The epics treated similar subjects, but elaborated them with greater care and ambition, and showed a special preference for the life of the outlaw gauchos, some of them men of flesh and blood, others only legendary figures. Three epics have won especial renown in this genre: Ascasubi's *Santos Vega*, del Campo's *Fausto*, and that great Argentine classic, *Martín Fierro* by José Hernández.

Fausto (1870) is the least interesting of these three works, since it is primarily a work of literary artifice. Its author, Estanislao del Campo (1834-80) was a city dweller in Buenos Aires, and 'the student must be put on his guard against taking for granted that del Campo's poem is a genuine, spontaneous gaucho song.' [15] *Fausto*, indeed, is best described as a *tour de force*, a parody of Goethe's masterpiece: A gaucho called Anastasio el Pollo goes to Buenos Aires and attends a performance of *Faust* at the old Colón Theatre; then he relates what he saw to a friend, using his own expressions and ridiculous comparisons. Some Argentine critics have called this poem an imitation of Goethe, which seems far-fetched; for it stands to reason that a gaucho could give only a rude imitation of the plot of *Faust*, without ever suspecting the philosophical meaning of the German author. Undoubtedly the poem has some lyrical stanzas of great beauty, which have won praise like Menéndez y Pelayo's 'this is good, wholesome, legitimate poetry'; but this can be considered a negative merit, since such passages reveal the cultured city poet. At best, *Fausto* is only a very weak mock-epic, in which the romantic temperament of del Campo belies his gaucho psychology.

More ambitious and at the same time more authentic in tone is *Santos Vega, or The Twins of La Flor* (1851, 1872), a poem of 13,000 lines, in which Hilario Ascasubi (1807-75) relates—in a very innocent manner—the life and deeds of a gaucho bandit and his final repentance and death in the bosom of the Catholic church. Ascasubi himself was primarily a man of action, and a leading foe of the tyrant Rosas, both on the battlefield and with the pen. During the siege of Montevideo, for instance, he published a series of gaucho ballads in pamphlet form, *Paulino Lucero, or The Gauchos of the Río de la Plata Singing and Fighting against the Tyrants of the Argentine Republic and the Eastern Republic of Uruguay* * (1839-51); again, after the defeat of Rosas in 1852, he returned to Buenos Aires and began publishing a periodical under the gauchesque title of *Aniceto el Gallo*. But Ascasubi's fame rests upon his *Santos Vega*, which is not so much an epic poem as a series of short stories and descriptive pictures of pampa customs: A *payador*, Santos Vega, enjoys the hospitality of a gaucho couple; to repay them, he relates the story of twin boys from the *estancia* of La Flor, one of whom becomes a gaucho outlaw. The work has no unity, little poetic value, and no social or philosophical purpose; but the author's minute descriptions of country life, customs, places, objects, people, all make of this poem a document of rare value. From a literary standpoint, the chief merit of *Santos Vega* does not lie in any particular intrinsic work, but rather in the way its author enlarged the gaucho genre; for, as Holmes has said: 'Ascasubi bequeathed to his literary successors the example and stimulus

* Ascasubi, *Santos Vega o los Mellizos de la Flor, Paulino Lucero, o los Gauchos del Río de la Plata Cantando y Combatiendo contra los Tiranos de las Repúblicas Argentina y Oriental del Uruguay.*

of a lengthy *romance* on gaucho life, and his expert use of gaucho terminology'—an example and a stimulus that were to bring forth their highest expression in *Martín Fierro*.

In *The Gaucho Martín Fierro* (1872),* by José Hernández (1834-86), the gauchesque epic reached its climax, and produced one of the classics of Spanish American literature. Hernández himself was something of an epic figure: 'His luxuriant, Jove-like beard, immense frame, and benign countenance were imposing, while certain details of his costume, such as the gaucho hat and sometimes the top boots, were in no wise ridiculous.' [16] An ardent politician, he was a member of the Federalist party —and a constant opponent of Mitre (the first constitutional President of a united Argentina) and of Sarmiento (the great educator), against whom he conspired, establishing himself in a Buenos Aires hostel and soliciting men and money for a rebellion. Indeed, Hernández took an active part in the uprising of the last gaucho insurrectionist, López Jordán. For in politics as in his famous epic, Hernández was on the side of the gaucho and the gaucho *caudillo* against the forces of 'civilization.'

It is perhaps this siding with the gaucho that gives *Martín Fierro* its epic proportions, and lends the protagonist heroic stature. Martín is a gaucho persecuted by the Argentine authorities because his views of life do not agree with those of modern society. He recognizes no rights of property. The pampa land, like the sky and the air, has no owner; the only tribunal capable of rendering justice—Martín Fierro's justice— is his own knife, his *facón*. Judges, mayors, army officers, police corrupt to the core, these are the mortal enemies of the gaucho. Martín Fierro fights this society that tries to displace the old order of things, and he becomes a moral force in Argentine history—the champion of liberty, a truly epic character. Speaking of this quality, Leopoldo Lugones says:

* Hernández, *Martín Fierro*.

Like all epic poems, *Martín Fierro* represents the heroic life of the race: it fights for liberty against adversity and injustice. Martín Fierro is a champion of that right which they have taken away from him; he is the Cid Campeador of that heroic cycle made immortal eight centuries before by the Spanish legends; he is a typical knight-errant helping fair maidens in distress. Another characteristic is his flight to the enemy's land when he is persecuted in his own! [17]

This kinship to the Spanish *epopeya* has been noted by other critics. As a matter of fact, *Martín Fierro* does have two distinctly Spanish antecedents—the *Romancero* and the picaresque novel. In the case of the former, the Spanish *romances* or popular ballads were of course the forerunners of the gaucho *romances*, and Martín the *payador* is their legitimate inheritor. In the case of the latter, Martín has at times some of the qualities of the rogue, but it is in two characters, in 'old man Vizcacha' and in Picardía that one finds 'all the tricks and philosophy' of the Spanish *pícaros*. But over and above all this, the purpose of *Martín Fierro* was the creation of an epic hero who embodies a national—that is, an Argentine —ideal. Hernández succeeded amply in this aim. All the other aspects of his work—description, narration, landscape—are subordinate to the fundamental one: the personality of his hero. To be sure, this gaucho poem lacks the robustness, the unity, the poetic loftiness, the philosophical import, and the grandeur of the *Iliad* or the *Chanson de Roland;* but in its own right, in the personality of Martín and what he stands for, it is a representative national epic.

Hernández has indeed created a very human hero—perhaps too human to be fully heroic—in the person of Martín Fierro, minstrel and outlaw. Martín, like a true *payador*, tunes his guitar and begins to sing his own story:

> I sit me here to sing my song
> To the beat of my old guitar;

> For the man whose life is a bitter cup,
> With a song may yet his heart lift up,
> As the lonely bird on the leafless tree
> That sings 'neath the gloaming star . . .[18]

As a good gaucho, Martín rejoices in his liberty and his solitude on the pampas:

> And this is my pride: to live as free
> As the bird that cleaves the sky;
> I build no nest in this careworn earth,
> Where sorrow is long, and short is mirth;
> And when I am gone none will grieve for me,
> And none care where I lie.[19]

Martín begins his history by recalling his happy early days in the *estancias:* the gauchos setting out to work with the dawn, buckling on their spurs and taking their soft saddle-skins; the day's tasks of breaking horses or guiding flocks on the plain; and finally, with nightfall, the merry gathering after supper by the kitchen fire.

But that golden age soon ceased, and the peace of the gaucho's hearth was succeeded by military persecution and frontier garrison duty. Martín goes on to tell of his miseries in the army, Indian fights, corporal punishment, delayed pay, and so on. At length he deserts and returns home to find that:

> Only a few bare poles were left.
> And the thatch and nothing more;
> Christ knows it was a mournful sight,
> It withered my heart up like a blight,
> And there in the wreck of my ruined home,
> To be revenged I swore.

From then on, Martín is an outlaw. The following stanzas give a picture of his existence as a runaway, in *pulperías* and dance-halls; his first crime, which he considers a 'legal fight' for his honor; his wandering over the pampas:

They call him a drunken gaucho beast
If he takes a spot of gin;
If he goes to a dance he's an upstart boor;
If he plays at cards he's a sharper sure;
He's a brawler if he defends himself;
If he doesn't—they do him in.

A hunted man now, Martín passes solitary nights on the desert, tracked by police riders. At length, the constabulary catches up and sets upon him, ten to one. But Martín triumphs in the fight, thanks to the help of Cruz, a former gaucho outlaw turned sergeant. Cruz and Martín become fast friends, companions in misfortune, and finally resolve to go beyond the frontier and join the Indians:

And one day when the sun's first ray
Made the plain like a sheet of gold,
Cruz pointed back where the eye scarce caught
The last ranch stand like a tiny dot.
And as he looked, two burning tears
Down the cheeks of Fierro rolled.

Such was the original poem of *Martín Fierro*. Seven years later, encouraged by the reception of his work, Hernández published a sequel entitled *The Return of Martín Fierro* (1879).* In this second part, Fierro and Cruz pass several years in an Indian village, until Cruz dies of the small-pox. Fierro then decides to return to civilization, and—after killing a cruel Indian chieftain and rescuing a captive white woman—he makes his way back across the desert. Returned to the settlements, Martín goes from ranch to ranch, seeking his old friends, and learning that the Law is no longer hunting him. Finally, at a gaucho gathering he meets two of his sons, and the boys tell their own stories—the older boy relating his unjust imprisonment, the younger telling of his association with the rascally old Vizcacha. Still another new arrival is then introduced, the young gaucho Picardía, who is none other than the son of

* Hernández, *La Vuelta de Martín Fierro*.

Martín's late friend Cruz. By this time, the story has lost its vigor and intensity and Hernández repeats himself. He introduces episodes that have nothing to do with the story, and finally the returned gaucho and the three boys part—the four could never earn a living together—and Martín ends the poem on this sentimental note:

> And if life fails me, this I know,
> When the news of my death is spread,
> The roaming gaucho, far away
> In the desert lands, will be sad that day,
> And a sudden ache in his heart will wake,
> When he knows that I am dead.

Martín Fierro was right. All the gauchos know his story and weep his death, the death of a whole race of gauchos of his type, destroyed by the machinery and wealth that is called 'civilization.' His name is even today a symbol of that virile life of the plains in which a gaucho was a free man, not a cog in an economic and social system; and with all his defects, he is a better representative of Americanism than the modern farmhand or the Syrian peddler who crosses the pampas that Martín used to roam. *Martín Fierro* is well known nowadays not only in the Argentine, but in all of Spanish America and in the Peninsula as well. Even the great Spanish intellectual, Miguel de Unamuno, used to recite the *Martín Fierro* to his students in the University of Salamanca, along with the *Iliad* and the *Odyssey*. The poem has been translated into several languages, and scholars all over the world have shown interest in its gaucho idiom and literary technique.

But perhaps the soundest estimate of its worth is to be found in the humbler homage rendered Hernández by his own compatriots of the Argentine pampas, as it is recorded in this typical scene related by Cunninghame Graham in his *A Vanishing Race*:

> In the long evenings, seated around the fire, passing the maté around, the adventures of Martín were sure to

be discussed. The gauchos seemed to take him as the embodiment of themselves and all their troubles, and talked of him as if at any moment he might lift the mare's hide which acted as door and walk into the hut. Those of the company who could read (not the majority) were wont to read aloud to the unlettered from a well-worn, greasy book, printed on flimsy paper in thin and broken type, after extracting the precious book from the recesses of their saddle-bags or from their riding boots. The others got it by heart and then repeated it as a sort of litany.

This, rather than the estimate of any university critic, would seem to be the true measure of *Martín Fierro:* Deriving from the folk-songs of the *payador*, this epic has succeeded so thoroughly in creating an embodiment of the gaucho and his struggle, that it is welcomed back by the gauchos themselves into a sort of folk literature.

The Gaucho in Formal Literature

Because gaucho folk-songs had reached their climax in the written epic, it need not be supposed that the development of the gauchesque genre ceased at this point. On the contrary, such was the success of *Santos Vega, Fausto,* and especially *Martín Fierro* with city audiences that writers soon saw the possibility of exploiting this new kind of literature. It was not long before the gaucho theme passed from poetry, with its reminiscences of folk-song, into prose, and the more formal literary mediums of the drama, the short story, and the novel.

Of course, as with the transition from oral to written verse, so here the change from poetry to prose did not take place at any one definite moment. Gaucho poetry continued to be written, notably by Rafael Obligado (1851-1920), who glorified the legend of Santos Vega: the invincible *payador* who, after years of supremacy in song, is vanquished by an unknown antagonist (really the Devil) and dies brokenhearted.

But the new forms were already supplanting poetry. Gaucho fiction made its first appearance, in a primitive 'dime novel' sort of form to be sure, in the works of the Argentine journalist Eduardo Gutiérrez (1853-90). Gutiérrez wrote a few dozen hair-raising novels, more accurately described as 'thrillers,' in which bad gauchos stabbed each other to death, kidnapped winsome lassies, and fought single-handed with whole police detachments. His books ranged from gauchesque tales to historical works to out-and-out crime stories; and some of them—like *John without Land* and *Juan Moreira*—would have been great 'box office' in the American moving pictures of twenty years ago, during the widespread vogue for lurid Western films. Perhaps the least objectionable of his novels is *Black Ant* (1881), his encounters with the law, his brutal and evil deeds, and his final regeneration in prison.* His greatest 'hit' was *Juan Moreira*, which appeared as a newspaper serial in 1880 and which instantly won the heart of the masses. Like Martín Fierro, Juan was a gaucho turned outlaw because of persecution, but in the elaboration of wild and impossible incidents, the novel was journalese rather than gauchesque. Gutiérrez cared more for gruesome plot and melodramatic effect than for authentic psychology; even the language of his gauchos was the corrupt slang of the city suburbs instead of the lusty talk of the real gaucho or the conventional speech of the epic poems.

Gutiérrez' harrowing thrillers were a crude beginning, to be sure. But the popularity of these early efforts at gauchesque fiction attested to the virility of the genre, which soon attracted writers of merit. Before the close of the nineteenth century, distinguished men-of-letters were composing gaucho novels. A movement had been initiated which was to last a half-century and produce a score of novelists, including a number of outstanding figures from Acevedo Díaz to Lynch, and at least one work with a claim to immortality, the gaucho classic *Don Segundo Sombra*.

* Gutiérrez, *Juan sin Tierra, Juan Moreira, Hormiga Negra*.

In the drama, at the same time, a similar development was under way. Once again, the prolific Gutiérrez must be given credit for initiating a movement of consequence: The stage presentation of his novel *Juan Moreira* scored a great hit for the Podestá Company in 1884; this performance is generally, though somewhat inaccurately, called the first gaucho drama. As a matter of fact, isolated gaucho plays had been given much earlier; and one anonymous piece, *The Romance of the Ranch Girl,** bears the surprising date of 1792. But with the dramatization of *Juan Moreira*, the gaucho was on the boards to stay. Other theatrical presentations followed in short order: an adaptation of the popular favorite *Martín Fierro*, versions of several novels by Gutiérrez, gaucho pieces composed especially for the stage. At the beginning, scenic arrangements of gaucho novels were introduced in the form of pantomimes in travelling circuses; later, as audiences favored this part of the show, special tents were arranged for these performances alone; and eventually regular theatres were created.

These, too, were rude beginnings, but they led to the flowering of the nationalistic and gauchesque theatre in the River Plate region. Reaching its apogee shortly after the turn of the twentieth century, this *teatro rioplatense* boasted such names as Martiniano Leguizamón (1858-1935), the author of many gaucho stories and the drama *Calandria* (1898),† and Roberto J. Payró (1867-1928), the gauchesque novelist and playwright. Payró's books, including the rural picaresque tale *The Marriage of Laucha* (1906) and *The Entertaining Adventures of the Grandson of Juan Moreira* (1910), were very popular in their day, and are still enjoyable for their unpretentious realism and good humor; and his plays, such as *On the Ruins* (1904), *I Want to Live By Myself* (1913), and *Fire in the Stubble* (1925), are among the most readable of the national-

* *El Amor de la Estanciera.*
† Leguizamón, *Calandria.*

istic school.* But the gaucho drama produced one illustrious figure who entirely overshadows the rest of the *teatro rioplatense*, and who oddly enough came at the beginning rather than at the culmination of the movement. The most important event in the history of the gaucho drama was the first performance—in Buenos Aires, in 1903—of a gaucho play called *My Kid, the Doctor*. The author, who until then had struggled in poverty and obscurity, was a young man named Sánchez, destined to be universally recognized as Spanish America's greatest playwright.

Florencio Sánchez

Indeed, Florencio Sánchez (1875-1910) ranks not only as the greatest, but quite literally as the only important dramatist of South America.[20] Like many another artist, his life followed the familiar pattern of early misery, fleeting triumph, and untimely death. A native of Uruguay, he went to Buenos Aires while still young, and started to work on a newspaper at the age of fourteen. His life was that of the true Bohemian; he dressed poorly, he ate little, he drank too much, and he struggled desperately to earn a pittance. From time to time he would scrawl off his plays on pads filched from telegraph offices. Then in 1903, when he was twenty-eight, came the production of *My Kid, the Doctor*, one of the most sensational successes in the history of the Argentine theatre. Sánchez was famous now, and his plays followed in rapid succession, twenty in the next six years, including *The 'Gringa'* (1904), *On the Skids* (1905), *Dead Men* (1905), *Our Children* (1907), *The Right to Health* (1907), *Family Life* (1905)—which rank among the best Spanish-language dramas of the Ibsenesque and nationalistic school.† But his years of

* Payró, *El Casamiento de Laucha, Las Divertidas Aventuras del Nieto de Juan Moreira; Sobre las Ruinas, Vivir Quiero Conmigo, Fuego en el Rastrojo.*

† Sánchez, *M'Hijo el Dotor, La Gringa, Barranca Abajo, Los Muertos, Nuestros Hijos, Los Derechos de la Salud, En Familia.*

prosperity and success were short indeed. In 1910 he set out
to visit Europe, going first to Italy—a land connected by strong
bonds to his native Uruguay—only to die there on February
23, at the age of thirty-five.

Sánchez' plays are characterized by great dramatic intensity
and completely real characters, and by his poetic feeling for
the land of the gauchos, which is on the verge of being destroyed by 'progress.' Thus in *My Kid, the Doctor*, he dramatizes the conflict between a gaucho father and his city-edu-
cated son—the battle between the old days and the new. Indeed the spirit of the pampas pervades all his works, whether
they deal with rural themes or with urban ones, as in *Dead
Men*. A careful examination of all his plays brings one to the
conclusion that such stories, such characters, such conflicts,
could never take place in conventionally organized countries,
but only in untrammelled, primitive, even barbaric ones. His
themes are never those of a 'soft' decadent society, but always
a product of primitive passions, of fatalistic attitudes, of basic
struggles. Naturally, dramas of this sort are directed against
many types of modern life: oppressors, parasites, knaves, hypo-
crites; while Sánchez' heroes, just as naturally, are reformers,
moralists, and particularly the victims of social institutions.
And all this flagellating realism is turned upon national subject matter, finding its surest theme in the basic problem of the
individualist *versus* convention, the rude gaucho *versus* the
city—the very clash that Sarmiento described as the struggle
between civilization and barbarism.

Yet for all the gauchesque and native elements of his theatre,
Sánchez' work is closely related to that of European authors.
This is perhaps the essential trait of his plays, that they represent the focusing of a skilled Old World technique upon the
American scene. For instance, it is possible to trace the strong
influence exerted by Ibsen on Sánchez. There are numerous
points of similarity in their plays. Sánchez, like Ibsen, applied
his best gifts to the *drame à thèse:* heredity, the rights of

woman, social problems, and even madness are themes common to both authors; like the Norwegian, Sánchez is a penetrating interpreter of modern psychology, though his tragedies are perhaps more direct and brutal than those of Ibsen. Another comparison suggests itself between the work of Sánchez and that of the great Spanish novelist Galdós. There is a great parallelism between the two, particularly in their manner of developing the struggle between good and evil, in all its gradations and all its terrible crudeness. One can even point out individual compositions, like Sánchez' *Family Life*, and Galdós' *Glory* which bear striking resemblances: In both appears the character of a strong man, who tries to guide his family on the straight path; routine and social conventions strive to destroy the original man; and parasitic relatives play an important part in both works. Similarly, one can find much in common in the writings of Sánchez and the Spanish playwright Echegaray; perhaps the influence of Ibsen is responsible for similar tendencies in the two authors.

Of course, it is not for his Ibsen-inspired stagecraft that Sánchez is most noted, but for his application of this technique to American themes. His plays mark, indeed, the fusion of indigenous subject matter with European literary methods; they exhibit a certain amount of refinement even in the most brutal tragedies. As such, Sánchez' work underlines an important phase in the development of the gauchesque genre. Previously, the man of the pampas, basically a primitive character, had been treated in equally primitive literary forms. But now the gaucho, his life, and feelings were no longer subject matter for verses improvised to the beat of a guitar, or popular epics sold in the *pulpería*, or harrowing thrillers printed in daily newspaper installments. The *gaucho*, the orphan of the plains, had become a theme worthy of accomplished writers— a subject that was to find its highest expression in the advanced technique of the modern novel.

THE GAUCHO NOVEL

THE earliest development of the gaucho novel—leaving aside the journalistic serials of Gutiérrez—took place not in Argentina as might have been expected, but in the neighboring Oriental Republic of Uruguay.[21] Even before the close of the nineteenth century, two writers of fiction, Acevedo Díaz and Viana, had produced distinguished works that, in a sense, foreshadowed the whole course of the gaucho novel. In the twentieth century a third, Zavala Muniz, explored in his three chronicles the whole subject of the gaucho's historical evolution, from the old heroic days to the era of outlaws, to the prosy modern times of gaucho farmhands.

The first of these *gauchescos*, Eduardo Acevedo Díaz (1851-1924), is generally considered the first nationalistic writer of Uruguay. Not only were there no Uruguayan novelists before him, but no subsequent author in his country has been quite able to continue in his footsteps as a writer on national themes. In his own life, Acevedo Díaz played an active (if not always well-rewarded) role in the formation of the new nation: a soldier of the revolutionary armies, he was at different occasions a politician, a diplomat, and an exile. And in his first three books, *Ismael* (1888), *Nativa* (1890), and *Cry of Glory* (1894), he covered the whole period of the Uruguayan Wars for Independence.* These works form a trilogy, which their author called 'a hymn of blood,' and they still rank as commendable works in the manner of the historical novel.

But Acevedo Díaz' masterpiece was his last book, *Soledad* (1894), which has had an effect on gaucho novelists to the present time. As a Creole or native novel, *Soledad* is a model work in its type; it has all the untamed landscape, the rude elemental characters, the epic sweep, the brutality and violence that are so characteristic of the South American scene. Its realism is absolute: the personages of the story, faithful to their

---

* Acevedo Díaz, *Ismael, Nativa, Grito de Gloria.*

simple unlettered natures, express themselves through actions rather than words. *Soledad*, perhaps because of this realistic nativism, has served as a pattern for numerous gauchesque novels, and later writers have paralleled not only the general form but even the most brilliant scenes of this work. For instance, the episode of the shearing is unusually vivid; its later counterpart is to be found in Zavala Muniz' first *Chronicle*. Similarly, the pampas fire—with all its details, even the lurid touch of the dead mare that is used to put out the flames—reappears in Lynch's novel, *Raquela*. Indeed, many of the most celebrated modern works of this genre, *The Gaucho Florido*, *The Chronicle of a Crime*, *The Romance of a Gaucho*, *Zogoibi*, have all followed in the path of Acevedo Díaz' trail-blazing novel, *Soledad*.[22]

Equally an innovator in his own way was another early Uruguayan gauchesque writer, the noted *costumbrista* Javier de Viana (1872-1925). Brought up among gauchos, he later went to the cities of Montevideo and Buenos Aires, where he was successively student, politician, and journalist; but his abiding interest remained in the pampas and the changing type of the gaucho. In his volumes of short stories, *Yuyos* (1912), and *Dry Wood* (1913), and in his novelettes, *Campo* (1896) and *Guri* (1898),* he composed extraordinarily realistic scenes of Uruguayan country life at the close of the past century, pictures full of local color and minute observation. The gauchos that he describes so painstakingly, unlike those of his countryman Acevedo Díaz, are no longer primitive and heroic figures. He paints the gaucho as an already half-degenerate being, whom the inroads of progress have transformed from a free nomad into a farm laborer or a bandit. Viana's gauchos still have certain robust qualities, but drink and poverty and illness have reduced them to the state of 'pariahs of the fields.'

Excellent as these stories are in their way, Viana's most im-

* Viana, *Yuyos, Leña Seca; Campo, Guri.*

portant contribution to the development of gauchesque fiction is his one full-length novel, *Gaucha* * (1899). In this work, the merits and defects of his technique stand out plainly: on the one hand, detailed realism in the description of the Uruguayan rural background, but on the other an artificial use of the naturalistic theories of Zola. This unfortunate combination appears even in the original conception of the book. Starting out with a real person and a fireside tale—a story Viana heard an old gaucho tell to an audience of farmhands drinking *mate* around the kitchen hearth—the novelist set to work. First he scrupulously explored the region, documenting his pages with details from life; but then he applied Zola's theories of heredity, creating a pathological character, Juana, whose psychological introversion is thoroughly out of keeping with her rustic personality. Despite this flaw, *Gaucha* remains even today a vigorous novel, written in a style rich with picturesque color and vernacular dialogue—a minor triumph of realistic regionalism.

Pure realism in the gauchesque genre, so auspiciously inaugurated by Acevedo Díaz and Viana, reached perhaps its strongest expression in the works of the contemporary Uruguayan novelist Justino Zavala Muniz (1897-   ). Zavala Muniz himself is as interesting and representative a character as any he has described; the son of a country storekeeper, and the grandson of a famous rural *caudillo*, he has repeatedly abandoned his desk for the life of action and his pen for the smoking pistol of the revolutionist. His works, which partake of this same dynamic quality, comprise three chronicles—*The Chronicle of Muniz* (1921), *The Chronicle of a Crime* (1926), and *The Chronicle of the Country-Store* (1930)—each of them analyzing a different period in the evolution of the gaucho, and each exhibiting the artistic progress of the author.†

* Viana, *Gaucha.*
† Zavala Muniz, *Crónica de Muniz, Crónica de un Crimen, Crónica de la Reja.*

The first *Chronicle* was composed by Zavala as a life of his celebrated grandfather, the *caudillo* or military leader Justino Muniz, who defeated the rival *caudillo* Saravia in countless battles. Impelled by affection for his illustrious forbear and a desire to clear his name from the stigma of treason, young Zavala started at the age of seventeen to collect personal reminiscences of the 'good old days'—memories and episodes that he finally brought out in *The Chronicle of Muniz*, a volume replete with the deeds of heroes and the violence of revolutionary action, set against the picturesque background of the beautiful ranch of Bañado de Medina. By way of contrast, the second *Chronicle* shows Uruguay in a later, less heroic period, when the *caudillos* have disappeared and the once respected gaucho has turned outlaw. One of these gaucho bandits, 'The Hawk,' moves through the pages of the novel like a nightmare-figure of horror and death, his face and hands stained with blood. Zavala Muniz frankly admires the brutal surrender of the gaucho to a life of crime—a point-of-view that lends a strange power to the whole book, though obviously, the reader will find himself surfeited by the excess of blood and brutal violence.

No such complaint can be made of Zavala Muniz' third and most mature book, *The Chronicle of the Country-Store*. Here, he has turned away from crime and battle to compose a sort of heroic-pastoral intermezzo. The scene is still Cerro Largo near Melo, where the youth Ricardo spends his days as a shop-keeper's assistant, listening to the gauchos who relate stories to pass the winter afternoons. In the tales they tell, the young man glimpses the heroic greatness of this vanished type now converted into a lowly 'hired hand'; but even in the latter-day peace and quiet of the ranch the gaucho reveals his greatness, humbly and nobly, by enduring patiently these dull prosy times, sustaining himself with the memory of a past gaucho glory.

As Zavala Muniz' *Chronicles* indicate, and as the whole

previous course of the gaucho novel had foreshadowed, the gaucho as a type had already begun to disappear by the first quarter of the twentieth century. At the same time, the gauchesque genre in literature was already nearing its end. Countless novels had exploited the subject [23] from every angle, almost invariably following a realistic technique. It remained only for two contemporary Argentine novelists to bring a psychological approach to the problem of the gaucho, a treatment that has produced the very finest novels of this field. One of these writers is Lynch, in whose stories, told with studied simplicity, the gauchesque genre reaches its perfect artistic balance. The other is Güiraldes, who has captured the heroic gauchesque spirit in the transcendent symbolism of *Don Segundo Sombra*—the *non plus ultra* of gaucho novels.

Benito Lynch (1885–1952) has brought a new and refreshing note to gaucho fiction.[24] The essential feature of his work is his unaffected naturalness—his ability to paint the gaucho sincerely, in a simple style, and without heroic trappings. This simplicity is equally characteristic of Lynch's own life. Of Irish extraction, he seems far more Anglo-Saxon than Argentinian: a tall rugged man, with a large bony face and bushy eyebrows, and a slow meditative manner of speaking. By preference, Lynch leads a quiet bachelor's existence, entirely apart from the littérateurs of Argentina, in the peaceful university city of La Plata. And just as his life reflects a complete serenity, so his latest literary style reveals the already consummate artist who has chosen voluntarily to limit his range and his ambitions.

This skill in self-limitation—deliberately choosing a simple technique, paying attention to homely details, keeping his characters within the narrow framework of unlettered countryfolk who express themselves in few words—is what sets Lynch apart from other writers on the gaucho. His stories are always in keeping with the rustic environment in which they are set, even when this fidelity to the truth mars the artistic merit of a story. Thus, in his first gauchesque novel, *The Carrion Hawks** (1916-17), he introduces just such a brutal and melodramatic ending as might actually occur in real life. The novel deals with the conflict between two characters who have the traits of the native *carancho* or carrion hawk: a cruel domineering father, tyrannical master of the ranch 'La Florida,' and his impetuous son who returns home after several years of university study in Europe. And Lynch solves the struggle by an unexpected double murder—which seems quite unlikely in the pages of a book, but which is perfectly in accord with the savage milieu of the pampas.

Lynch, with this urge to interpret rural life as it really is, has won renown for his masterful descriptions of country scenes. The kitchen, the fields, the life of farm animals, the casting of a spell according to the directions of an elderly medicine woman—such bits of local color appear constantly in his novels, never detracting from the flow of the story, but so vividly done that they stamp Lynch as Argentina's leading *costumbrista*. Episodes like the ranch fire in *Raquela* † (1918), to take one example, can safely be ranked, for coloring and movement, among the very finest things that have ever been written in South America. Here, for instance, is one memorable detail—the flight of the wild creatures from the spreading flames:

> A veritable army of red partridges began to cross the patio. It was a compact column, hundreds of birds hurrying in the same direction, silently and sadly, stupefied by the danger to such a degree that they seemed like tame chickens.
> Not only partridges filed across the patio, fleeing from the menacing fire, but also all sorts of representatives of the lesser fauna . . . We saw foxes, skunks, prairie rats . . . and even snakes and vipers. All that heterogeneous population, all that mysterious world that bustles in the

* Lynch, *Los Caranchos de la Florida.*
† Lynch, *Raquela.*

straw of the *pajonales*, and that in ordinary daily life we sense rather than see—all of it was filing through the patio of the ranch, noiselessly and precipitously, just as whole villages flee before the advance of the enemy.[25]

But Lynch's work is outstanding for still another trait, even more noteworthy than his descriptive talent: his unusual ability to create living characters. This is nowhere better seen than in *The Englishman of the Bones* * (1924), the touching love story of a young English scientist (a 'bone digger') and a gaucho girl. The heroine Balbina—a girl of 18, black haired, ingenuous, and untamed, whose feelings change gradually from prankish malice and downright hate to gratitude, fondness, and desperate adoration—is Lynch's best creation. Even the final tragedy, when 'Mister James' leaves and Balbina takes her own life, seems the logical and inevitable doing of the characters themselves. Lynch's tendency to let his personages govern their own destinies without interference by the author reaches its climax in *The Romance of a Gaucho* † (1930), a novel written entirely in the gauchesque idiom. Here, he has achieved an extraordinary effect by suppressing all external description and using instead the device of the gaucho jargon itself. This characteristic mode of speech, based on archaic Spanish and full of strange ellipses and virile metaphors, lends itself remarkably to the story: the love of the gaucho Pantaleón for the Señora Julia, a married woman as fine-souled and noble as she is young and pretty. Written as it is in *habla gauchesca*, this novel, perhaps more than any other, exhibits Lynch's sincerity. A gifted writer and observer, he has personally watched the tragic disappearance of the men of the pampas, and he has dedicated his best efforts to preserving on paper figures of the gauchos as they really were.

For the gaucho is today a vanishing type. The nomadic orphan of the plains is rapidly being supplanted by Spaniards

---

* Lynch, *El Inglés de los Güesos.*
† Lynch, *El Romance de un Gaucho.*

and Turks; and even those gauchos that have survived now trim their beards and work as hired hands on ranches. Perhaps it is for this reason that the greatest of all gaucho novels is not a work of realism—not even of psychological realism like Lynch's—but instead the obviously stylized portrayal of Güiraldes' *Don Segundo Sombra*. Ricardo Güiraldes (1886-1927) died at the early age of thirty-nine, just when his masterpiece was being acclaimed by press and public.[26] His brief life is chiefly significant as a background for the composition of his one great book, with its frankly autobiographical elements. Güiraldes' own existence—his many years passed in the ranch of La Porteña coupled with his wide culture and his travels abroad, his change from a gaucho's boyhood to the manhood of a cultivated gentleman—this simple pattern underlies the action (it can hardly be called plot) of *Don Segundo Sombra*. In this same connection, his earlier books are interesting largely because they contain elements—though only elements—of the traits which were to distinguish his gaucho masterpiece. Thus, *Raucho* (1915) studies the character of a youth removed from his early rural environment; *Tales of Death and Blood* (1915) and the posthumous *Six Stories* (1929) exhibit a strange penetration of native Argentine themes; *Xaimaca* (1923) reveals elements of nostalgia; and *Rosaura* (1922) is written in that advanced technique which is such a feature of Güiraldes' work.*

But none of these books exhibits any of that dazzling originality which was to make the appearance of *Don Segundo Sombra* in 1926 an event in the history of Spanish American letters. This unique book has won a permanent place as an Argentine classic, both for its merits as a work of art and for its perfect interpretation of the gaucho. Don Segundo, as Güiraldes has created him, is not so much a human being of flesh and blood, as a myth—the ideal gaucho, the symbol of the

---

* Güiraldes, *Don Segundo Sombra, Raucho, Cuentos de Muerte y de Sangre, Seis Relatos Porteños, Xaimaca, Rosaura.*

pampas. The author himself informs the reader that this character, by his very name, is a *sombra*, a shadow; and he writes thus in his very first picture of Don Segundo:

> Motionless, I watched him move away, the silhouette of man and horse strangely enlarged against the luminous horizon. It seemed to me that I had a phantom, a shadow, something that passes and is more of an idea than a real being; something which drew me with the force of a hidden pool sucking the current of a river into its depths.[27]

Above everything else, this Don Segundo is a complete man, master of himself in every situation, possessor of his soul. His nobility derives from his concept of liberty, which compels him to lead a life of solitude and anarchic individualism, and to wander ceaselessly across the plains.

Güiraldes has presented his mysterious ideal gaucho in a story that is almost a symbolic tale. A young lad—whose name does not appear in the book, but who is obviously the author himself—is the narrator. The boy lives in the house of his aunts, in an Argentine town, as though in a prison, remembering his happy childhood on his native ranch. But on one memorable day, his whole life is changed: he sees the shadowy figure of Don Segundo, and runs away to follow his hero and become a plainsman. Bruised, rain-soaked, exhausted by the unaccustomed labors of the pampas, the youth is finally 'adopted' by Don Segundo. Five years pass, and he becomes a thorough gaucho, travelling the highways with Don Segundo, who not only instructs him in the difficult arts of cowpunching and horsebreaking, but also develops his imagination with tales of witches and devils. The pair wanders constantly, for Don Segundo can never remain still: his feet devour leagues of pampas, his course is always onward, his best conversation is the soliloquy. At length comes the news that the boy's father (whom he never knew as such) has died, leaving him estates to look after; the youth, settled on his ranch, becomes interested in books, and changes gradually from a gaucho to a man of culture. But his foster-father Don Segundo, sure that his protégé is now a man, leaves for the life of the endless horizons. The farewell is heartbreaking; but from this 'death' of the *gauchito* created by Don Segundo emerges the literary *Don Segundo Sombra* created by Güiraldes.

As a novel, *Don Segundo Sombra* can perhaps best be compared to *Don Quixote*. Like Cervantes' immortal work, it belongs to that purely Spanish type of novel in which the chief interest lies in the character portrayed, and the action is hardly more than a series of episodes. Nor does the resemblance end here. For Don Segundo, like Don Quixote, is a knight of the ideal; an ideal of simple manliness and freedom. Here perhaps lies the secret of Güiraldes' work: he has sought to ennoble a historic national character so often caricatured in circus pantomimes and bandit novels—and he has amply succeeded. For the shadowy figure of Don Segundo will forever stretch across the pampas, not as a picture drawn from life, but as a legendary symbol of a heroic type that was.

For the gaucho, another 'vanishing American,' has already made his contribution to the life of the New World. Always considered a backward social element, it was nonetheless he who initiated Argentina's commercial greatness, when the first gaucho traded his first cowhide at the *pulpería*. The gaucho fought the Indian for two hundred years and kept him away from the civilized centers established in the plains; the gaucho was the soldier in the armies of Belgrano and San Martín, which played such an important role in winning independence from Spain. But above all the gaucho gave his native land something greater, a regional literature that has served as a model of spiritual and cultural independence for all of Spanish America. Gaucho literature has given its best: in poetry, *Martín Fierro;* in the drama, the plays of Florencio Sánchez;

and in the novel, *Don Segundo Sombra*. And as the gaucho has disappeared, so will his literary ascendancy. But the example of the gauchesque genre remains as a rewarding chapter in literary history: an example of those new and native forces that have wrought the transformation from the imitation of European models to that literary Americanism which dominates the contemporary field of Spanish American letters.

5

The Spanish American Novel

THE REALISTIC NOVEL

A CHAPTER on the prose fiction south of the Río Grande cannot begin better than by stressing one fundamental point: the extraordinary significance of the modern Spanish American novel. Beyond question, the novel is the most important literary expression of twentieth-century South America; and modern Spanish American novelists rank—for vigor, originality, and stylistic mastery—alongside their most distinguished fellow craftsmen in the modern world. Yet this novel is chiefly interesting not for its intrinsic merit, high though that assuredly is, but as a reflection of the culture of an entire continent.

First of all, the contemporary novel is a sign of Spanish America's passion for producing literature. Indeed, literary activity is of such vital importance in the lives of Latin Americans that it may be said to occupy a position similar to that of economic interest in the lives of North Americans. For if the southern continent has not been prolific in industrial leaders, bankers, economists, and scientists, it has nevertheless brought forth excellent men of letters. Few outsiders have even a faint idea of the great number of poets, literary critics, and especially novelists, flourishing in those lands. And almost no foreign critic is aware of the way literary creation is cultivated, entirely out of proportion to other cultural outlets of

the Spanish American republics. In politics, they oscillate between primitive tyrannies and theoretical democracies; in education they slavishly try to put into practice the theories of
European educators like Lunacharsky and Decroly, and Americans like John Dewey, though they are invariably equipped
with a pitifully inadequate school budget. Thus, despite their
feverish desire to accomplish something in all branches of
intellectual endeavor, Latin American countries have succeeded in a strictly limited number of fields; a few of their
jurists and anthropologists are well known abroad, but they
have achieved positive distinction only in history and philology, in the fine arts, and above all, in literature. This remarkable literary fertility finds its strongest expression today in the
contemporary novel.

But the novel is significant for still another reason. Spanish
American novels, or at least a large number of them, are of
the realistic type. That is to say, their authors have tried to
reproduce and interpret, according to varying canons, the life
that they found in the world about them. Thus, in the nineteenth century, Spanish American novelists described the internal struggles of the young republics, the formation of a
stratified society, the growth of great cities, and the tragedy
of individual lives drawn into the slum-life of poverty and
degradation. And in the twentieth century, they have observed
some of these same phenomena, but generally they have written with a widening perception of man in his struggle against
primitive nature, of men working in mines and plantations
and factories, of sensitive spirits unable to cope with modern
life, of simple souls engaging in a revolution they cannot
understand. In its treatment of such subjects the realistic
novel becomes a precious record from which to study the life
of the Spanish American continent.

This documentary value is especially noticeable in the
earlier novels of the realistic school. From a strictly literary
point of view, these nineteenth-century Spanish American

novels often have little value, except as forerunners of the modern regional novel. But they do afford a priceless picture of life in those times. Of course, reality appeared too in the works of the romantic novelists, and of other writers. Thus, Isaacs' famous novel *Maria*, and Mármol's *Amalia*, both afford descriptions of American psychology, customs, and manners of life; and even Ricardo Palma, in his *Peruvian Traditions* with its anecdotes of the colonial era, nonetheless preserves the flavor of things American. But when realism as a movement made its appearance, the American scene acquired for the first time a place of importance in the novel.

The greatest Spanish American realist of the past century was unquestionably Alberto Blest Gana (1830-1920), whose ambition was to become 'the Balzac of Chile.' Blest Gana had a wide acquaintance with French literature; in fact, he was for a long while the Chilean Minister to France, and he lived in that country for some fifty years, rearing his numerous family there, and dying in Paris. And the influence of French realism was the dominant one on his novels. As he tells the story himself: 'One day, reading Balzac, I burned all the poems of my adolescence and swore to be a novelist.' Thereafter, Blest Gana was the commentator of Chilean life after the pattern of *The Human Comedy*, recording, in detailed documents, the transformation of Chilean society from an energetic world of pioneers to a lax degenerate society. To be sure, he never attained to the stature of his French master; he was too fond of intrigue, too given to spoiling the unity of his novels with a needless multiplicity of characters, too prone to caricature the ridiculous traits of his chief personages, too lacking in depth and stylistic distinction. Withal, Blest Gana was a careful observer of national life, and a good painter of social customs. Thus, to understand the formation of the aristocracy, the middle class, and the lower class in Chile, to observe how the government functioned in the early days of the Republic, to witness popular action and popular speech at close range, one need only turn to the novels of this conscientious realist.

For example, in his masterpiece, *Martín Rivas* (1862), Blest Gana has used a simple story—that of a middle-class young man who marries a girl of the aristocracy—to paint a full-scale and animated picture of Chilean society in the 50s. He has sketched this society minutely and from every angle: the great role played by politics and money; the struggle between liberals and conservatives, between *pipiolos* and *pelucones;* the division of classes into *rotos* (lower class), *gente de medio pelo* (middle class), and *gente decente* (plutocracy); the influence of French culture among the wealthy, their rampant opportunism, and their moral laxitude. The pages of *Martín Rivas* are filled, too, with priceless descriptions of private parties, popular festivals, political gatherings, church ceremonies, markets, in such abundance that it would be hard to find anywhere a better picture of the city of Santiago in the middle of the last century.

In *During the Reconquest* * (1897), Blest Gana again portrays the city of Santiago, this time as it was from 1814 to 1818, those tragic years in the life of the young nation when the victorious Spaniards, after defeating Generals Carrera and O'Higgins, subjected the country to the most brutal despotism. Sinister and ridiculous Spanish leaders, heroic patriots, picturesque *rotos*, and all sorts of feminine characters move through the pages of this book. More than a novel, *During the Reconquest* stands out as the epic of a nation, a great fresco painting (as one critic has remarked) of the Chilean soul struggling for its independence. The antithesis of this heroic age is painted by Blest Gana in *Transplanted* † (1904), in which decadent Chileans are shown wasting the strength of their ancestral blood in Paris. These emigrés have gone abroad to be absorbed into a life of luxury and ostentation, hoping to marry their children to titled Europeans. Blest Gana merci-

* Blest Gana, *Durante la Reconquista.*
† Blest Gana, *Los Trasplantados.*

lessly describes the petty intrigues, the endless efforts, the undignified acts by which the newcomers try to 'crash' the Parisian salons, only to be scorned by the authentic nobility and nicknamed *rastaquoueres*, a derogatory word coined especially in ridicule of the American visitors. And he dramatizes their tragedy in a melodramatic fashion: The heroine Mercedes, a rich Chilean young lady, rejects the good Patricio, with whom she is in love, and marries a German Prince Rösprinbruck to please her family; realizing that she has made an irreparable mistake, she commits suicide during her honeymoon. The weaknesses of such a story are those of Blest Gana as a novelist: his milieu is excellent, his moral aim commendable, but the symbolism of his work as a whole is trite and unconvincing.

No other Spanish American realist ever attained to the stature of Blest Gana, though the school was not lacking for devotees both in the nineteenth and the twentieth centuries. Many of them, however, were imitators of Spanish rather than French realism, avowed followers of Pérez Galdós. Thus the *novela galdosiana* had a Chilean disciple in the person of Luis Orrego Luco (1866–1948), who in his *New Idyll* (1900) attempted to sketch high society, and in *Great House* (1908) portrayed the entire period of the *resurgimento* with sketches of aristocratic life, business affairs, social gatherings, amorous intrigues, and even crimes.* Even more influenced by Galdós was the Argentine novelist Carlos María Ocantos (1860–)— best known for his *León Zaldívar* (1888), *Quilito* (1891), *Missy Jerome* (1898), *Don Perfecto* (1902)—who has written on every imaginable theme from drug addiction to the harmful influence of Argentinisms on the Castilian language.† Another follower of Spanish literary tendencies was the Colombian Tomás Carrasquilla (1858–1941), who in his first book, *Fruits of My Native Land* (1896), described the mountain

---

* Orrego Luco, *Un Idilio Nuevo, Casa Grande.*

† Ocantos, *León Zaldívar, Quilito, Misia Jeromita, Don Perfecto.*

folk of Antioquia, a theme to which he returned in his master-piece, *The Marchioness of Yolombó* (1928); and who, in his fertile and penetrating criticism of Colombian society, shows himself a member of the school of Pérez Galdós.*

Still another type of Spanish American realism appeared in the work of the naturalists who flourished at the turn of the century. Faithful to the principles of Zola's experimental novel —that everything human is the result of the physiological organism, which in turn is determined by heredity and environment—they produced a number of works that introduced hitherto taboo subjects and settings. On the one hand, these novels were little but imitations of Zola in their use of psychopathology, insanity, and sordid material. But on the other, they created a sensation by their denunciation of Spanish America's real social cankers: the exploitation of mine workers, peasants, and city laborers; the general venality of government officials; the appalling conditions of tenement life; the frightening increase of social disease and the uncontrolled development of prostitution. Perhaps the best known of these naturalistic novelists was the Mexican Federico Gamboa (1864-1939), who won continental renown with his *Santa* (1903), the Spanish American prototype of Zola's *Nana*.

Naturalism obviously did not paint a pretty picture of Spanish American life. But it did open the eyes of novelists to the world about them. Later writers were to shake off the clichés of both naturalism and realism, the desire to prove a 'scientific' point, or the wish to paint a vast canvas that would include the entire 'human comedy.' But the way had been prepared for the novelist to treat every aspect, however brutal, of human existence. Thus realism and naturalism led directly to the Americanist novel of the twentieth century: to the novel of the city, first of all; and later—here Zola's *Earth* was a stimulus—to the still more interesting novel of the land.

* Carrasquilla, *Frutos de mi Tierra, La Marquesa de Yolombó.*

THE NOVEL OF THE CITY

THE city novel in Spanish America [1] derives directly from the naturalistic novel of the past century. South American novelists have devoted themselves to describing primarily the seamy side of metropolitan life: slums, tenements, centers of vice, waterfront districts, and so on *ad infinitum*. Hence it is no wonder that the two leading exponents of the city novel— Manuel Gálvez in Argentina, and Joaquín Edwards Bello in Chile—are conspicuous for their old-fashioned techniques. Thus, Edwards Bello might have become Chile's greatest novelist were it not for his *demodé* realism; his earlier books have all the defects of the naturalistic and realistic schools— overemphasis on propaganda, and a tendency to observe human beings according to certain *a priori* concepts; and his best works show a decided preference for the more sordid aspects of 'life in the gutter' that are generally associated with Zola. Similarly, Gálvez, for all that he protests his independence from naturalism, has nevertheless strong parallels with Zola; true, his work is more romantic and emotional, and his compassion for the unfortunate is closer to Dickens or Daudet; but in his concept of the novel, and his execution of this concept, Gálvez' work reminds one of the *roman experimental*.

All the same, Manuel Gálvez (1882-   ) is one of the leading novelists of Argentina, and indeed of Spanish America.[2] A native of Paraná, Gálvez has spent most of his life in Buenos Aires, where he studied law at the University, founded the magazine *Ideas*, and held the post of Supervisor of Secondary Education. Apart from trips to Europe, the chief events of his existence have been connected with the publication of his books and the storms of controversy provoked by them. For his novels, like Zola's, often partook of the character of exposés; for instance, his important first book, *The Normal-School Teacher* (1914), vivisects the pettiness of provincial minds and the moral smallness of the educational profession,

while his celebrated best-seller *Nacha Regules* (1919) describes
the miseries of existence in the brothels of Buenos Aires. And
like Balzac, he set himself a mammoth task: to put modern
Argentina on paper, showing its rapid growth, its greatness,
its defects. Thus, in *The Teacher*, he describes the monotonous
life of La Rioja, a city of the interior; in *Soul Sickness* (1916),
his scene is the great unfeeling metropolis of Buenos Aires,
in which a writer struggles desperately and finally dies; in
The Shadow of the Convent (1917), he shows the ancient
conservative city of Córdoba, and the struggle between narrow clericalism and nascent liberalism.*

In his novels Gálvez has used Argentine society as a labora-
tory, much as Zola had done with the society of Paris, eventually turning the novel from its channel of aesthetic purpose
into the lake of sociological propaganda. But whatever his
shortcomings as an artist, his picture of modern South American life is truly a remarkable one. No phenomenon seems to
escape the interest of this writer; he gives copious data on
such problems as marriage, divorce, free love, corruption in
education and politics, the death-hold of capitalism upon
society, and the despair of the masses in its grip. In his pages,
the reader finds himself in the salons of Argentine society;
in the waiting rooms of Ministers of State; in the offices of
school directors; in the country mansions of landowners; in
cloisters; and even in the gloomy recesses of meat-packing
houses, jails, and fishermen's hovels.

No less complete is the picture of Chilean city life given by
Joaquín Edwards Bello (1888-   ), who in *Esmeraldo's Cradle*
(1918) and especially in his famous book *The 'Roto'* (1920)
revealed himself as the novelist of the Chilean *roto* or city
urchin.[3] Although his greatest achievement has been in the
painting of slums, Edwards Bello gives a realistic if somewhat
caricatured picture of all aspects of Santiago and Valparaiso

* Gálvez, *La Maestra Normal, Nacha Regules, El Mal Metafísico,
La Sombra del Convento.*

life. In his earlier novels—*Useless* (1910) and *The Monster* (1912)—he paints the external aspects of these cities with their boarding houses, churches, brothels, and gambling dens. And in his more recent book, *Valparaiso, the Windy City* (1931) he returns to external description,* giving pictures of Santiago, Concepción, and Talcahuano, as well as of Valparaiso proper. He paints this city as a commercial metropolis, with all its ancient landmarks obliterated by the earthquake; a materialistic society where wealthy foreigners are lionized, where banks, companies, and mines prosper though never by fair and legal means.

But Edwards Bello's best pictures of Chilean city life are to be found in his two novels on the *roto*, the man-of-the-lowest-class, the urban type who corresponds to the rural peon. As studies of character, these books are necessarily limited by their subject, the ragged *roto* being psychologically an elementary type, whose two necessities are food and liquor; as social documents they rank high. In *Esmeraldo's Cradle*, for instance, Edwards Bello has probed deep at both ends of the social scale, to give sharply etched pictures of Chilean city dwellers. He dashes off his portrait of high society with a few superficial jabs, painting ridiculous young men-of-the-world, lazy society misses, the vain elegance of the Racing Club; while on the other hand, he gives a most minute and realistic picture of Esmeraldo's 'cradle,' the brothel La Gloria. It is this same den of vice—peopled by the same characters, Esmeraldo, his mother Clorinda, who runs the house, the women of the establishment, the gambler Fernando, and so on —that is the setting of *The 'Roto.'* Indeed, La Gloria is the true protagonist of the work, the festering center that incubates vice and crime and tragedy in the midst of the big city.

This type of city novel has had other devotees in South America, notably among writers whose forte lies in some other

* Edwards Bello, *La Cuna de Esmeraldo, El Roto; El Inútil, El Monstruo, Valparaíso, la Ciudad del Viento*.

field and who have attempted an occasional study of urban life. Such, for example, is *Juana Lucero* (1902), by the Chilean escapist Augusto Thomson [4] ('d'Halmar'), a book which treats the most sordid aspects of city existence. Again, the distinguished novelist Eduardo Barrios,[5] in *A Lost Soul* (1917), has painted the city from a somewhat different point of view, showing the tragedy of a sensitive spirit in a materialistic environment. Here, Barrios has described every Chilean institution: church, home, army, military school, *liceo*, club, library, tenement house, et cetera; but his work, as always, is chiefly outstanding as a psychological study. Again, the Cuban Carlos Loveira (1882-1928), while primarily a writer of social propaganda, has given occasional pictures of city life. Of all Spanish American writers, Loveira is perhaps the one who most closely resembles Zola; and in his *Juan Criollo* (1927) he has shown vivid naturalistic cross-sections of Havana, where his hero endures a life of hunger and misery in the slums, only to end as a wealthy deputy with a fine house and luxurious automobiles.*

Another celebrated writer who has dissected Spanish American city life is the Venezuelan Rufino Blanco Fombona (1874-1944), who in *The Man of Gold* † (1920) has written a biting indictment of political life in Caracas. Politics rather than fiction writing has been Blanco Fombona's main interest: an active figure in Venezuelan affairs, he has several times been a political prisoner and is best known for his impassioned campaign against 'Yankee imperialism' in Spanish America. So it is quite understandable that his *Man of Gold* should be one of the most vivid and detailed pictures ever drawn of the Spanish American politician. This character, the *hombre de oro* himself, is not the aggressive tyrant, but rather that indispensable figure, the political puppet. And Blanco Fombona has devoted a whole novel to explaining the process by which an

* D'Halmar, *Juana Lucero*; Barrios, *Un Perdido*; Loveira, *Juan Criollo*.
† Blanco Fombona, *El Hombre de Oro*.

elderly miser is manipulated into the position of becoming dictator—a sordid behind-the-scenes account of petty intrigues, scheming politicians, moronish and debauched generals, and a general atmosphere of venality and corruption.

In general, however, the city as a subject for fiction has attracted relatively few contemporary Spanish American novelists. Apart from those mentioned here, only writers of lesser importance [6] have devoted themselves to this genre. The reasons for this are not hard to find. To begin with, South American cities do not present any very remarkable traits to distinguish them from urban centers in other parts of the world; they are either of the type of sleepy steeped-in-convention provincial capital to be found in some parts of Europe, or of the modern commercial metropolis that is identified with the United States. And the more sensational aspects of this city life form an extremely limited picture—poverty, degradation, bureaucracy, political venality—that is fully covered in a few novels. Spanish American rural life, on the contrary, is in many cases still violent and primitive and everywhere marked by highly original aspects. It is natural, therefore, that by far the greater number of modern writers should be attracted to the far-richer novel of rural and semi-savage regions.

THE NOVEL OF THE LAND

THE very phrase 'novel of the land' suggests the observation that the land itself is the chief actor in a good many Spanish American novels. In itself, this does not of course guarantee any great originality. For example, the Chilean short-story writer, Mariano Latorre (1886–1955), has painstakingly studied and written about the rural regions of his native land—only to produce works that resemble those of the Spanish novelist Pereda. But where South American writers have chosen to do books on the uncivilized parts of the continent, like the still-unexplored forests of the Amazon basin, the results have been remarkable.

The novel of the *selva*, to take a striking case, has been cultivated in many countries from Bolivia to Brazil. The greatest book of all this jungle fiction, and the one which will best serve as a prototype for the rest, is that extraordinary novel *The Vortex* * (1924), by José Eustasio Rivera (1889-1928), a gifted Colombian poet and novelist who, by a strange whim of fate, died prematurely of pneumonia in New York, the greatest city in the world.[7] The 'vortex' in his novel is of course the tropical forest itself, which Rivera, during his brief life as poet, lawyer, and civic figure, had the occasion of visiting as a member of the Venezuela-Colombia Boundary Commission. His journey took him across the valleys of the Casanare, the Meta, the San Martín, and the Vaupés; he travelled along the Orinoco, the Río Negro, the Casiquiare; he lived among the river Indians, and he was lost for a while in the *selva*, where he suffered the torments of thirst and mosquitoes and ants and fever; and while he was convalescing from beri-beri, at his journey's end, he wrote his masterpiece, *The Vortex*.

In this novel, the vast tropical forest comes to life, all its horrors transmuted by Rivera's poetical imagination: He describes dark cities of trees, which no human being has ever entered; trees covered with living nets of parasitic plants, and these in turn covered with millions of insects and larvae; trees that talk and move as if endowed with magic life. And this *selva* has its myriad inhabitants: howling tribes of monkeys; swarms of ants that descend unexpectedly over all living beings, devouring them in a few seconds; blind alligators in their stagnant waters. Even more important, the entire forest is never static for a moment; it is frightfully alive, in all its monstrosity of gestation, decay, violence, and death—with no room for romantic visions:

> Here there are no amorous nightingales, no Versailles-like gardens, no sentimental panoramas! Here are the

* Rivera, *La Vorágine*.

croakings of hydropic toads . . . the trickle of putrefied springs. Here, the aphrodisiac parasite that covers the ground with dead bees; the multitudes of flowers, contracting themselves with sensual palpitations and sticky sweat, that intoxicate one like a drug; the malignant liana whose fuzz blinds animals; the *pringamosa* that inflames the skin, the seed of the *duruju* that looks like a prismatic globe and contains only caustic ashes . . .

Here, at night, unfamiliar voices . . . The sound of the ripe fruit falling . . . the dropping of a leaf . . . And when the dawn sheds its tragic glory over the forests . . . the constant noise of the shrieking wildfowl, the snorts of the wild boar, the laughter of the ridiculous monkey . . .[8]

Here, indeed, is a magnificent background for fiction—and it is this savage setting itself that governs the story of Rivera's novel. For he shows how this forest dominates the human beings who drag themselves through its depths; how it attacks their minds and bodies, incubating fevers and insanity; how with its thousand tentacles it seizes men and transforms them into wild beasts.

Thus, Rivera has painted the tragedy of rubber exploitation in the midst of this tropical *selva*, the plight of Indians and half-breeds, enslaved by European adventurers and hurled by the thousands into this green hell to toil and to die. Sometimes they try to flee, and perish in the forest; sometimes they commit suicide by drinking the thick liquid of the rubber trees. Rivera has written a terrible exposé of these conditions, describing the horrors of the *caucheros* in all their brutal intensity, with a violence and passion that may be judged by the following excerpts:

I have three hundred trees to take care of, and it takes me nine days to lacerate them; I have cleaned them of creepers and lianas; I have opened a path towards each of them. On trudging through this army of giants, to fell the ones that don't shed latex, I often find tappers stealing my rubber. We tear each other with fists and machetes; and the disputed latex is splashed with red. But what does it matter if our veins increase the supply of sap? The overseer demands ten liters a day, and the lash is a usurer that never forgives.

And what if my neighbor dies of fever? I see him stretched out on the leafy mold, shaking himself, trying to rid himself of flies that will not let him die in peace. Tomorrow I shall move away, driven elsewhere by the stench. But I shall steal the latex he gathered. My work will be so much lighter. They'll do the same with me when I die . . .

As I gash the dripping trunk, as I channel it so that its tears may flow into the tin cup, clouds of mosquitoes that protect it suck my blood, and the miasmas of the forest dim my eyes. Thus both the tree and I are suffering, are tearful in the face of death; and both of us struggle until we succumb.[9]

Equally powerful, in its natural setting and in the violence of the human passions it engenders, is the novel of the prairies, which finds its highest expression in *Doña Bárbara* (1929), by the Venezuelan Rómulo Gallegos (1884-   ).[10] A well-known educator in his native country, Gallegos has also had a brief and unsuccessful political career; literature, however, has been his ruling passion since early manhood, and he early started his labors in this field as a journalist and short-story writer. It is in the novel, however, that Gallegos has achieved world fame, and he ranks today as one of the greatest of Spanish American novelists. As an interpreter of the tropics, his only peer is Rivera, in *The Vortex*. By way of contrast, Gallegos has none of Rivera's romantic delirium; he writes instead with a classic serenity, even when his subject is the *selva* itself, in *Canaima* (1935). Here, too, the tropical forest dominates human beings who plunge into its depths seeking gold or rubber; what is more, a spirit of evil, 'Canaima,' lurks in the woods, in the tempests, in the hearts of the wild beasts and the eyes of the serpents, waiting to take possession of the imprudent man who ventures into its domain.

But it is in his pictures of the Venezuelan *llanos*, the vast tropical prairies stretching far into the interior, that Gallegos shows his mastery. Unlike the *selva*, these prairies preserve all the charms and serene beauty of nature; it is only men who destroy one another in the clash between civilization and barbarism that takes place in this setting. Gallegos shows the reader the Venezuelan *llano* in a many-dimensioned picture: he describes the landscape proper in memorable passages filled with vast horizons and splendid tropical dawns; he paints the life of the *llanero*, the rodeo, the march across the quagmires, the alligator hunt; and to all this he adds a flavor of mystery, injecting into his narratives all sorts of popular legends of ghosts and demons and souls in torment. Here, for example, is the explanation of 'the familiar':

> According to an ancient superstition . . . it was the custom in those parts, whenever a new ranch was being established, to bury an animal alive between the jambs of the enclosure, so that its spirit, a prisoner of the land, might watch over the ranch and its owners. From this it got the name of Familiar, and its apparitions were considered lucky omens. The Altamira familiar was a water bullock which, according to tradition, don Evaristo Luzardo had buried at the gate of the sheepfold. And it used to appear between two lights, pawing in the midst of a marsh, from which it raised a great dust;—a marsh, incidentally, that no-one had ever seen from near by, because it used to disappear along with the familiar whenever anyone tried to come near it . . .[11]

Gallegos' interpretation of the prairie is both profound and affectionate, and he shows it under countless different guises: now through minute descriptions of coffee plantations in *The Climber* (1925); now in the theme of *Cantaclaro* (1931), where he tells the story of a troubadour of the plains, a singer of those errant ballads that are the soul of the *llanos*.*

This background of the Venezuelan prairies, with their vast

* Gallegos, *La Trepadora, Cantaclaro*.

haciendas that are breeding-places of crime and revolution, forms the setting of Gallegos' great novel *Doña Bárbara*. Gallegos knows the psychology of these haciendas perfectly: the decadent land ownership, the adventurous Indian and mulatto servants, the bandits and rural parasites. But well as these elements are handled, Gallegos' real power appears in his treatment of the central character—*Doña Bárbara*, a woman of strong character though devoid of moral sense, a perfect incarnation of the *caciquismo* or 'bossism' that is a phenomenon of these plains. Raised among smugglers and brutally wronged in her youth, Bárbara takes revenge upon men in general; as Doña Bárbara—the very name is symbolic of barbarism—she becomes the *cacica* of a huge ranch on the plains north of the Orinoco. Here, surrounded by criminals, enlarging her holdings daily by every manner of dishonest dealing, possessing beauty and wealth and power, she bends men to her perverse will. Some she has assassinated; some she converts into blind tools of her own evil purposes; some she destroys with liquor and indulgence. Gallegos has created an unforgettable person in his *cacica*, and this character and the vivid background of the Venezuelan prairie combine to make of *Doña Bárbara* a true Spanish American classic.

Yet despite the great originality of the novel of the prairie and the novel of the *selva*, the Spanish American rural novel has taken still other interesting forms. Just as the landscape itself seems to become a protagonist in the pages of Rivera, and to a lesser degree in those of Gallegos, so rural man himself —not as an individual, but as a hero *en masse*—is the protagonist of a whole series of novels. From Mexico to Argentina, the great masses of peasants, miners, soldiers, and fishermen have afforded untouched literary material that opened new vistas to rural novelists. The previous romantic novel and the bourgeois novel limited their interest to the aristocracy and the middle class; but the novel of the land discovered a host of new characters: Indians, mestizos, mulattoes, Negroes, 'forgotten men' of all sorts.

Nowhere has this novel of the mass personage found richer expression than in the novel of the Mexican Revolution—a prolific genre which, from the literary point of view, partakes of the spirit of revolt.[12] In Mexico, the revolution played havoc with all traditional concepts of government and culture. On the one hand, the Indian, galled by the oppression of a pseudo-democracy which had done little to improve his situation, ultimately revolted against church, landowner, and government; while on the other, his interpreter the Mexican novelist staged a parallel rebellion against previous forms of art, descending to 'the people' for his characters. Hence, although Zapata, Obregón, and Carranza occasionally appear, the favorite protagonist of these novels is the most popular hero of the revolution, Pancho Villa. A representative work of this type is *The Eagle and the Serpent* * (1928) by Martín Luis Guzmán (1887-   )—who has crowded his chronicle of Pancho Villa's deeds with incredible adventures and episodes, until what is in fact a historical narrative reads like a novel. Other examples of this 'descent to the people' by novelists of the Mexican Revolution may be seen in *The Indian* (1935) by Gregorio López y Fuentes (1895-   ), and in the books of Michoacán of José Rubén Romero (1890–1952).

But the true masterpiece of this genre, *The Underdogs* † (1915–16) by Mariano Azuela (1873–1952), gives perhaps the best picture of the 'mass personage,' selecting its hero from the anonymous leaders of the revolutionary movement.[13] It goes without saying that Azuela knew his Mexican Revolution at first hand. Born in Lagos de Moreno, young Azuela was violently anti-Porfirio Díaz, and upon the success of Madero's revolution he became the political leader of his home town. Later he served in the revolutionary armies that fought against Vic-

* Guzmán, *El Águila y la Serpiente.*
† Azuela, *Los de Abajo.*

toriano Huerta; during the brief period of the Convention, he was Director of Public Education for the State of Jalisco; and finally, upon the triumph of Carranza, he fled to El Paso, whence he returned to Mexico City without ever taking any further part in politics. Apart from this brief revolutionary experience and his long career as a writer-of-fiction—he has published some dozen novels and two novelettes—Azuela's third occupation has been medicine, a calling which he has followed with great devotion. Indeed, something of the physician's objectivity is to be seen in his masterpiece, *The Underdogs*.

This novel, already acclaimed as a classic and translated into numerous languages, explains the Mexican revolutionary process by a case in point. A peasant, Demetrio Macías, is insulted by soldiers and his house is burnt down. He takes his rifle and flees to the open country; and some of his friends, tired of their life, follow him. In a few weeks he becomes the leader of a small band. Successful encounters with the federal forces increase the number of his followers until he has a good-sized army—at which point the former peasant bestows upon himself the title of general. He ultimately becomes a real factor in the destiny of his country, but he is betrayed by his powerful rivals. His army disintegrates, and in a last battle his faithful band is destroyed and he is killed.

The Underdogs is thus a cold analysis of those Mexican revolts which to the author's mind have neither purpose nor significance. That this is Azuela's meaning can be clearly seen in passages like the following, where Luis Cervantes points out to his chief the futility of revolutions:

'But you've only a handful of men down here; you'll only be an unimportant chieftain. There's no argument about it, the revolution is bound to win. After it's all over they'll talk to you just as Madero talked to those who had helped him: "Thank you very much, my friends, you can go home now . . ."

'Well, that's all I want, to be left alone so I can go home.'

'Wait a moment, I haven't finished. Madero said: "You men have made me President of the Republic. You have run the risk of losing your lives and leaving your wives and children destitute; now I have what I wanted, you can go back to your picks and shovels, you can resume your hand-to-mouth existence, you can go half-naked and hungry just as you did before, while we, your superiors, will go about trying to pile up a few million pesos . . ."'

Demetrio nodded and, smiling, scratched his head thoughtfully . . .

'As I was saying,' Luis Cervantes resumed, 'when the revolution is over, everything is over: Too bad that so many men have been killed, too bad that there are so many widows and orphans, too bad that there was so much bloodshed.[14]

Tragically enough, Azuela is perhaps right in his conclusions; for just as Demetrio is betrayed, so is the Mexican betrayed by unworthy generals and even by opportunist labor leaders.

At any rate, Azuela has told his classic story of the revolution with vigor and realism. His style is fragmentary, nervous, at times even incorrect, but always full of color and life. He uses the indispensable number of words to express his meaning, and no more. And this manner of writing is perfectly suited to his subject, allowing the great human drama of the revolution to stand out stark and unadorned. Azuela's chief merit is that he has seized the essence of this drama so remarkably: The blind struggle of these men who have abandoned their wives and their children, who sometimes remember the joys of home—but only to go on, because their guns are loaded, and there are plenty of women and guitars in the next town, and anyhow they don't know how to stop fighting. Azuela has summed up the tragedy in this scene of Demetrio's homecoming:

Demetrio Macías' wife, mad with joy, rushed along the trail to meet him, leading a child by the hand. An absence of almost two years!

They embraced each other and stood speechless. She wept, sobbed. Demetrio stared in astonishment at his wife who seemed to have aged ten or twenty years. Then he looked at his child that gazed up at him in surprise. He wanted to hold him in his arms but the frightened child took refuge in his mother's skirts.

'It's your own father, baby! It's your daddy!'

The child hid his face with the folds of his mother's skirt, still hostile.

Demetrio handed the reins of his horse to his orderly and walked slowly along the steep trail with his wife and son.

'Blessed be the Virgin Mary, Praise be to God! Now you'll never leave us any more, will you? Never . . . never . . . you'll stay with us always?"

Demetrio's face grew dark. Both remained silent, lost in anguish. Demetrio suppressed a sigh. Memories crowded and buzzed through his brain like bees about a hive.

A black cloud rose behind the sierra and a deafening roar of thunder resounded. The rain came pelting down, shattering the white roses clustered like sheaves of stars clinging to tree, rock, and bush over the entire mountain-side. In the shelter of a rocky hut the couple sought refuge.

'Demetrio, please. For God's sake, don't go away! My heart tells me something will happen to you this time.'

Again she was racked with sobs. The child, frightened, cried and screamed . . . Gradually the rain stopped; a swallow . . . fluttered obliquely against the last silver threads of rain, gleaming suddenly in the afternoon sunshine.

'Why do you keep on fighting, Demetrio?'

Demetrio frowned deeply. Picking up a stone absent-mindedly, he threw it to the bottom of the canyon; then he stared pensively into the abyss, watching the arch of its flight.

'Look at that stone; how it keeps on going . . .' [15]

Apart from the novel of the Mexican Revolution, the 'mass personage' has appeared in a great number of works that come under the general classification of the Indianist novel.[16] This type of book has been most cultivated in those west-coast countries—Bolivia, Peru, and Ecuador—which have a predominantly Indian population. Two principal lines of approach have been followed by these novelists writing about the aboriginal races: some have chosen to see only the picturesque or archaeological aspect of Indian life, while others have dedicated themselves to the writing of impassioned protests against the abuse and exploitation of the native by his white overlords. The *novela indianista* has followed both of these courses throughout much of its development. Thus, the early chivalric vision of the Indian in *Cumandá* and similar romantic novels was rudely shattered in 1889; for in that year the Peruvian Clorinda Matto de Turner (1854-1909) provoked a sensation with her *Birds without Nest*, which openly denounced the brutal enslavement of the Indians. Still later, Abraham Valdelomar (1888-1919) ignored ugly realities, and in his exquisite volume of Inca legends, *The Children of the Sun* (1921), initiated a whole series of novels * devoted to ancient lore.[17]

Quite in keeping with this dual tradition, the most celebrated of all Indianist novels—*Race of Bronze* † (1919) by the Bolivian publicist Alcides Arguedas (1879-1946)—is a true cry of protest, and at the same time a work rich in picturesque color and folklore. In the first half of his famous book, Arguedas relates the odyssey of some Bolivian Indians from the *altiplano* or high plateau, as they travel to the valley to sell their products—an epic voyage across mountain torrents and treacherous quicksands, a journey enlivened by all sorts of typical native episodes and Andean landscapes. But the second half of the novel exposes the suffering and destruction of these Indians by the greed of the *patrones;* a sombre narrative that

*Matto de Turner, *Aves sin Nido;* Valdelomar, *Los Hijos del Sol.*
† Arguedas, *Raza de Bronce.*

gives the reader a veritable feeling of anguish as he contemplates the martyrdom of the enslaved 'race of bronze.'

More recently, the indigenous theme has been almost completely appropriated by a group of militant novelists who have devoted themselves to exposing the ungodly aspects of Indian slavery—often with more righteous indignation than literary skill. These young writers, most of them Ecuadorians, exhibit a decided disrespect for grammar, style, syntax, and even common sense. Their literary masters are Dostoievski, Proust, Gorki, John dos Passos, and Hemingway, whose formulas they apply to the indigenous scene with very odd results. And they mix socialism with psychopathology to such an extent that some of their native characters seem to be Freudian cases rather than real Indians. Yet their books have the unquestionable merit of exhibiting a real and frightful state of affairs—the same horrible cruelties of promoters in the Putumayo region of Ecuador that were denounced to the world by Sir Roger Casement. It was here that rubber companies conducted the most sanguinary massacres of the twentieth century, ejecting Indians from their lands, hunting them like rabbits in the forest, and killing them or forcing them to kill one another in the most barbarous manner. No wonder, then, that nothing is too black or too crude for the pages of these writers; and that the majority of them are rampant Marxists, who tend to forget that the aim of the novel is (or ought to be) primarily aesthetic and not political or sociological. The best representative of this new type of Indianist novel in Ecuador is Jorge Icaza (1902-   ), whose *Huasipungo* (1934) depicts the burning of the native ranches and the assassination of the Indians, at the order of some North American promoters. This book is in a sense the epitome of a whole genre—violent, bestial, bloody, black as a nightmare.

It is a decided relief to turn from the works of these chroniclers of horror to the novels of a gifted young author who ranks today as the outstanding writer of *novelas indianistas*,

Ciro Alegría (1908–), the leading contemporary novelist of Peru. Using the same theme as the Ecuadorian novelists, the destruction of an Indian village by the greed of white men, Alegría has composed a work of rare color and power in his prize-winning book, *Broad and Alien is the World* (1941). In an earlier novel, *The Serpent of Gold* (1935), Alegría displayed his familiarity with the life of Indians along the Marañon River: their struggles against inhospitable nature, their superstitions, and the subtle sense of humor that is such a feature of their daily life.* But in *Broad and Alien is the World* he has produced the culminating work of the modern *novela indianista*.

In this remarkable book, Alegría portrays the life of the Indian village of Rumi: the daily routine of humble folk living contentedly with their little *chacaras* (cultivated fields), their habits of work, their oral traditions and religious beliefs, their way of toiling the land in the communal system typical of Peruvian Indians from time immemorial, their rare treasures of dignity and kindness. Alegría creates his picture of this village with great charm and a minute knowledge of Indian ways; his hero is never any one individual, but rather the entire little group, the community of Rumi. And he writes with fervor and force, as he narrates his tragic story: how the ambition of a white landlord, who wishes to extend his properties, destroys the peaceful settlement in connivance with the law, the army, and even the local church. The fearful brutalities of *The Vortex* are repeated here, and in the end the community is wiped out; some of its members die resisting the invasion, others are enslaved in the rubber plantations, others become outlaws, and still others disappear in the big cities. Even a final attempt to move the remains of the *comunidad* to arid lands is a failure, and Rumi is utterly destroyed.

Broad and Alien is the World thus follows a pattern simi-

* Alegría, *La Serpiente de Oro, El Mundo es Ancho y Ajeno.*

lar to the other great Indianist novel, *Race of Bronze*. Both novelists first give a rich picture of native life; then they show the enslavement and destruction of the Indians by the white man. An obvious conclusion suggests itself: the *novela indianista*, at its best, involves a fusion of the two trends which have characterized the genre as a whole. It is not enough for the novelist to express sympathy or even violent fury at the suffering and exploitation of the Indian, without at the same time possessing an equally strong feeling for the positive features, the picturesque folkways and the ancient traditions and values of American aboriginal life. When it combines these two trends, the Indianist novel becomes—as in *Broad and Alien is the World*—one of the highest expressions of the Spanish American novel of the land.

THE NOVEL OF ARTISTIC ESCAPE

NOT all modern Spanish American novelists, however, are concerned with the realistic interpretation of the native scene. A good number of them, and they include some of the most distinguished writers of the continent, have preferred to turn aside from the problems of daily life, and devote their energies to different forms of purely aesthetic literature. This movement, too, has its origins in the nineteenth century. For just as the regional novel traces back to the realistic and naturalistic works in vogue from 1880 to 1900, so current 'artistic' literature stems from the great movement of modernism that flourished at that same period.[18]

Like modernism also, these artistic novels reflect a real aspect of Spanish America's culture. At first glance it seems curious to find so many volumes of delicate beauty and charm—works of fantasy, studies of sentiment, analyses of the subconscious—all of them directed to a limited audience with refined aesthetic sensibilities. But this corresponds to a real phenomenon in the life of lands below the Río Grande: The culture of these nations is still an aristocratic one, with educational opportunities limited to the few rather than open to the many; and cultured persons do tend to form an intellectual elite. The process of democratization is already well underway in literature, as is strongly evidenced by the realistic novel. But the phenomenon of 'Arielism' does exist; novelists do compose exquisite books that are read by a relatively small circle. Their work, far from being considered unrepresentative, should be regarded, like the poetry of the modernists, as a manifestation of the Spanish American creative genius.

A good many of these artistic novelists (like their *modernista* forerunners) are frank escapists, writing by preference about far-away lands or past times. Spain has exercised a peculiar attraction for these craftsmen, whose books on the enchantment of old Spanish cities or on Spanish life in past centuries often have an exotic flavor not found in the novels of natives of the Iberian Peninsula. Three writers are particularly known for their portrayals of Spain, each admirable in its way: 'With *The Glory of Don Ramiro* by Larreta and *The Spell of Seville* by Reyles, *The Passion and Death of Pastor Deusto* [by 'd'Halmar'] forms a veritable trilogy of South American novels of Spanish motif. If the Argentine [Larreta] succeeds by the rich choice of vocabulary, if the Uruguayan [Reyles] excels by the dexterous construction of his work, the Chilean ['d'Halmar'] triumphs in greater poetic force and in more daring conception.' [19]

The last named of these three, the Chilean Augusto Thomson, 'd'Halmar' (1880–1950), has followed a literary evolution typical of many escapists. At first he tried his hand at crudest realism tinged with Tolstoyan philosophy, attempting to practice his principles in a vegetarian literary colony; but later he became Consul of Chile in Calcutta, and plunged into oriental exoticism in his volumes of mysterious and atmospheric travel sketches, *Nirvana* (1918) and *Smoke Shadow in the Mirror* (1924). Finally, in *Passion and Death of Pastor Deusto* (1924), he composed an exotic novel with Seville as a background;

here, he paints the beautiful Andalusian city, its fantastic types, its churches and cafés and religious processions—all of this done with an intense joy of life, a passionate fondness for the city itself, and an impeccable literary form.*

Similarly, the Argentine Enrique Rodríguez Larreta (1875-) has essayed an interpretation of the Spanish spirit in his world-famous novel *The Glory of Don Ramiro* (1908). Rodríguez Larreta—himself a man of means and onetime diplomat—later attempted unsuccessfully to write on a native American theme, in his gauchesque novel *Zogoibi* (1926), a work that has been severely criticized.† His masterpiece remains *The Glory of Don Ramiro,* where he has undertaken a study of historical psychology, in an elegant and ornate style. His theme is the conflict of the human soul which, in its longing for greatness, vacillates between the ideals of the conquistador and the monk, of power and renunciation. For the polish of its style and for the excellence of its reconstruction of Spain in the days of Philip II, *The Glory of Don Ramiro* ranks as one of the finest historical novels ever written in the Spanish language.

Perhaps the outstanding South American writer on Spain is Carlos Reyles (1868-1938), Uruguay's leading novelist.[20] His masterpiece, *The Spell of Seville* ‡ (1935), is conceded by foreign and Spanish critics alike to be one of the best books ever written on that city. Reyles came by his fondness for Seville quite naturally. His mother was an Andalusian, and Reyles himself was a markedly Spanish type: small build and rapid movements, strong aquiline nose and bony features, tiny steel-bright eyes. What is more, at eighteen young Reyles was left a millionaire by his father, and was thus enabled to travel to Europe and especially to Spain, which he visited often. His

* D'Halmar, *Nirvana, La Sombra del Humo en el Espejo, Pasión y Muerte del Cura Deusto.*
† Rodríguez Larreta, *La Gloria de Don Ramiro, Zogoibi.*
‡ Reyles, *El Embrujo de Sevilla.*

independent means also made it possible for him to devote his life almost entirely to literature, writing critical articles, short stories, and particularly novels. In his later years, after his fortune was gone, the Uruguayan government created a lectureship especially for him at the University of Montevideo.

Like d'Halmar, the escapist Reyles showed a strong influence of Zola in his early work, notably in *Beba* (1894), a novel laid against the background of an Uruguayan stock farm, and demonstrating the hereditary evil effect of consanguinity in animals and human beings. To be sure, Reyles' work offers a depth of psychological analysis quite unlike the *roman experimental*—notably in his celebrated *Race of Cain* (1900), where he plunges deep into the psychology of an abnormal character who seeks evasion in a life of strange refinements and ultimately murder and suicide. Reyles has also, like the escapist Rodríguez Larreta, written on the native gauchesque theme, both in *Out of the Soil* (1916), a somewhat deterministic study of rural life resorting also to the use of heredity; and *The Gaucho Florido* (1932), which, while not exactly a failure, is one of those works that miss their mark.*

The Spell of Seville—also known as *Castanets* in English— is however quite different in technique from Reyles' other books. A novel of extraordinary plastic beauty, of warm sensuousness, of lyric enthusiasm, it has none of Reyles' usual methods of analysis; here, Seville, the city itself, dominates everything, creating its own characters who go through life governed more by instinct than by reason. The main characters of the story are the very incarnation of all that is Sevillian: Paco Quiñones, the gentleman bullfighter; and La Pura, the famous dancer; and the chief action takes place in the café El Tronío—where, naturally, the hero and heroine of Seville meet and fall in love. But Pitoche, the singer and guitarist and erstwhile lover of La Pura, tries to regain her affections.

* Reyles, *Beba, La Raza de Caín, El Terruño, El Gaucho Florido.*

Spurned, Pitoche draws a knife on the bullfighter, who dis-
arms him and starts to strangle him; but the dancer, whose old
love has returned in a flash, seizes the knife and stabs Paco in
the shoulder. The denouement is rapid: the gentleman bullfighter is nursed back to health by his fiancée, whom he marries, and the conscience-stricken dancer finally leaves Seville
to expiate her crime.

For its style alone, apart from all its other excellences, *The
Spell of Seville* ranks as a masterpiece. Reyles has been able to
combine classic Spanish prose with the salty Andalusian popular speech; and his descriptions of Seville's cathedrals and processions, and Holy Week streets filled with flowers and man-
tillas and Cordoban hats, are a positive delight to read. Most
remarkable of all, however, is the way in which he has been
able to evoke the very soul of Spain, for in the words of the
noted essayist Unamuno: 'Never has anyone written of the
Spanish soul with such novelty and profundity.' This special
power of Reyles, an Uruguayan, to evoke things Andalusian,
may be seen from the following account of the characteristic
singer or *cantaor:*

> A *cantaor* without suffering is like a guitar without
> strings. People think that the Ay's and the quaverings are
> arrogant adornments, agilities, vocal flourishes. Nothing
> falser; they are moans, and for that reason, according to
> the way each *cantaor* suffers, he presses and shapes bal-
> lads to give them the form of his complaint and the
> taste of his tears. El Chato de Jerez, when he sang all
> alone, would cry; and Conchiya la Peñaranda, many times
> upon coming off the stage, used to be seized by violent
> fits of tears that would tear her soul out. For you see
> we're not machines for giving out sounds, like tenors are,
> but creatures who suffer, and, so as not to suffer, sing.[21]

Spain, however, is not the only theme that has appealed to
South American writers seeking the exotic. Some novelists
have been able to produce an atmosphere of strangeness and
mystery by using American materials, like the famous Chilean

Pedro Prado (1886–1952) [22] in his fantastic story *The Queen of Rapa Nui* * (1914). Here, Prado has set his tale in a remote and isolated possession of Chile, tiny Easter Island near Oceania. His characters include only three 'civilized' men, the rest being islanders, Coemata Etú, the tiny queen, Inú, the warrior, Coturhe Ururiri, the wise man; and his narrative gives a picture of island life—tribal assemblies, dances, funerals—in a charming and simple example of exotic narration. Still another phase of exoticism on American themes is to be seen in the work of Gustavo Martínez Zuviría, 'Hugo Wast' (1883-)—a writer of popular escape fiction, adventure novels, and historical romances in the manner of Dumas—whose books, while not poorly written as one would expect from their great number, are not concerned with any aesthetic aims whatever.

Perhaps the most skilful creator of this sort of American exoticism is Horacio Quiroga (1878-1937), one of the greatest short-story writers of the Spanish language. Though born in Uruguay, Quiroga passed many years in the Argentine jungles of the Chaco and Misiones; and from these experiences he drew his remarkable tales in which tropical forests, rivers, trees, and animals all blend in a picture of rare imagination and artistic beauty. Influenced in his youth by Poe and Baudelaire, and later by Kipling, Quiroga found his true path in tales of primitive nature and hallucinating fantasy. Some of his stories show Misiones types and settings; others, like his *Jungle Tales* (1918), deal with the *selva* and have animals for protagonists; still others, like *Tales of Love, Madness, and Death* (1917), are fanciful and pathological, with characters impelled by wild passion or insanity; finally, some are philosophical and symbolic. Perhaps most fascinating are his animal stories, such as the weird tale of the cranes 'with their red stockings,' or his masterpiece *Anaconda* (1921).† In this story, Quiroga de-

* Prado, *La Reina de Rapa Nui.*

† Quiroga, *Cuentos de la Selva, Cuentos de Amor, de Locura y de Muerte, Anaconda.*

scribes the fearful battle-to-the-death between snakes and poisonous vipers, humanizing these creatures, and superimposing a remarkable aesthetic and philosophic interpretation upon the reptilian struggle. In this unique type of work, Quiroga had demonstrated the extent to which a writer can go in creating a masterful exotic fantasy out of purely American materials.

The native trend, which is noticeable even among these writers of exoticism, is in itself highly significant. It appears even more strongly in another type of artistic novel which looms large today in the attention of Spanish American writers of fiction. This is the novel of psychological or philosophical tendencies—a genre that has nearly as many devotees as the very realistic novel of the land, and a type of book which, for all its penetration into the realm of the subconscious or the aspirations of the human soul, often reveals a background of very healthy Americanism.

THE PSYCHOLOGICAL AND PHILOSOPHICAL NOVEL

By far the greater number of Spanish American artistic novels are not at all escapist in purpose. Rather, they are concerned with real life, which they study not in its vast social aspects but in the microcosm of one individual human being. These psychological and philosophical novelists, since it is not their intention to flee from reality, often present their character studies against realistic American backgrounds. For instance, a Chilean big city is described in detail by Barrios, as a setting for the tragedy of *A Lost Soul;* and country life is shown with malicious realism by Prado in his philosophic fantasy *Alsino.* Plantations, rural courtrooms, military academies, saloons—farmers, magistrates, politicians, artists, peons—all the places and characters of the realistic novel are found in these works. Yet these things appear invariably as the mere outward setting for a drama that takes place within the mind or heart or soul of the central character. In this respect, contemporary psychological novelists might be likened to the 'New Worldists' of the modernist movement, who use real American materials for some aesthetic purpose. For, like the authors of escape fiction, these writers of psychological and philosophical novels invariably exhibit their relation to the modernist school of Rubén Darío.

Hence it is not surprising that the first important psychological novelist in Spanish America—the Venezuelan Manuel Díaz Rodríguez (1868-1927)—was also a famous modernist.[23] Like so many other modernists, Díaz Rodríguez went to Paris and was deeply impressed by his travels in France and Italy, which he described in his *Travel Sensations* (1896). His first works of fiction, short stories later collected into *Tales in Color* (1898),* were published when the modernist movement was at its height, in journals of the new school.[24] And, like most modernists, he felt in his own life the drama of the artist's struggle in a hostile materialistic world—a story he has told in the autobiographical *Broken Idols* (1901). In this novel, Alberto Soria, a young Venezuelan who has lived in Paris and become a sculptor, comes home to fight against the 'barbaric' life of his native land; longing to regenerate his country, and to attain perfection as an artist, he achieves only failures and a wish to flee to a more civilized environment. The story is that of the author himself, with an important difference: Díaz Rodríguez did achieve the artistic perfection that he sought, and his three novels, *Broken Idols*, *Patrician Blood* (1902), and *Peregrina, or The Enchanted Well* (1922), established his fame, beside that of Rodó, as the great master of modernist prose.†

Such being the case, Díaz Rodríguez wrote exclusively artistic novels, though the American scene is often present in his pages. In *Broken Idols*, the city of Caracas is of course the setting for the sculptor's tragedy; in *Peregrina*, Díaz Rodríguez

---

* Díaz Rodríguez, *Sensaciones de Viaje, Cuentos de Color*.

† Díaz Rodríguez, *Idolos Rotos, Sangre Patricia, Peregrina o el Pozo Encantado*.

has sought instead to capture some of the charm of the Venezuelan landscape. Nature seems to play a determining role in this book, subtitled *A Novel of Rustics in the Valley of Caracas:* the solemn majesty of Mount Avila, the freshness of the streams that flow down from its summit, the ever-renewed greenness of the valleys, the snow-like panorama of blooming coffee-plantations, the fresh grace of ferns and orchids.

But Díaz Rodríguez' greatest achievement is his remarkable study of psychopathology in *Patrician Blood*. The story opens with the drowning of the heroine Belén, just as she was leaving for Paris to meet young Tulio Arcos, whom she had married by proxy. Tulio becomes ill at the news, and recovers only to be pursued by a strange vision of his beloved in the sea:

> It was always the same strange sensation of water, the same gentle vibrating descent on a transparent hammock, the same fantastic voyage between mountains and valleys at the bottom of the ocean, to the purple undersea hill on whose summit reposed the beauty of Belén, like an open lily on a mountain of roses. And Tulio was always conversing, or thought he was conversing, with his bride, as long as the dream didn't vanish or she didn't turn into rigid white coralline.[25]

The hallucination grows stronger, heightened by the suggestive force of everything green—young leaves, emeralds, and especially water. In time, the attraction of the sea becomes greater; the vision has become permanent, and Tulio travels through the Mediterranean on a fantastic honeymoon lived in the realm of the subconscious. At length he embarks for Venezuela, and when he reaches the spot where his beloved was drowned, he leaps into the sea to rejoin the siren. Written as it is in Díaz Rodríguez' matchless style, with polished images and poetic rhythm and brilliance of color, *Patrician Blood* is still, after nearly half a century, a masterpiece of weird imagination and psychopathology.

Even more bizarre in its psychopathological implications is the work of the contemporary Guatemalan writer Rafael Arévalo Martínez (1884-   ), whose life-story is nearly as fantastic as his strange tales.[26] His death was announced in 1920, and a number of his friends composed epitaphs to his memory; yet, according to latest advices, Arévalo Martínez is still very much alive, and in recent years has been Director of the National Library of Guatemala! Here is his personal history, as told by himself:

> As for biographical data, I can only say that I was born in 1884, that I was married in 1911, that I have seven children, a body incredibly emaciated (I weigh 94 pounds), and that I have had a chronic neurasthenia since I was fourteen years old. And nothing more.[27]

To these meager details can be added the spiritual autobiography that Arévalo Martínez has set down in a number of his books—*One Life* (1914), the novel *Manuel Aldano* (1926), and the fanciful *Nights in the Palace of the Nunciature* (1927) —where he describes his education, his neurasthenic abnormalities, and his Christian faith.[*]

Arévalo Martínez' strange personality has found literary expression in a series of novelettes that are unique for their use of a weird psychological theory. According to this writer, individuals have traits best represented by some particular animal; and in keeping with his theory he has created the 'psychozoological tale' in *The Man Who Resembled a Horse* (1915) and *Mr. Monitot: The Animals of the Tropics* (1922). These character studies are as unforgettable as they are bizarre: [†] Mr. Monitot, who arrives at the Theosophical Society, a huge timid man, balancing himself from leg to leg, like an elephant; Miss Eguilaz, short, pretty, and plump, with her perpetual white

---

[*] Arévalo Martínez, *Una vida, Manuel Aldano, Las Noches en el Palacio de la Nunciatura.*

[†] Arévalo Martínez, *El Hombre que Parecía un Caballo, El Señor Monitot.*

feathers (the dove); and her suitor Mr. Reinaldo, long and thin, with his fascinatingly ugly face and hypnotic eyes (the serpent). Perhaps the most remarkable of these characterizations is that of the *caudillo*—the tiger—Don José Vargas, handsome and proud and boundlessly cruel, dressed in white linen, with light eyes and blond hair, and an enormous solitaire on his carefully tended hand.

Perhaps the best known of Arévalo Martínez' extraordinary creations is the 'man who resembled a horse'—in reality a well-known Colombian poet. This character, 'Mr. Aretal,' is described as having a strangely equine aspect:

> Mr. Aretal stretched his neck like a horse; Mr. Aretal used to fall like a horse—he would slip suddenly with his left foot, and his haunches would almost touch the ground . . . Mr. Aretal was gesticulating as he sat in front of his gold pieces, and all of a sudden I saw him move his arms the way pure-blooded horses move their hoofs . . . Mr. Aretal used to see the way horses do; when he was intoxicated with his own words . . . he would tremble like a high-strung animal . . . and incline his head and turn it sideways and look that way . . . Mr. Aretal used to approach women like a horse. In sumptuous gatherings he couldn't stand still. He used to draw near a pretty woman . . . with elastic motions, his head held low and to one side, and then trot all the way around the room.[28]

But Arévalo Martínez carries his analysis still farther; his 'Mr. Aretal' has not only the physical appearance of a horse, but the character of a horse as well. Fantastic as this notion seems, it is a remarkable analysis of an incomplete human being: as gifted and remarkable as a racing thoroughbred, and at the same time with no more moral fibre than a four-footed animal. Here perhaps lies Arévalo Martínez' greatest power—not in his richly worked style or in his Poe-like gift of evoking mystery, but in his human sympathies and his strangely intuitive and compassionate understanding of his fellow-man. He feels a sort of Christian pantheism that makes all created things one; and like a literary St. Francis he experiences a true affection for Brother Tiger, Brother Horse, Brother Serpent, and Sister Dove.

Farther removed from the field of fantasy and closer to real life are the novels of the Chilean Eduardo Barrios (1884-   ), whose works nonetheless stamp him as a master of abnormal psychology.[29] The son of a Chilean father and a Peruvian mother, Barrios has lived in nearly every country in Latin America, and has engaged in countless occupations; he was a prospector in Collahuasi, he delivered machinery to an ice-factory in Guayaquil, he sold stoves in Buenos Aires and Montevideo, he travelled with a circus and even appeared as a weight-lifter; finally, he settled permanently in Chile, where he has been at different occasions Director of the National Library and Minister of Education. Barrios has followed no fixed norm—save that of being, as he says himself, 'a man of sentiment.' It is mainly for his understanding of sentimental abnormalities, which he has analyzed in a remarkably transparent style, that Barrios' work is remarkable. His three novels—*Sentimental Madness* (1915), *A Lost Soul* (1917), and *Brother Ass* (1922)—study feelings that range from the affections of a child to the mystical torments of a monk, and place Barrios among the greatest living masters of emotional writing.[*]

The American note is by no means absent from Barrios' work. Thus, in *A Lost Soul*, he gives much emphasis to the Chilean city environment, the hostile setting in which the abnormally sensitive hero—a weakling patterned after Frédéric Moreau in Flaubert's *Sentimental Education*—lives out his tragedy of frustration and maladjustment. And in *Brother Ass*, Barrios has written charming atmospheric pictures of a monastery set in a thoroughly Chilean landscape, with the rough earth of the garden, the olive trees, and the old well,

[*] Barrios, *El Niño que Enloqueció de Amor, Un Perdido, El Hermano Asno.*

the vistas of tree tops and far-away roofs. Yet in his pages, as in those of other psychological novelists, the American scene appears merely as a background for the detailed study of characters.

Barrios excels in painting abnormal personalities; not exactly neurotics, but rather human beings whose emotional nature is overwrought, and who end in insanity or spiritual disintegration. Possibly the most extraordinary of these sentimental characters is the child protagonist and narrator of *Sentimental Madness*. This slight volume, a novelette rather than a novel, purports to be the diary of a boy of ten who falls in love with Angelica, a young woman who is a friend of his mother, and ultimately loses his reason. Barrios himself thus explains the theme of this remarkable study of abnormal psychology:

> Have you ever heard a bird sing at night?
> It sometimes happens that a beam of moonlight . . . penetrating through foliage, falls upon the branch where a little bird is perched asleep, and wakes it. Of course, this isn't the dawn, like the bird imagines—but it sings.
> Afterward, if the fledging is what's known as a strong and well-balanced little bird, it discovers its mistake, and buries its beak once more between its warm feathers, and goes back to sleep.
> All the same, there are some birds, restless and frail creatures, who are quite bewitched by the moonbeam. And having sung, they hop about in bewilderment and start to fly . . . Only, as the day hasn't dawned, they soon get lost in the dark, and either drown themselves in a lake illumined by the pale beam of light, or pierce their breasts against the thorns of a rosebush . . .
> What is that poisonous beam that wakes certain souls while it is yet night, and robs them of the dawn and drowns them in an existence of shadows? [30]

Equally supersensitive is the hero of Barrios' *A Lost Soul*, Lucho Bernales, who instead of going mad under the blows of harsh realities and sentimental tragedy, drags on his existence, drifting from saloon to saloon in an alcoholic stupor.

In *Brother Ass*, however, Barrios surpasses himself as a delineator of unstable emotions and master of an incredibly beautiful and simple prose style. The title of the work is taken from St. Francis of Assisi's term for his body, 'brother ass'; and the story tells the inner struggles of Brother Lázaro, the narrator, and of Brother Rufino, the 'saint' of the monastery. Brother Lázaro passes through an emotional crisis when he meets María Mercedes, the sister of his youthful sweetheart, but he ultimately finds peace in the cloister; whereas Brother Rufino, tormented by his mystical longings for perfection and humility, ultimately succumbs to madness. For its skill at painting characters and feelings, and for the magic of its transparent and evocatory style, *Brother Ass* is unquestionably one of the most beautiful emotional novels ever written.

Even more perfect in its way is the work of another Chilean, perhaps the greatest writer of artistic novels in Spanish America, Pedro Prado (1886–1952).[31] This novelist, who is also a poet of distinction, has passed most of his days in the peaceful family life of his spacious country villa on the outskirts of Santiago. Here, from 1915 to 1916, he presided over the celebrated group of 'The Ten,' an association of painters, poets, musicians, and architects. Chile's leading stylist, if not the leading stylist of all Spanish America, Prado is known for his essays, parables, and poems in prose, but especially for his novels, of which the most celebrated are *A Rural Judge* (1924) and *Alsino* (1920), and for his prose tragedy *Androvar* (1925).* These books are studies of remarkable characters, but their purpose is less psychological than philosophical, and they stamp Prado as a philosophical novelist of great distinction—a title that can be claimed by few other writers of Spanish America.

In Prado's work one hardly knows which to admire more, the moral elevation of the thought or the limpid perfection of

* Prado, *Un Juez Rural, Alsino, Androvar* (*tragedia en prosa*).

the style. His writing frequently reaches the level of poetry, yet at the same time he is fond of realistic bits of description, which give a strangely Chilean atmosphere to his symbolic stories. In *Alsino*, for instance, he describes a farmhouse kitchen, sooty and dim with the vapor of cooking food, and smelling of the garlic and onions hung from the rafters.

Yet it is never the background or even the characters themselves that preoccupies Prado; his chief concern is always with ideas and the building of a personal philosophy. Thus in *A Rural Judge*, Prado analyzes the dilemma that confronted him as a district judge who tried to administer justice by the dictates of his conscience. The judge's decisions are shown as clashing with the rigid legal code; his moral interpretations of justice are wasted on rascals and rogues; he finds it impossible to do individual justice, for if you punish a man for a crime, you punish at the same time his mother, his wife, and his children; to be just, he feels that he should reward good at the same time that he punishes evil. Finally, unable to satisfy his own conscience, he resigns. The problem here is the tantalizing one of human limitations, which Prado has explored still further in *Androvar*. In a strange combination of fancy and reality, he has created the parable of the master Androvar, his wife, and his disciple Gadel—an extraordinary triangle, in which three souls are supernaturally fused and penetrate the mysteries of death itself.

Prado's masterpiece is *Alsino*, which some critics have classified as a fairy tale, some as an allegory, and some as a work of transcendent symbolism. *Alsino* is the simple saga of a Chilean country boy who longs to fly, and by his efforts to do so falls from a tree and becomes a hunchback. In time, however, his hump grows into a real pair of wings; Alsino flies under the blue sky, over valleys, mountains, and rivers; he descends to earth and comes into contact with ugly and cruel reality; he is mistaken for an angel, he is arrested, his wings are clipped and he is exhibited in a cage, and finally he is blinded by a girl who tries to win his love. He starts to fly once more, only to fall wounded into the bottom of a ravine, where he hears the voices of the springs and the trees; the fox comes to lick his wounds, the wild creatures bring flowers, fruits, and meat, and the wild doves lull him to sleep. In his death agony, Alsino feels one last impulse to fly; at a terrific altitude, he folds his wings and his body ignites:

> A league before reaching the earth, there remained of Alsino only impalpable ashes. Lacking the weight to continue falling, they floated like snowflakes till dawn. The breezes at daybreak set about scattering them, and at length they fell—but the slightest wind blew them upwards again. And so, dispersed and imponderable, they have remained for a long time now, and will continue to remain, floating like mist in the invisible air.[32]

The symbolism of *Alsino* is clear: the little hunchback with wings is man, longing to soar above the ugliness of life into the regions of the infinite, and yet fatally bound to earth.

Alsino is unquestionably the highest expression of the psychological and philosophical trend in Spanish American fiction —a trend which, next to the rural novel, has attracted the greatest number of writers. For apart from the outstanding figures of Díaz Rodríguez, Arévalo Martínez, Barrios, and Prado, many other excellent novelists have devoted their efforts to this sort of book. In the field of child psychology, for instance, it would be hard to surpass Teresa de la Parra (1895-1936), author of the charming *Memories of Mamá Blanca* (1929), a volume of childhood reminiscences in the form of short stories. Again, María Luisa Bombal, in *The Woman in the Shroud* (1938), has produced a work of rare power; full of mystery, in the situation of the dead woman who remembers her life; and beauty, in the vivid perfection of a style rich in sense impressions of color and smell and taste; and psychological depth, in the story of a life lived intensely through varying experiences of love and hate and suffering and maturity. Finally, the philosophical tendency is represented by Eduardo Mallea (1903-   ), the author of *Tales for a Despairing Englishwoman* (1926), *European Nocturne* (1935), *The City by the Motionless River* (1936), *History of an Argentine Passion* (1937), and one of the most interesting writers of contemporary Spanish America.* As the titles of his books indicate, Mallea is very Argentinian and very European at the same time. More of an essayist than a novelist —even his novels seem a series of short essays thin-linked together by a thread of plot—Mallea combines artistic expression with philosophical implications. His style is always pungently lyrical, and he excels in descriptions of the city (not the country) landscape. Mallea's ideas are the very antithesis of Prado's serenity, for he feels a constant anguish in this anarchic hour of human destiny; in his confusion, he oscillates dangerously between an aristocratic rightist and a demagogic leftist attitude. His is the tormented groping of what Gertrude Stein has called 'a lost generation.'

The number and quality of these writers—from Díaz Rodríguez to Mallea—attest to the important place of the psychological novel in contemporary Spanish American fiction. In social significance, such novels of course rank far below urban and particularly rural works; yet in literary merit, they often surpass more realistic compositions. It is not necessary, however, to draw any comparisons between realistic and artistic novels. The very greatest realistic works—like *Doña Bárbara*—are of course works of art, and contain elements of a psychological and symbolic, rather than purely external realism. While the best artistic novels—like *Alsino*—are rich in their profound penetration of real problems in human life. Perhaps it is more judicious to say that the realistic trend is certainly the dominant one in the contemporary Spanish

* De la Parra, *Las Memorias de Mamá Blanca;* Bombal, *La Amortajada;* Mallea, *Cuentos para una Inglesa Desesperada, Nocturno Europeo, La Ciudad Junto al Río Inmóvil, Historia de una Pasión Argentina.*

American novel, but that this literary production is completed and rounded out by the artistic novel. Taken as a whole, modern Spanish American novels give a full and satisfying picture. On the one hand the novel of the city and the novel of the land present a powerful and vivid study of the outside world —the savage forces of nature, the 'mass personage,' the squalor of slums and tenements. And on the other hand, the psychological and philosophical novel affords a brief but intense glimpse into the realm of the subconscious, the personality, the emotions, the soul—those mysterious forces that compose that other reality, the world within.

Brazilian Literature

THE PORTUGUESE COLONIAL PATTERN

AT the risk of appearing elementary, it is necessary to preface a study of Brazilian literature with a schoolroom observation: The people of Brazil speak *Portuguese*, a Latin language similar to Spanish.

So simple a fact as this has served, alas, as a barrier to the wider appreciation of Brazilian letters. On the one hand, it sets Brazil apart from the neighboring countries; for this nation takes pride in speaking Portuguese, and its people refuse to be classified as Spanish Americans even if Portugal was once a part of Philip II's Empire. Yet on the other hand, when an all-inclusive term like 'Latin Americans' is proposed—a most acceptable literary denominator, as it covers both Spanish and Portuguese, and serves to emphasize the important influence of French letters—the Spanish-speaking nations raise equal objections. For very few Spanish Americans have taken the trouble to learn Portuguese or to familiarize themselves with Brazilian culture, following the similar attitude of Spain in regard to Portugal. The situation is doubly unfortunate, and whenever a Spanish American critic undertakes the study of Brazilian letters—as for instance, M. García Mérou—the writers of both countries are greatly indebted to him.

This mutual indifference is thoroughly illogical and unfortunate, for the literary development of Brazil follows much the same stages as that of Spanish America. Brazilian culture owes its origin to factors quite like those that prevailed in the rest of the New World: a vast virgin land peopled by aborigines, brought under the control of a dominant European race. And just as the neighboring lands were subjected for centuries to Hispanic norms, so Brazil underwent a long shaping in the parallel Portuguese colonial pattern.

The conquest of Brazil, starting with Alvarez Cabral's discovery, was illumined by the same blaze of heroic adventure as marked the Spanish conquest. In that era, the Portuguese had a character quite similar to that of their neighbors, the Spaniards. They were a restless conquering people; they had achieved a position of world prominence for their nation; their culture, while not equalling the brilliance of the Spanish Golden Age, was nonetheless at its apogee; and their literature boasted some of the most distinguished figures in European *belles lettres*—names like Gil Vicente, Sá de Miranda, Bernardim Ribeiro, and the immortal Camões.

These Portuguese conquerors found, too, a great untamed land with all the beauty and horror of primitive nature. And with no less zeal than the Spaniards, they proceeded to explore and subjugate it, pushing their frontier ever inland, to discover a land of immense tropical forests crossed by the Amazon River and its tributaries, and steep rocky mountains that form a great interior plateau of what Cunninghame Graham calls 'wooded, back-lying highlands.' Much of this country remains unknown and unexploited even today, for Brazil's twentieth-century population of some fifty millions occupies a small part of her vast area—an area larger than that of the United States, and covering about half of the southern continent. Obviously, such a natural setting—of tangled rain-soaked jungles, and fertile river-valleys, and temperate highlands with legend-inspiring deposits of diamonds and emeralds—such a background of tropical wilderness could not fail to exert a strong influence on the culture of Brazil. And its impress has been strongly felt in literature, where the *selva* plays so prominent a part in the modern novel, and the inland plateau or *Sertão* has, since colonial times, been of extraordinary importance in Brazilian letters.

The Portuguese colonial period also witnessed the formation of Brazil's racial mixture, a factor of peculiar social and cultural importance. The first conquerors found none of the fabulous monsters that were supposed to inhabit the legendary island of 'Brasil,' but only tribes of extremely primitive people: the Tupis, the Ges, the Cariris, the Caribas, and others not yet classified, who lived in a period of rudimentary agriculture, hunting, and fishing, constantly warring among themselves. After the coming of the Portuguese, this Indian strain was either destroyed by the sword, alcohol, or disease, or else assimilated to produce the *mestiço* element who were known by the name of *mamelucos*. A third racial component was added in the African slaves imported in the sixteenth century into Brazil (as into the rest of America). The crossing of these Negroes with the Portuguese produced the *mulatos*, a group which in the second century of the colony attained great importance in the sociological formation of Brazil, and which has continued to increase till present times. Only in the twentieth century has fresh European immigration—especially German, Italian, and Portuguese—altered the picture. It is axiomatic that this process of racial mixture, largely accomplished in colonial times, has likewise shaped the Brazilian people and hence their literature.

Apart from these basic factors in the formation of Brazil during the colonial period—the conquest, the natural setting, and the resulting racial mixture—the Portuguese colonial pattern has had yet a stronger influence. As with the domains of Spain, the colonial era was centuries long, and strict. Brazil, as an independent entity, is therefore a very young nation. And one can detect in her make-up, as does the perhaps too-severe Brazilian critic Afrânio Peixoto, all the defects and qualities of young nations:

> A great pride in the land that they repute to be the best in the world . . . and a nativism that dominates literature to such a point that they cannot see any defects in it . . . Little imagination . . . and even less concentration, but great verbal power. Many orators, poets, journalists, who distinguish themselves by their fluency, verbosity, and dramatic ability. Few thinkers, narrators, investigators; no philosophers . . .
>
> The young men have great ambitions and little patience for the slow acquisitions of work; from this springs pessimism, discontent, bitter criticism of those who do something. As in North America, so there is in Brazil an endless multitude of 'Babbitts' with an almost equal number of critics. More critics than creators in any line of activity . . . At any rate there is pride, egolatry, a yearning for utopia, a certain idealism and generosity, qualities which given time will produce something worthwhile.[1]

COLONIAL LITERATURE

PORTUGUESE American colonial literature—like its Spanish counterpart—was not at first divorced from the literary production of the mother country. The first writings about the conquest likewise, naturally enough, took the forms of the history and the epic. Distinguished Portuguese historians journeyed to Brazil to record its living history; and a few travellers, dazzled by the beauty and originality of the new land, wrote descriptions of it. Thus, such writers as Father José de Anchieta, Soares de Souza, Manoel da Nobrega, although born in Portugal, are mentioned in the history of Brazilian literature. Parenthetically, one should remember that the same thing is true of Spanish American writers, like Bernal Díaz and Ercilla. Such is the case of the first colonial poet in the Portuguese language, Bento Teixeira Pinto (1540?-1618?), author of the epic *Prosopopéa* (1601), in which American nature and the American man appear for the first time in Portuguese poetry.

Continuing the parallel still further, the seventeenth century witnessed, in the literature of Portugal, the same triumph of Gongorism in poetry and *conceptismo* in prose that characterized the literature of Spain. This affectation spread equally to the life of the Portuguese colony. And as in the Spanish colonies, so in Brazil too, ornate elegance was chiefly cultivated in a metropolitan center: the city of Bahía. The Brazilians, enriched by their large estates, dedicated themselves to a life of luxury that was not inferior to that of European capitals. Bahía became in consequence a great center of wealth and intellectual activity, and a literary flowering occurred as a matter of course. The Bahía writers studied Latin, Italian, and Portuguese poets with interest, but their true inspirations were Quevedo and 'the Prince of Darkness.' Around this time, there appeared too a strong feeling of patriotism and a tendency of Brazilian writers to mention with affection the peoples and customs and flora of the new land. This did not, however, indicate new literary modes of expression, any more than did similar examples of patriotism and American subject matter in Spanish colonial writers, like Balbuena with his poem *The Greatness of Mexico*. For Gongorism was the mode of the day, and this affectation invaded (as it did elsewhere) not only literature, but all the realms of art and even religious oratory.

In this last field, the outstanding figure was the famous Jesuit Father Antônio Vieira (1608-97), the very one to whom the illustrious Mexican poetess, Sor Juana Inés de la Cruz, addressed her *Critique of a Sermon*. Although born in Portugal, Father Vieira spent fifty years of his life in Brazil, and many of his pedantic and grandiloquent sermons deal with Brazilian topics. He was indeed a daring defender of the Indians, and some Brazilian critics like to read in his thought as well as in his style a new element that is not Portuguese. Be that as it may, Father Vieira expressed, in his fiery sermons directed against the Dutch, the patriotism of his time and the strong bond of union between colony and mother land. Here, for example, is a passage from his *Sermon for the Good Success of the Arms of Portugal against Those of Holland:* *

> Let us imagine then (even that which if imagined and fancied causes horror); let us imagine that Bahía and the rest of Brazil fall into the hands of the Dutch; what is going to happen if such an event occurs? They will enter the city with the impetuosity of conquerors and of heretics: they will respect neither condition, nor sex, nor age; with the sharp edge of the scimitar they will strike everyone alike; the women will weep seeing that their chastity is not respected; the old men will weep seeing that their age is not regarded; the nobles will weep seeing that their position in society is not considered; the religious and the venerable priests will weep seeing that not even their sacred tonsures can protect them; finally all will weep, and most of all the innocent ones, for not even those will heretical cruelty respect (as it has not on other occasions).[2]

But whether one regards Father Vieira as typically colonial or characteristically Peninsular, the main fact remains that he was a spectacular orator who acquired a universal reputation in his time. As such, he became the leading exponent of a Brazilian literary school, which employed as dominant elements hyperbole, antithesis, repetition, and Latinisms. Followers of this tendency were the Jesuits Antônio de Sá (1620-78) and Eusébio de Mattos (1629-92). Disciples also of Vieira in their sententious and ample style were the historians Sebastião da Rocha Pita (1660-1738), author of the *History of Portuguese America* (1730); and Nuno Marques Pereira (1652-1728), whose *Narrative Compendium of the American Pil-*

* Vieira, *Sermão pelo bom sucesso das armas de Portugal contra as da Holanda.*

grim (1728) was very popular during colonial times and has since been acclaimed as the first novel of Brazil.*

The century was no less prolific in ornate poetry than in elaborate prose—and here again the masters were the Spaniards Góngora and Quevedo. The most important Brazilian poet of the time, Gregório de Mattos (1633-96), was a spiritual brother of Quevedo, not only in his technique but also in his temperament. A Bohemian through and through, he might almost be called a native François Villon. The son of rich landowners, he was afforded the luxury of being sent to study in Portugal, where he received the degree of Doctor of Laws at Coimbra. There he lived several years and attained posts of distinction; but having fallen into disgrace, he returned to his native country in 1679. In Bahía, Mattos next secured several positions in the Church, but because of his unstable life and the many satires he wrote, he was persecuted by his enemies and ultimately abandoned by his friends and his wife. Finally he was banished to Angola in Africa, where the governor took pity upon him and sent him back to Pernambuco in the east of Brazil. There he lived for some time among Bohemians, until his death in 1696.

Mattos was a combative satirist for whom poetry was a type of stiletto. He criticized Bahía society with the same mordant wit that Juan del Valle Caviedes, the contemporary Peruvian, turned upon Lima society of the same time. Both poets are disciples of Quevedo, and use poetry as an instrument of social reform; both attack money, courtesans' vices, the ignorance of physicians, the hypocrisy of churchmen, the vanity of the nobles; both have read Góngora with profit, so that their compositions have earmarks of the great Cordoban bard. Being this type of poet, it is small wonder that Mattos has provoked much discussion among latter-day critics, whose judgments are often contradictory and partial. Thus,

* Rocha Pita, *História da América Portuguesa;* Marques Pereira, *Compêndio Narrativo do Peregrino da América.*

Mattos is not, as Silvio Romero insists, the genius of native literature; nor is he, as Veríssimo claims, a perverted neurotic. Possibly Edison Lins is right in asserting that Mattos' poems show no signs of revolt against the moral degradation of the colony; yet it is equally true that Mattos was the enemy of venality in politics, and that he would not lavish praise on certain powerful individuals. Again, Mattos' defenders are perhaps wrong when they see him as a champion of the abolition of slavery, for the poet himself belonged to the slave-owning class.

Without becoming involved in these disputes over Gregório de Mattos' character and motives, it is however quite possible to form a judgment of him as a satirist and a poet. In his verse, Mattos is at times an excellent lyrist; he possesses an elegant form and a strong sense of color, and is at once sensuous and refined. Even if he is excessively erotic in his love poetry, vulgar in his popular poetry, and coarse in his satire, Mattos expresses at times the tenderness of the religious bards, and the sweetness of poets who, like Fray Luis de León, sing of the quiet pastoral life. In some of his sonnets, there are reminiscences of the work of his contemporary, Sor Juana Inés de la Cruz. All in all, Gregório de Mattos was not a great poet, but he had a perfect command of the Portuguese language, which he enriched with new words and idiomatic forms. As a satirist, despite his debts to Quevedo and Góngora, he holds the very highest position in Portuguese colonial literature.

Manuel Botelho de Oliveira (1636-1711) is another of the poets of Bahía who has saved himself from oblivion. A good Latin and Italian scholar, well educated in Coimbra, he was the author of an artificial Gongoristic poem, *Music of Parnassus* * (1705), which has survived chiefly for its lengthy descriptions of the fruits and cereals of Brazil.

* Botelho de Oliveira, *Música de Parnasso*.

This nascent Americanism or 'Brazilianism' was all but smothered in the general literary formalism of the succeeding era. Portuguese colonial literature of the eighteenth century was but a feeble echo of that artificial poetry popular in Italy, France, and Portugal during the foundation of the Academies. Bahía was of course the center of this movement, and under the protection of the Viceroys a number of Brazilian Academies were established: 'The Academy of the Forgotten Ones,' 'of the Happy Ones,' 'of the Select Ones,' 'of the Renascent Ones,' and the 'Arcadia across the Sea'! Fortunately for the modern reader, the great bulk of this arcadic poetry has been lost: fanciful idyllic verses in Latin, Spanish, Italian, and Portuguese; songs of praise and love, satires and elegies, flattering sonnets dedicated to kings, princes, and noblemen. Only two names of the school are remembered today: Manoel de Santa Maria Itaparica (1704-c.1768), author of the *Eustachiad* * (1769), an epic poem on the life of St. Eustachio; and Antônio José da Silva (1705-1739), *o judeu* or 'The Jew,' who composed plays and operettas of a strongly national flavor, and whose tragic life ended when he was burnt at the stake by the Inquisition in Portugal.

The extreme artificiality of this arcadic school can best be appreciated if one contrasts it with the Brazilian life of the period—the famous and virile era of the *bandeirantes*.[3] For in Brazil, the heroic spirit of discovery had not disappeared as elsewhere; on the contrary, it was prolonged in this eighteenth century of energetic interior conquest, when the *bandeirante* explored the hinterlands (*Sertões*) in an epic struggle against the Indian and Nature. But none of the 'audacity of the *bandeirantes*, running after gold nuggets, silver mines, and precious stones . . . with their brutality of "supermen of the desert" . . .'—none of this appeared in the

* Santa Maria Itaparica, *Eustachidos*.

poetry of the Academies. So it is small wonder that Bahía gradually lost its prominence as a literary city, and that the hub of poetic activity shifted, in the second half of the century, to the inland mining center of Minas Geraes. Here, in the *mineira* school, Brazilian poetry enjoyed a brief but brilliant period, featured by such outstanding names as da Gama, Durão, da Costa, Peixoto, Gonzaga, and Alvarenga, and marked by the revival of the epic, the genre most attuned to the heroic conquering spirit of the age.

The greatest figure of this *mineira* group, and indeed of the whole century, was José Basílio da Gama (1741-95). Like many other Brazilians, he studied in Portugal and later in Rome, where he became a member of the literary society *Arcadia Romana*. He lived in Portugal for many years, and his masterpiece, *The Uraguay*,* was published in Lisbon in 1769. The work is a composition in blank verse describing the war of Spain and Portugal against the Paraguay Indians in 1756, a struggle to which the natives had been incited by the Jesuits. Historically, the theme is one of limited value, though da Gama attracted much attention for his indictment of Jesuit policies. To the modern reader, however, the work is chiefly interesting for its purely literary merits.

As a narrative in verse, *The Uraguay* is the work of a true poet. It exhibits a well-balanced development and a simplicity of expression that are rare in Brazilian literature. And it contains, apart from the account of the war, brief but effective descriptions of the new land, which da Gama was the first to treat as an integral part of artistic expression. Thus, he makes frequent references to the beauty of the Brazilian landscape:

> Here all these vast expansive plains
> Are spread with boggy woven reeds
> And small hard rushes parched with heat . . .

* Da Gama, *O Uraguay*.

> And whitish houses, temples high
> Far in the distance are discerned
> Among the verdure's greenish shade . . .[4]

No less interesting is his information on Indian customs and usages, which gives this composition an atmosphere of realism.

Nor was this skilful use of native material da Gama's only excellence. He had as well the gift of imagery and he was at times an exquisite lyric artist capable of poetical expression, synthesizing a great thought in a single verse. Lines of beauty abound in *The Uraguay*—such as the following:

> And eyes now rolling in cold death . . .

> Death was so lovely in her face! . . .

> The eyes where love had reigned one day,
> Full of death.

Furthermore, the whole poem has an intimate *saudade*—that untranslatable Portuguese term that implies nostalgic sadness. It reflects the landscape emotionally through the temperament of an author who believes in the inborn goodness of the Indians. Episodes like the death of Lindoya—a beautiful Indian girl poisoned by a serpent, like a native Cleopatra—are written with a melancholy tone that announces the appearance of a new poetic sensibility. Indeed, it would not be hazardous to say that Basílio da Gama is one of the earliest forerunners of romanticism in Latin America.

Even more noteworthy for his use of native elements is da Gama's contemporary, Santa Rita Durão (1722-84), author of the celebrated epic poem *Caramurú* (1781), which some critics have called the *Lusiads* of Brazil. Durão too was born in Minas Geraes, and studied abroad; he obtained the degree of Doctor of Theology at the University of Coimbra, and then joined the Order of St. Augustine. He also lived in Portugal most of his life; there he wrote his epic, and there he died. But the resemblance between the two poets was merely external. Durão had none of his compatriot's lyricism; he had no gift for the poetic atmosphere, the refined twist of the phrase, the charming image. His work is overloaded with religious emphasis and platitudes and literary formulae. More than a poet, he was a novelist in verse, and a keen observer of native customs.

It is above all for his ability to produce a truly Brazilian epic that Durão can claim enduring fame. His *Caramurú* relates the discovery of Bahía by Diogo Alvares Correa about the middle of the sixteenth century. Diogo Alvares—so Durão tells the tale—is shipwrecked near Bahía with six friends; the other survivors are devoured by the cannibal Indians, but Diogo is luckily too ill to tempt them. Gradually, he wins mastery over the savages. He kills a bird with a shotgun saved from the wreck, for which deed the terrified natives name him *Filho do trovão* or 'Son of Thunder,' and *Caramurú* or 'Dragon of the Sea.' Soon, the aborigines are under his command, and he marries Paraguassu, daughter of a native chieftain. Next follows a visit to Europe, made jointly by Diogo and his beloved Paraguassu. As they leave Brazil, five Indian maids swim after the boat until one of them, Moema, is drowned and the others turn back:

> The light goes from her eyes, she gasps and trembles,
> With pale complexion, moribund appearance,
> And loosing the helm with lifeless fingers,
> Amid the salty foam, sinks to the bottom.
> But on the surge of sea which roars and rages,
> She turns to loom once more from the depths, and saying
> 'Ah, cruel Diogo!' with grief overpowering,
> Then seen no more she sinks beneath the water.[5]

The rest of the journey is equally eventful—notably the stopover in France, where Paraguassu is baptized and takes the name of Catharina, after her godmother Catharine de Medicis. When the pair returns to Bahía, the Tupinambá Indians hail Paraguassu as the heiress of their empire. But Paraguassu is now the Christian maiden Catherine, and more occupied with visions of the Virgin than with ruling her savage subjects. In the final stanzas of the poem, Thomé de Souza is sent by the King of Portugal to colonize Brazil, and Catherine renounces her legal rights as Princess of the Tupinambás in favor of João the Third. Whereupon this monarch orders Diogo and Catherine rewarded for their services:

> And finally the righteous king doth publish
> In favor of Katrina and Diogo
> A royal honorable declaration
> Which destines many honors to his merit.
> In recompense of loyalty, affection,
> With which the crown was trusted by the lady,
> He then commands the colony to honor
> Diogo Alvares Correia de Viana.[6]

In addition to its narrative excellence, this epic is remarkable for its use of indigenous material. Critics have praised the nativism of the poetry, which is illustrated in many passages and episodes: the picture of the shipwreck, of the anthropophagous savages, and of the ceremonies of a native sacrifice, all in the first Canto; the account of an Indian village in the second; and finally, the incident of Moema, and the descriptions of sugar cane, tobacco, tapioca, the pineapple, the coconut, the chameleon, et cetera. Yet too much stress should not be placed on this so-called 'Indianism.' It is no more genuine than the artificial chivalric atmosphere that prevails in the sixteenth-century epics of Ercilla and Oña, or the pseudo-Indianism of the romantic novel represented in Spanish America by Mera's *Cumandá* and in Brazil by Alencar's *Iracema*. Thus, Diogo is an unreal character out of a romance of chivalry, and the platonic Paraguassu is an unlikely Indian,

> Of color white as whitest snow,
> And where not of snow, then of rose.

Nevertheless, *Caramurú* is a work that lives on in Portuguese much as the *Araucana* continues to be read in Spanish; and while the Brazilian epic lacks the merits of Camões' great *Lusiads*, it still holds a very high place in Portuguese epic poetry.

The other poets of the *escola mineira* were of a more lyric sort, if the term lyric can properly be applied to their often formalized and meaningless versification. Typically Arcadian, for example, was Cláudio Manoel da Costa (1729-89), author of the worthless epic *Villa-Rica* (pub. 1839); an artificial pastoral poet, with but a single string to his lyre, he wrote elegant and empty love-sonnets that show influences of Camões, Ronsard, and Petrarch.

Yet this eighteenth century of Academies and unrealities was drawing to a close, as was the whole decadent colonial era. There were already rumblings of the social upheaval that lay ahead, and these revolutionary stirrings affected even the poets of the *mineira* group. In 1789, the intolerable administration of Cunha Menezes, the Governor of Minas Geraes, led to an attempted rebellion—the famous *Inconfidência Mineira*, of which several poets were the heroes and victims. The evil Governor himself was described, by the fiction of setting the action in Chile, in the famous anonymous poem *Chilean Letters* * (1786). This satirical work has been attributed [7] to Thomaz Antônio Gonzaga (1744-1807), who was himself one of the conspirators. Gonzaga's experience, indeed, is typical of the lot of his fellow poets; and he has immortalized its sentimental aspects in his celebrated book *Marilia of Dirceo* † (1792). As a good Arcadian, Gonzaga ('Dirceu') fell terribly in love with 'Marília,' but just as they were about to be married, he was caught as one of the members of the *Inconfidência* and exiled to Angola, where he died many years later. In *Marilia of Dirceo*, the poet confesses his eter-

* *Cartas Chilenas.*
† Gonzaga, *Marília de Dirceu.*

nal love for his Marilia—in a bucolic mood during his happy life in Brazil, and with the deepest sorrow after his exile.

Another illustrious *Confidente* was the poet Ignácio José de Alvarenga Peixoto (1744-93), who also died an exile in Africa. Of his voluminous works, only a few poems have survived, including some sonnets of merit. Finally, one must mention Manuel Ignácio da Silva Alvarenga (1749-1814), a lyric poet of the closing years of the colonial era. Alvarenga dedicated his verses to Glaura, and in consequence suffered for years in prison, where he was cast by his enemies. He wrote satires, and poems of love in which the subjective note is mingled with a real feeling for the native landscape. Hence, he deserves to be called the last of the 'Arcades' and the first to offer certain romantic elements in his poetry. For Brazil— like the colonies of Spain—underwent the transforming influences of Independence and romanticism in the nineteenth century. The eighteenth century came to its end in a whirlpool of political revolutions and spiritual upheavals. The Portuguese colonial period and the domination of the mother country in life and literature were drawing to a close, and a new era of romantic emancipation lay ahead.

INDEPENDENCE: THE BIRTH OF BRAZILIAN LITERATURE

BRAZIL, like the other nations of South America, achieved her political independence in the early part of the nineteenth century. This was accomplished, however, not by a violent revolution, but through a number of gradual stages. As early as 1808 Brazil yielded to the new trend by opening her ports to European commerce, thereby breaking the commercial monopoly of Portugal. The same year that saw the economic liberation of the colony witnessed still another event of importance: in 1808 Brazil enjoyed its first newspaper, the *Rio de Janeiro Gazette*, as a result of the establishment of the first printing press, the *Imprensa Régia*. Ideas of independence became of course the order of the day, but a succession of historical events retarded Brazilian liberation until 1822, the year in which Dom Pedro of Portugal became the first Emperor of a theoretically free nation.

In literature, too, the process of emancipation was a slow and long-drawn-out affair. No violent changes occurred for the first thirty years of the century, primarily because no literary genius appeared. Poetry remained lifeless and static, still under the influence of the Minas-Geraes school; it was even more artificial than the compositions of the Academies. Many insignificant versifiers continued to write sonnets and odes in which there was no soul, no vibration of passion, no voice of the land: emphatic, empty, stiff rhetorical excercises designed to please the vanity of their pompous authors.

Only two figures of merit stand out in this interval of stagnation, two vigorous writers who had none of the mediocrity of their generation—José Bonifácio de Andrade e Silva (1765-1838) and Antônio Pereira de Souza Caldas (1762-1814). José Bonifácio, indeed, has won from posterity the title of 'father of Brazilian Independence.' Probably the best-endowed mind of his time, he was a scientist, a politician, a great orator, a moralist, and a poet. Being a man of haughty temperament, he soon turned against the Emperor and ultimately against his own country; as a result, he was exiled and began writing poetry after he was sixty, violent verses of patriotism, liberty, and hatred, under the influence of Byron.[8] Less violent, but no less disillusioned, was his contemporary Souza Caldas, a poet of pseudo-classic tendencies, and by far the most readable writer of the period. Souza Caldas' life was sad and bitter, and his poetry is mainly subjective and pessimistic. He composed an *Ode to the Savage*,* in which one can detect traces of Rousseau and Chateaubriand; and, like Chateaubriand, he too failed to find consolation in his mundane art, and turned to Catholicism. He exhibits also some vague similarities with

* Souza Caldas, *Ode ao Homem Selvagem*.

Lamartine, and all in all he might be considered a distant forerunner of Brazilian romanticism.[9]

Yet despite this mediocrity in literary production, a general ferment was under way. The years of the Independence period were turbulent and somewhat chaotic, in the midst of which the young country was struggling to assert its national will and create an autochthonous expression. Centuries of colonial domination had, of course, impressed a thoroughly Portuguese character on all aspects of cultural life. Yet the spiritual essence of Brazil was quite different from the genius of the mother country. Here was a new people, a strange mixture of three discordant races, a nation destined to be another colossal melting pot in a New World. Above all, here was a young nation seeking new outlets of every sort.

With the advent of its independence, Brazil ended its isolation and plunged into the currents typical of modern European life. New cultural centers were founded on foreign models: the Botanical Garden, the National Library, the National Museum, the Academy of Fine Arts. After the introduction of the printing press, the first books were published: *Marilia of Dirceo* by Gonzaga, and *The Uraguay* by Basilio da Gama. There occurred a positive renovation in thought, and prose writers of merit appeared in the fields of natural science, philosophy, history, and jurisprudence. For this was the age of national independence, and it called for a great deal of independent thinking. Above all, the new generation sought to avoid everything Portuguese; Portugal represented despotism in politics and classicism in literature, and the younger thinkers and writers naturally turned to other lands for inspiration.

Foreign influences thus had an early role in the shaping of Brazilian culture, much as in the nations of Spanish America. The cultures of France and England and Germany early began to exert a strong sway on the new nation; a French artistic mission was invited to the country; and the younger writers sought new models in the literatures of France, England, and Spain. The favorite foreign authors were of course the great writers among the European pre-romantics and romantics—Chateaubriand, Mme de Staël, Rousseau, Lamartine, Musset, Hugo, Byron, Scott, and Espronceda—and romanticism soon found ardent Brazilian exponents. The reason for this is easy to perceive. Brazil, like the other Latin American countries, furnished a fertile field for the introduction and development of the romantic movement. Romanticism emphasized the cult of primitive man and virgin nature, both of which were important elements in the new land; it upheld ideas of defiance and liberation from ancient ties, notions which could not fail to find sympathetic echoes among young patriots and nationalists. So it is not surprising to find romanticism taking strong hold in the former Portuguese colony, just as it had in the neighboring republics of Spanish America. And it is thoroughly understandable that Brazilian national literature should have its beginnings in the exuberant floods of verse and the colored idyllic prose of the romantic era.

BRAZILIAN POETRY

AT the outset, and for a period of half a century, Brazilian poetry bore the distinguishing characteristics of romanticism. It had, to be sure, a twofold parentage: on the one hand, the European romantic poets, and on the other the native verse of colonial times. But in the main, it followed the principal patterns of the European school: the early sentimentalism and religiosity of Lamartine, the later *mal du siècle*, even the grandiloquence of some of Victor Hugo's moods. Thus, for example, Brazil's first romantic, Domingos José Gonçalves de Magalhães (1811-82), wrote verses that were mainly reminiscent of Chateaubriand and Lamartine. Still a classicist in his first book, *Poems* (1832), he turned towards a new expression in his *Poetic Sighs and 'Saudades'* published in Paris in 1836.*

* Magalhães, *Poesias, Suspiros Poéticos e Saudades*.

Magalhães was typically representative of that lachrymose poetry so popular in Europe at the beginning of the century, a poetry that found consolation for human sadness in religious faith. Also a poet of the natural beauties of his country, Magalhães attempted an interpretation of the Indian soul in his celebrated poem 'Confederation of the Tamoyos,' which served as an example of traditional inspiration to later romantics like Gonçalves Dias and Alencar. For Brazilian romanticism was not at all a period of sterile imitation. On the contrary, it expressed the natural exuberance of the Brazilian temperament, and was marked by figures of brilliance—notably Gonçalves Dias, Brazil's first great poet.

Antônio Gonçalves Dias (1823-64) was not only Brazil's greatest romantic poet, but also—as his compatriots would say —a true Brazilian. In his veins ran the blood of three races, white, Indian, and Negro, a factor that gives him a distinctive Brazilian personality. Carvalho observes that the racial mixture in this poet was always in conflict with itself: the Indian in 'The Tymbiras,' 'Song of the Tamoyos,' 'Y-Yuca Pyrama'; the Negro in 'Slave'; and the Portuguese in 'Sextains of Friar Anthony.' * At any rate, it oriented his interests, for Gonçalves Dias was not only a poet but a distinguished ethnologist, who devoted many years to the study of Indian languages. But despite his intellectual accomplishments, Gonçalves Dias led the life of a true romantic: he passed a restless and sorrowful existence, and finally died in a shipwreck.

Gonçalves Dias exhibits in his works a Christian romanticism, shaded by soft landscapes and a vague melancholy. He is a true poet of nature, a pantheist who always suffers from that nostalgic feeling the Portuguese call *saudade*—an emotion that is intensified when he was far from his native land, as in this 'Song of Exile':

* Gonçalves Dias, *Os Tymbiras, Canção dos Tamoyos, Y-Yuca Pyrama, Escrava, Sextilhas de Frei Antão.*

There are palm trees in my homeland
Where a 'sabia' is singing,
But the birds who warble here
Do not sing as in my country.

There are more stars in our heavens,
And more flowers in our meadows;
In our forests is more life,
And our life has more affection . . .

God grant that I may not die here
In this place, without returning,
And without enjoying pleasures
Which I find not in this country,
And the palm trees I would see
Where the 'sabia' is singing.[10]

Human sentiments touch him too, and he has written beautiful poems extolling love and friendship, in stanzas like the following:

That which causes grief incurable,
That which causes torment, that which kills,
Deeper that cruel grief, than bitter death,
Is to die in life, and on the breast
Of the woman whom we worship,
In the warm heart of the friend.[11]

Sometimes, however, Gonçalves Dias turns to a less profound though charming form of writing, one which reminds the reader of the ingenuous songs of medieval poetry. Of this sort is his 'Green Eyes':

They are green, green eyes,
They are eyes of sea green
When it's calm at sea;
Eyes the color of hope.
Eyes for which I died.
Those eyes—ah, woe is me!
Since I saw them I've lost
My identity! [12]

But Gonçalves Dias' most enduring note is that which he expresses in his *American Poems*,* a work which stamps him as the national poet of Brazil. In 'Y-Yuca Pyrama' there is more real native emotion than in the celebrated 'Tabaré' of Zorrilla de San Martín, the Uruguayan poet who seems to be the disciple of the Brazilian. And in 'The Tymbiras,' Gonçalves Dias has sung the tragedy of the Indian race in stanzas of robust lyricism and extraordinary vigor, as may be seen in these lines from the *Introduction:*

> . . . I conjure up the spirit
> Of the savage warrior! Grim his appearance;
> Severe and almost mute, with slow steps,
> He walks, uncertain—the bipartite bow
> He supports in his hands, and from his naked shoulders
> The broken quiver hangs . . . the spilled
> Now useless arrows indicate
> The sorrowful march and the unsteady steps
> Of him who, in the land of his fathers, in vain
> Seeks refuge, and flees human contact.[18]

This virile Americanism and even this melancholy love of nature were altogether abandoned by the succeeding group of Brazilian romantics. These poets, the neurotic Manoel Antônio Alvares de Azevedo (1831-52) and his accomplished disciples—Casimiro de Abreu, Fagundes Varella, Laurindo Rabello, and Junqueira Freire—were all afflicted with sentimental pessimism, early disillusion, in a word with the *mal du siècle*. The critic Afrânio Peixoto has characterized them well in a few lines:

> These young men, contaminated by literature, suffered from 'Weltschmerz' or 'mal du siècle' and were singled out by Destiny for tragic ends. A homicidal literature was this that carried off Franco de Sá at twenty, Alvares de Azevedo at twenty-one, Junqueira Freire, Casimiro de Abreu, and Dutra e Mello at twenty-three . . . Martins

* Gonçalves Dias, *Poesias Americanas*.

Penna at thirty-three, Fagundes Varella at thirty-four, Laurindo Rabello at thirty-eight . . . If the orgy was intellectual for some of them under the influence of Byron, as in the cases of Alvares de Azevedo, for others it was a reality similar to that of Edgar Poe and Alfred de Musset, and for still others like Fagundes Varella it became sheer alcoholism. If Baudelaire chewed hashish, Junqueira Freire ate camphor; tuberculosis, a romantic illness, carried off Casimiro de Abreu . . . ; and Alvares de Azevedo died at twenty of hypochondria, a Byronic ailment.[14]

A healthier trend was manifested by yet another romantic group under the leadership of Antônio de Castro Alves (1847-71). Socially minded, Castro Alves was the champion of the abolition of slavery and of republicanism in Brazil, two noble ideals that unfortunately have little to do with poetry as an art. To move the recalcitrant spirit of the time, Castro Alves needed great verbal power, fiery eloquence, and profound emotional force—and he possessed all of these. But he was grandiose and bombastic; and he usually soared on the blue immensity of his own grandiloquence, like an Andean condor. Hence his poetry and that of the few minor poets who followed him are referred to as the *condoreira* school, a school that began by imitating the Victor Hugo of the *Châtiments* and ended in a conflagration of fiery metaphors. With all his shortcomings, Castro Alves has been hailed by a few critics as the greatest romantic poet of his country. The judgment is a partisan one, but Castro Alves, with his qualities of color and brilliance of form, and his passionate enthusiasm for lofty causes, does illustrate the aspects of romanticism that are dearest to the Brazilian soul.

Perhaps because of this affinity to the national temperament, romanticism as a movement was extremely persistent in Brazil. The romantic fire had largely burned itself out by 1870, when Brazilian poetry turned towards the new formulas of Parnassianism: emphasis on metrics, the substitution of perfection in form for intimate confession, a visual impression of beauty, a metallic clacking of the line, and in general a dazzling brilliancy. Yet Brazilian poets were loath to abandon the exuberance of the last romantics; and today it is not easy to classify with the Parnassians such figures as Machado de Assis and Guimarães. Luis Guimarães, Jr. (1845–98) perfectly illustrates this overlapping of tendencies. His books, *Bouquets* (1869), *Filigrees* (1872), *Sonnets and Rimes* (1880),* reveal the artisan of form so characteristic of the Parnassian, and at the same time they exhibit everywhere that delicate nostalgia typical of the romantic. It is this very fusion of different elements that lends particular interest to the work of one of the greatest names in Brazilian letters, Machado de Assis.

Joaquim Maria Machado de Assis (1839-1908) has been called by one of his countrymen, José Veríssimo, 'the highest expression of our literary genius; the most eminent figure of our literature.' Machado de Assis exhibited Parnassian tendencies, as may be seen from the titles of his books—*Chrysalids* (1864), *Barques* (1870)—but his work resembles rather that of Rubén Darío, the great poet of Spanish America.† Thus Machado, like Darío, had a many-sided talent: a writer of a refined temperament, he modernized Brazilian poetry while remaining almost a classic writer himself: he witnessed the intense suffering of humanity, but he preferred to express his sorrow with a charming smile; he had the melancholy make-up of the romantic, but his culture would not allow him to become too verbose in the expression of his emotions.

Few poets in the Portuguese language have attained more elegant diction and imagery than Machado de Assis displays in poems like 'Blue Fly,' a composition that recalls the best of Darío's immortal *Prosas Profanas*:

* Guimarães, *Corimbos, Filigranas, Sonetos e Rimas*.
† Machado de Assis, *Crisálidas, Falenas*.

It was a blue fly with wings of pomegranate gold,
  Daughter of Cathay or Hindustan,
Springing from a deep flesh-colored rose among the
  leaves,
  On a certain night in summer time.
And she buzzed and flew about, and flew about and
  buzzed,
  Shining in the splendor of the sun
And the brightness of the moon. She shone much
  brighter than
  Diamonds of the Great Mogul would shine . . .

Yet to this external perfection of form, Machado de Assis adds
a deep, if skeptical, understanding of human aspirations. He
introduces the figure of a man who watches the blue fly,
learns her symbolic meaning, and sees an oriental vision of
himself between her wings; but at length comes the tragedy:

Then the man, extending forth his callous coarsened hand,
  Only used to carpenters' rough work,
With a gesture laid a hold of that resplendent fly,
  Curious to re-examine her . . .

He examined her to such a point, in such a way,
  Torn and tarnished, nauseated, vile,
She succumbed. And thus that subtle and fantastic thing,
  Thus that vision vanished from the man.

Now today when he goes by, with cardamomum and
  Aloe on his head, and stylish airs,
It is said he has gone crazy, that he does not know
  How it was he lost his bright blue fly.[15]

In philosopical atmosphere, then, Machado de Assis actually
surpassed the great Nicaraguan, as he did too in his penetrating sense of humor. Here, for instance, is one of his masterpieces of insight: *Vicious Circle*, a bit of subtle philosophizing
generally acknowledged to be one of the most beautiful sonnets ever written in Portuguese:

Dancing in the air a restless firefly was lamenting:
'Would to God I were that vivid yellow constellation,.

Burning in the everlasting blue, an endless candle!'
But the constellation, gazing at the moon, resenting:
'Would that I could imitate that pure transparent clearness
Which, from a fretted Grecian column is admired
By a lovesick beauty sitting at a Gothic casement.'
But the moon was gazing at the sun with bitter feeling:

'Wretched I! O had I that colossal brightness,
Immortal clarity that sums up light and splendor.'
But the sun, his rutilant and golden head inclining:
'What a weight upon me is this aureole of genius.
And how wearying this blue immeasurable umbel.
Why was I not born to live my life a firefly, humble?' [16]

Parnassianism, which found only a partial devotee in
Machado de Assis with his sentimental and philosophic over-
tones, was soon adopted in earnest by a number of distinguished Brazilian poets. Three writers are generally mentioned
as the outstanding Parnassians of Brazil: Olavo Bilac, an artist
of tropical color and oriental splendor; Raymundo Correia,
whose exquisite craftsmanship never quite obscured his under-
lying despair; and Alberto de Oliveira, who polished and re-
polished his verses in an effort to attain absolute perfection
of form.

Olavo Braz Martins dos Guimarães Bilac (1865-1918) is not
only the greatest name in the Parnassian poetry of Brazil, but
at the same time one of the outstanding poets of the Portuguese language. From the French Parnassian writers—Gautier,
Hérédia, Leconte de Lisle—he learned the magnificent or-
chestration of his verses. In his voluptuous, purely sensuous attitude, he was an exponent of the lush moods of the tropics, a
lover of color and music and exotic visions. He was also a
spontaneous natural poet, with the vigor of a Santos Chocano,
whom he resembles at times; but unfortunately Bilac possessed
only a strength of word and phrase, not of a continuous inward force. His imagination was limited; and though certain
of his volumes, like *Poems* (1888) and *Afternoon* (1919),

have a compelling beauty, he lacked the powers of synthesis
and of spiritual elaboration of his materials.*

For Bilac was above all the poet of external form—not of
form rough-hewn as in nature, but the polished and perfected
form of the craftsman. Thus he writes in his 'Profession of
Faith':

> I don't want divine Jupiter,
>   Herculean, handsome,
> To be carved from sacred marble
>   With the quarry hammer . . .

—explaining instead his true preference:

> More than mass extraordinary,
>   Which is so amazing
> A fine artist's reliquary
>   Really is what tempts me.[17]

He was a true artist, who believed the poet should shape his
verses with patience and care, in the search for technical perfection:

> Twist, perfect, polish, heighten
>   Every phrase; and then in fine
> On the molded golden verses,
>   Like a ruby set the rhyme.[18]

To this fondness for outward form, Olavo Bilac brought no
transforming inner vision, but he did express a pantheistic
emotion of universal love. This love, in his verses, progresses
from its most human aspect of erotic passion to the higher
forms of metaphysical intelligence, so well expressed in his
'Listening to the Stars':

> 'Now (you will say) to listen to the stars at night!
> I'm sure you've lost your reason!' I will say to you,
> However, so to hear them, often this I do—
> I waken and I open windows, pale with fright.

> And we converse all night, while sparkles in the sky
> Just like an open canopy, the Milky Way . . .

* Bilac, *Poesias, Tarde.*

And I will say: 'To understand them, you must love,
Since only he who loves (and he is one of few),
Can hear and truly understand the stars above.' [19]

Less sensuous and more inwardly tormented was the work
of Raymundo Correia (1860-1911), the most refined poet of
the Brazilian Parnassian school. Correia was a fine craftsman
too, a disciple of Gautier whom he equalled in technical skill;
and his verses abound in spontaneous charm and primeval
freshness. Yet, deeper in his songs one finds a note of utter
despair, a morbidity and a strange richness of imagery reminiscent of Baudelaire. His artistic sensibility, his intuition of
beauty, his philosophic skepticism, his feeling for nature, all
these made him one of the truest poets that Brazil has produced. Few writers can evoke, for example, such a sense of
complete desolation as Correia has created in this 'Saudade' on
a dead city:

Here in days gone by the hymns resounded;
Many royal coaches on these pavements
And within these squares, today abandoned,
Passed by in a grand display of splendor.

Flowery arches, light of reddish torches,
Festive guns, and bright unfurling banners,
Spiral fireworks, trumpets, and confusion
Of multitudes of people, of bells ringing—

All has passed!' But in these blackened arches,
In these frightful elevated turrets,
On their frigid stones someone is sitting.

And his tearful eyes of melancholy
Look about, and weep like Jeremiah
On Jerusalem of many dreams.[20]

The third important Parnassian was Alberto de Oliveira
(1859-1937), never a truly popular poet, but one who in his
sensibility, his melancholy, and his tenderness, truly expressed
the national spirit. Oliveira's lyric enthusiasm, an almost child-

ish exultation, revealed a romantic aspect in his work. Yet in
his aim for perfection of form and his great efforts to polish
his style he was a true Parnassian, as may be seen from his
lines to 'The Sky of Curitiba':

> What a sky of silver, carmine! What a star of daybreak
>   and of dawn!
> And now the sun! And now the day! A loud sonorous
>   voice says: Sing!
> Birds sing near by, and like the birds, the forest sings,
> Where insects suck the cherished nectar, and the river
>   sings.
> The sky of Curitiba makes me sing!
>
> What a sky of carmine, bronze! The sun now enters
> Radiant, immense. It is the hour of peace, the hour of
>   myrrh and incense,
> Pray! a voice says. And a bell cries in the air.
> The angels pray, perhaps. And on a solitary cliff a pine
>   is lost in thought.
> The sky of Curitiba makes me pray!
>
> What a sky of ebony and flame! All nature sleeps. The
>   city sleeps.
> And I alone before the vastness of the night, I think and
>   suffer, lift my glance to stars.
> Then, Dream!: a voice says, of that which is above.
> Ah, what a sky of calmness and of light!
> The sky of Curitiba makes me dream! [21]

With these three figures—Bilac, Correia, and Oliveira—Brazilian Parnassianism had given its best. Towards the close of
the nineteenth century, the inevitable reaction against the
movement set in, as it had elsewhere. Poets were bored with an
art that was always impassive and objective, with a poetry of
mere description and form that fulfilled no mystic longings.
Inner visions had to be expressed, shapeless ideals and intimate
feelings had to take form. For such purposes symbolism was
indispensable: a poetry of vague suggestions and a musical
atmosphere, a soft poetry full of nuance, tenderness, reminis-

cence, transparency, translucency. Soon a new school of symbolists held the center of the poetic stage.

Brazil's outstanding symbolist was João da Cruz e Souza (1862-98), a Negro poet from Santa Catarina. In his books—*Shields* (1893), *Lanterns* (1900), and *Last Sonnets* (1905)—he spoke for his race, feeling all their oppression and trying to liberate himself from earthly bondage by soaring into metaphysical regions.* He had the sombre moods of Baudelaire, whom he imitated; he constantly voiced the tragic sentiment of his life; and he expressed a subconscious premonition of better things in some remote unknown. Cruz e Souza was far from being a great poet, but in his disorganized verses one sees the end of an epoch and the beginning of a daring new trend. Others of this school included Bernardino da Costa Lopes (1859-1916), the author of *Chromos* (1881), *Pizzicato* (1886), *Heraldries* (1895), *Sinhá Flor* (1899), *The Vale of Lilies* (1901), still a Parnassian, but one who resembles the symbolists in his simple musical poems on every-day life; and Mario Pederneiras (1868-1915), whose volumes of delicate poetry—*Nocturnal Rounds* (1901), *Stories from My Home* (1906), *Whims of Dreams and Life* (1912)—exercised a decisive influence on the contemporary writers of his country, particularly because of his introduction of free verse.† Finally, one must mention Alphonsus de Guimarãens (1873-1921), who in his books of religious poetry—*Dona Mystica* (1899), *The Seven Sorrows of Our Lady* (1899), *Kyrie* (1902), *Pastoral Letter to Believers in Love and Death* (1923), and *The Burning Chamber* (1899)—showed himself to be a true disciple of Paul Verlaine.‡ Like Verlaine, he passed with facility from bacchanalian excesses to the liturgical mood. Most of his verses

* Cruz e Souza, *Broquéis, Faróis, Ultimos Sonetos.*

† Costa Lopes, *Cromos, Pizzicato, Brasões, Sinhá Flor, Val de Lírios;* Pederneiras, *Rondas Nocturnas, Histórias do meu Casal, Ao Leú do Sonho e à Mercê da Vida.*

‡ Guimarães, *Dona Mystica, Septenario das Dôres de Nossa Senhora, Kiriale, Pastoral aos Crentes de Amor e da Morte, Câmara Ardente.*

were composed under the stress of tragedy, with the constant thought in mind of his beloved's death—and he sought consolation in lines like these 'To the Hands of the Virgin':

> Hands envied by the lilies, chosen hands
> To mitigate the sufferings of Christ,
> Whose bluish veins seem fashioned of the same
> Pure astral essence as the holy eyes . . .[22]

But the final reaction against this school—and indeed against all the poetry that had preceded it—came in the twentieth century, with the movement known as Brazilian modernism. This modernism (not to be confused with the *modernismo* of Spanish America) was officially launched in São Paulo in 1922, with a daring lecture by Graça Aranha; the crux of the movement was the destruction of things old, the idea that modernity was more important than beauty itself, that a poet must be original at all costs. This soon degenerated into chicanery and stupidity; some 'modern poets' went to such extremes of nationalism that they founded the *Revista de Antropofagia*—the *Cannibalistic Review*, whose tenet was to revert to the Indian, to the anthropophagous, and destroy all foreign elements in Brazilian literature. Yet the school created by Graça Aranha has produced a number of excellent contemporary poets, of whom by far the outstanding is Jorge de Lima, one of the brightest names in current Brazilian literature.

Jorge de Lima (1895–1953) is one of the most complete personalities in the modern lyric poetry of his country. A restless creative genius, he possesses a temperament that is constantly renewing itself. He began his poetic career as a Parnassian, only to break away from this type of conventional writing into the most versatile forms of expression; he has written sociological, communistic, and even mystical poetry; and in addition, his verse ranks with the work of the modern revolutionary novelists, Lins do Rego, Amado, and Veríssimo, as an authentic interpretation of the very essence of Brazilian life. Of his dozen odd books, perhaps the most significant are *Poems* (1925), *New Poems* (1927), *Banguê and the Negress Fulô* (1928), *Selected Poems* (1933), and *Time and Eternity* (1935),* in collaboration with the great poet Murilo Mendes. And of his many contributions to Brazilian poetry, perhaps his outstanding is the creation of Negro verse, a genre broadly cultivated today in those Latin American countries that have African racial elements. Representative of his work in this field is the famous and powerful poem 'That Negress Fulô,' of which the following stanzas give only a glimpse, for the poem must be read in its entirety to appreciate its sensuous evocations and ultimate tragedy:

> Now, it happened that there came
> (That was many years ago)
> To the home of my grandfather
> A handsome negro woman.
> She was called negress Fulô!
>   That negress Fulô!
>   That negress Fulô! . . .
>
> That young negress Fulô,
> She stayed, then, as a servant,
> For to watch over Sinhá,
> And to starch for Sinhô.
>   That negress Fulô!
>   That negress Fulô!
>
> O Fulô! O Fulô!
> (It was the voice of Sinhá)
> Come to help me, O Fulô,
> Come to fan my body,
> For I'm perspiring, Fulô!
> Come to scratch my itch,
> Come to give me a rub,
> Come to swing my hammock,

* Lima, *Poemas, Novos Poemas, Banguê e Negra Fulô, Poemas Escolhidos, Tempo e Eternidade*.

Come to tell me a story
For I'm sleepy, Fulô!
    That negress Fulô!

One day there was a princess
Who lived in a castle,
Who possessed a dress,
With the little fishes of the sea.
On a duck's leg did she come,
On a chicken's did she go.
The King-Sinhô commanded me
To tell you five more stories.
    That negress Fulô!
    That negress Fulô . . .[23]

Among other contemporary poets, a great deal of attention
has been attracted by Mario de Andrade (1893–1945), who has
won the name of 'Pope of Futurism.' The very titles of his
books—*There is a Drop of Blood in Every Poem* (1917),
Hallucinated Pauliceia (1922), *The Slave who isn't Isaura*
(1925), *Macunaima* (1928), and *Sorrows for Sale* (1930)—
indicate the idiosyncrasies of this writer, who in every volume
attempts a new and radical mode of expression.* Other modern poets, however, if one may venture a personal evaluation,
are more likely to stand the test of time. They are, in the
order of their importance: Manoel Bandeira (1886–   ), the
sincere and subjective author of *Ashes of Hours* (1917) and
Libertinage (1930); Emílio Moura, the bard of Minas Geraes;
Augusto Frederico Schmidt (1906–   ), whose verses show
a social preoccupation in *Song of the Freeman* (1930),
or a tragic note in *Songs of Night* (1934);† Carlos Drum-
mond Andrade (1902–   ), a bitter and revolutionary poet;
Guilherme de Almeida (1890), a writer of great technical skill;
and Cecília Meirelles (1901–   ), Gilka Machado (1897), and

* Andrade, *Há uma Gota de Sangue en Cada Poema, Pauliceia Desvai-
rada, A Escrava que não é Isaura, Macunaima, Remate de Males.*
† Bandeira, *Cinza das Horas, Libertinagem;* Schmidt, *Canto de Liberto,
Cantos da Noite.*

Murilo Mendes (1901-   ), the neo-Catholic poet who, after having been a Marxist and a Surrealist, today expresses himself in a most limpid voice. There are others, too—young singers endowed with enthusiasm and ability, faithful aesthetic interpreters of their nation, of a Brazil that holds out the promise of one of the most original artistic expressions of the modern world.

BRAZILIAN PROSE FICTION

NOT the least element in this literary panorama of modern Brazil is the contemporary novel, a remarkable interpretation of the national spirit. Brazilian novels rank today with the most interesting produced anywhere; they are especially noteworthy for their intense nationalism, their almost complete attention to the native scene. But before examining these vigorous modern works, it is best to review some of the main writers and currents of the preceding century, in order to trace the development of this nationalistic trend in Brazilian prose fiction.

The Brazilian novel began with the idyllic outpourings of the romantic era: that period characterized, in all Latin American countries, by a chivalric portrayal of the Indian and a Chateaubriandesque feeling for nature.[24] In Brazil, these traits are represented by the very greatest of the country's romantic novelists, José de Alencar (1829-77). His novels of Indian theme—*The Guarani* (1857), *Iracema* (1865), *Ubirajara* (1875), and *The Ipê Trunk* (1871)—illustrate the interpretation of the indigenous soul as writers conceived it in those times.* They give an adulterated picture of the native: a poetical warrior covered with showy plumage, and speaking the language of a heroic knight; a maiden in an ecstatic attitude of Platonic love. But at the same time, his pages are filled with the clear splendor of the Brazilian forests, waterfalls, rivers, and meadows—all this revealed with a poetic charm

* Alencar, *O Guarany, Iracema, Ubirajara, Tronco de Ipê.*

and an insight into natural beauty as profound as Alencar's penetration of human behavior was shallow. Thus *Iracema*, his masterpiece,[25] is an extraordinary combination of spiritual candor and beauty of style, a mixture of European romantic formulas with nascent Americanism. The story is pure romantic idyll, the tale of a Portuguese conqueror, Martim Soares Moreno, and his unfortunate love for the Indian maiden Iracema, who adores him till the day of her death. Yet at the same time, *Iracema* is a book of great symbolic significance, a synthesis of that crossing of bloods which underlies the racial formation of Brazil and the rest of the Latin American continent. Alencar, despite his romanticism, initiated a national trend, for he described the American landscape and the American man (however idealized), and he gave prominence to Brazilian subject matter and problems.

Still other romantic novelists—Macedo, Silva Guimarães, Távora, and the Viscount Taunay are generally included in the classification—added new directions to this incipient nationalism. Even Joaquim Manoel de Macedo (1820-82), the weakest of the group, wrote descriptions of Brazilian popular life and manners; unfortunately, his novels—*The Brunette* (1844), *The Blond Boy* (1845), *Rosa* (1849), *Vicentina* (1853), and *The Foreigner* (1855)—are written in a sugar-coated sentimental tone that is not pleasing to modern taste.*

More important was the contribution of Bernardo da Silva Guimarães (1827-84), who cultivated the regional novel, a genre that has remained important in Brazilian fiction. The background of Silva Guimarães' books is the *Sertão*, that Brazilian hinterland explored in colonial times by *bandeirantes* in search of mines and slaves; these *bandeirantes*, having exhausted their mines, remained to populate the desert *Sertões*, living a wretched existence far from the centers of civilization. Silva Guimarães did not introduce the *sertanejo* in Brazilian

* Macedo, *A Moreninha, O Moço Louro, Rosa, Vicentina, O Forasteiro.*

fiction—Alencar had already done that in *The Gaucho* (1870)
—but he popularized the type in a series of novels: *History and
Legends* (1872), *The Hermit of Munquém* (1871), *Maurício*
(1877).* Later writers followed his lead, including Franklin
Távora, Coelho Netto, Affonso Arinos, and several contemporary novelists; and of course Euclydes da Cunha, who in his
celebrated *The Sertões* composed a masterful description of
these authentic Brazilian sons of the land. These are the types
one finds in Guimarães works, a trifle more real than any that
had preceded, but nonetheless stereotyped characters against
the pleasing background of their native landscape—*The Semi-
narian* (1872), *The Indian Alfonso* (1873), and *The Slave
Isaura* (1875).† Likewise a regional novelist, Franklin Távora
(1842-88), stands as a transitional writer between romanticism
and realism. Descriptions of the *Sertão* and its types appear in
his most important works: *Cabelleira* (1876), which may be
considered the first regional novel of the North, and which
marks the appearance of the picturesque rural bandit of those
regions; *House of Straw* (1866); *Man of the Forest* (1878), in
which he shows a great affection for the *caboclo;* and *Lourenzo*
(1881).‡ In these works, Távora has given the first true pictures of the life of the Northern hinterland, without avoiding
its disagreeable aspects of misery and ignorance.

Even more realistic was Alfredo d'Escragnolle, Viscount
Taunay (1843-99), a forerunner of Brazilian realism, though
he is always classed with the romantic novelists. A soldier in
the wars against Paraguay between 1864 and 1870, he reflected
the changed national point of view that resulted from this
campaign. After the war, a new critical conscience was born
in Brazil; men of letters began to think about the fundamental
issues of their country, and many of them struggled for the

* Silva Guimarães, *História e Tradições, O Ermitão de Munquém,
Maurício;* Alencar, *O Gaúcho.*

† Guimarães, *O Seminarista, O Indio Affonso, A Escrava Isaura.*

‡ Távora, *Cabelleira, Casa de Palha, O Matuto, Lourenço.*

abolition of slavery and the establishment of a republican form of government; science and philosophy oriented the education of the younger intellectuals, who began to examine their own nation with searching eyes. From this mood there came a new tendency towards realism in literature—the Brazilian man had to appear alive, of blood and bone, and the landscape had to show sombre tones as well as bright—a new trend of which Viscount Taunay was the earliest representative. A historian as well as a novelist, he is remembered for his *Retreat of Laguna* (1871), a description of the Matto-Grosso campaign; but his real masterpiece is *Inocência* * (1872), a story of love, jealousy, and vengeance in the Matto-Grosso.[26] To the modern reader, the plot of this work seems trite: the spurned lover of Inocência murders the young doctor who had gained her love; yet the work has a great simplicity of form—and much humor in characters like Dr. Meyer, the naturalist who is in Brazil collecting butterflies, and who, two years after the tragedy, presents the Entomological Society of Magdeburg with a new specimen of lepidoptera, the *Papilio Inocentia!* But the chief merit of Taunay's work lies in its Brazilianism; though his books deal with the Matto-Grosso, he is not so much a regional novelist as a nationalistic writer who had travelled throughout Brazil and was thoroughly conversant with all aspects of his country's life.

What had been only glimmers of reality in the works of Taunay and Távora soon developed into a full-fledged realistic and then naturalistic movement.[27] Under the influence of Zola, Brazilian novelists plunged headlong into sociological research, psycho-physiological phenomena, and auto-analysis. Pure realism of a skeptical sort, rather than the formulas of naturalism, marked the novels of the poet Joaquim Maria Machado de Assis. In his most important works of fiction, *Braz Cubas* (1881), *Quincas Borba* (1890), and *Dom Casmurro*

---

* Taunay, *Retirada da Laguna, Inocência.*

(1900), Machado de Assis is a cynical philosopher who portrays life as it is, without cringing at evil or rejoicing at goodness. *Quincas Borba*, for example, is set in Rio de Janeiro, and tells the story of a wealthy and eccentric philosopher who dies leaving his friend Rubião as sole heir; included in the legacy is a dog who bears the donor's name, 'Quincas Borba.' In time, Rubião loses everything—the woman he loves, his fortune, his friends, his mind—everything, that is, except the one thing he constantly neglected: his faithful dog. This is sophisticated writing, very much like that of Anatole France; and indeed, Machado de Assis is so profound in his treatment of character that he may be considered Brazil's first psychological novelist. The other Brazilian novelists who flourished at the close of the nineteenth century had little of this ironic realism; on the contrary, the more eminent ones—Azevedo, Ribeiro, Pompeia, and de Souza—were exponents of the naturalistic theories of Zola.

Thus, Aluízio Azevedo (1857-1913), the official creator of naturalism, was a direct and often brutal writer. Too deeply influenced by the *roman experimental*, he occasionally allowed his descriptions of slums and his discussions of social problems to retard the movement of his novels. Otherwise, he was a great novelist—a keen observer, a vigorous interpreter of national life, a bold painter of popular customs, and above all a shrewd critic of society, as may be seen in his most celebrated novel, *The Mulatto* (1881).* The very plot of this book is in itself a daring comment on Brazilian life: Dr. Raymundo da Silva, the illegitimate son of a landholder and one of his Negro slaves, comes to the city of S. Luis do Maranhão in Brazil, following his education in Portugal, intending merely to settle some business. While here, he stays with his paternal uncle and falls in love with the latter's daughter, Anna Rosa. Because of Raymundo's race and origin, his sweetheart's relatives

---

* Azevedo, *O Mulato*.

and friends oppose the marriage; 'the mulatto' is finally murdered at the order of a priest, and the girl is married off to the head clerk at her father's store. The whole book is an exposé of a society deeply rooted in tradition and conforming only outwardly to a standard of morals set by the church. Other novels by Azevedo—*Boarding House* (1884), *The Man* (1887), *The Screech Owl* (1889), and *The Tenement* (1890) —illustrate still further his mastery of naturalistic formulas, and constitute the most faithful pictures of Brazilian society in those times.*

Quite as faithful a disciple of Zola was Júlio Ribeiro (1845–1890), who, in his novel *Flesh* † (1888), carried to extremes the elements of erotic love, physiological processes, and vulgarity of expression. *Flesh* is the story of a young girl, Lenita, and her growth into a creature of passion. Born in the country, well educated, she goes to the city at the age of fourteen, there to become a successful figure in society; upon her father's death, she goes to live at the estate of an old friend of the family, Colonel Barbosa; there she falls in love with Manoel, the colonel's son, and one day—after being bitten by a rattlesnake, and believing she is about to die—she confesses her feelings to him. From then on, the novel is little more than a series of orgies, climaxing in the inevitable tragedies of satiation and suicide.

Realism of a different sort is exhibited by Raul Pompeia (1863-95), a sensitive introvert; and by H. M. Inglez de Souza (1853-1918), a writer of great descriptive powers. Pompeia's single autobiographical novel, *Athenaeum* ‡ (1888), amounts to a realistic *tour de force*. Written in a very labored form, it relates the sufferings of a child who leaves the affectionate environment of his home to enter a school; Pompeia's style is bitter and ironical, as he describes the stupidity of the

---

* Azevedo, *Casa de Pensão, O Homem, O Coruja, O Cortiço.*
† Ribeiro, *A Carne.*
‡ Pompeia, *Atheneu.*

Director, and the cruel pedagogical methods which fail to take into account child psychology. Unlike his contemporaries, Pompeia was a subtle poet, and had he lived a few years earlier he would have been a romantic. Inglez de Souza, on the other hand, might well have been the greatest of Brazilian naturalists, if he had paid less heed to the clichés of this Zolaesque literary school. His works include *The Story of a Fisherman* (1876), *Colonel Sangrado* (1877), *The Cocoa-Planter* (1888), and *The Missionary* (1888), his most important novel and a book unjustly forgotten by Brazilian readers.* *The Missionary* is a vividly told and dramatic tale of a priest, who, wishing to convert a wild tribe of Indians to the Catholic faith, is himself converted to a licentious life by a native girl. Inglez de Souza has been able to create very real characters, but again one must lament the handicapping influence of the naturalistic stock-in-trade, overemphasis on a deterministic philosophy, excess of description and minute detail, and the so-called scientific 'attitude.'

Yet with all its shortcomings, naturalism made a valuable contribution to the Brazilian novel: By the end of the nineteenth century, reality became permanent in literature, and the writers of the twentieth century were to inherit this wealth of discovery. They received, in addition, fresh guidance on the realistic and nationalistic road, from two great figures at the turn of the century: Euclydes da Cunha, who was to set an indelible seal of regionalism on Brazilian literature; and Graça Aranha, who was to become the prophet of Brazilianism at the expense of foreign influences.

Euclydes da Cunha (1866-1909) is the author of the most celebrated book in Brazilian literature, *The Sertões* (1902).† This extraordinary work describes that Northern hinterland of Brazil that lies between the Rivers São Francisco and Mercúrio

* Inglez de Souza, *História de um Pescador, Coronel Sangrado, O Cacaolista, O Missionário.*
† Da Cunha, *Os Sertões.*

—its landscape, geography, geology, climate, and flora; its inhabitants with their racial characteristics and the relation they bear to their environment. All these factors are analyzed from a scientific standpoint, but *The Sertões* has also its historical aspect. For the book also discusses the failures and successes of five expeditions sent by the federal government to overcome a rebellion in the interior, and the vicissitudes of the famous Antônio Conselheiro. But how much importance does Euclides attribute to this bloody struggle? It appears only as a background for presenting the inhabitants of the hinterland. Primarily, the reader sees the *Sertões,* and he learns to understand the psychology of the *caboclo* who inhabits those regions, the descendant of the original *bandeirantes,* in a mortal clash against the invader of his land. To write such a book, an author needs much scientific knowledge and years of study; yet Euclydes da Cunha was able to achieve this technical preparation without sacrificing his literary gifts. *The Sertões* is, from start to finish, a masterpiece of artistic spontaneity and fresh poetical expression.

The other writer who studied his nation from a scientific point of view at this same period was Graça Aranha (1868-1931), the author of *Canaan* * (1901), a book which has done much to develop an interest in Brazilian literature all over the world.[28] Aranha was a man of broad European culture, acquired not only in books but from his long trips abroad as a diplomat. Yet from 1920 on, he was the apostle of modernism in Brazil, of that radically nationalistic and anti-European reform in literature; and in 1924, as the Brazilian Academy would not accept his militant ideas on art, he resigned from that institution. Graça Aranha was undoubtedly a man of great cultural impulses, and a first-rate stylist. His *Canaan* is a *roman à thèse,* a novel of ideas, in which the formation of the Brazilian nation is discussed by two newly arrived

* Aranha, *Chanaan.*

young Germans. Unfortunately, the theories it expresses are not too original—they deal mostly with the old problem of the mixing of bloods, and they are uttered in a somewhat Messianic style by Herr Milkau and Herr Lentz. Consequently *Canaan* is somewhat disorganized and uneven, but this lack is more than compensated for by its incomparable descriptions of landscape and native customs. Indeed, for its beauty of style and racial emotion, *Canaan* well deserves the position that has been accorded it by most critics—that of the most representative Brazilian novel.

The influence of these two writers, Graça Aranha and Euclydes da Cunha, following after the realistic movement, was quite decisive. They fixed the national character of Brazilian literature—a Brazilianism that has dominated almost all modern novelists, be they writers of fantasy like H. M. Coelho Netto (1864-1934), whose *The Sertão* (1896), and *Black King* (1914) combine natural settings with a vivid imagination; or realists like Afrânio Peixoto (1876-   ), whose *Maria Bonita* (1914), *Fruit of the Forest* (1920), and *Sinházinha* (1929) present the social and psychological position of Negroes, mulattoes, and half-breeds in the rural society of his country.* Indeed, twentieth-century Brazilian novels are definitely nationalistic in character; and their chief purpose seems to be the interpretation of the very essence of their country's soul, in a way that it has never been interpreted before.

The Contemporary Novel

THERE is in the Brazilian novel of today such an exaltation of life that this genre almost partakes of the lyric poem and the drama. Life bursts, in these novels, with a tropical force, with the unrestrained impetus of native forests and majestic rivers.[29] Sometimes the novelist is a refined city-dwelling artist, master of all the creative subtleties of European techniques. But more

* Coelho Netto, *O Sertão, Rey Negro;* Peixoto, *Maria Bonita, Fruta do Mato, Sinházinha.*

often he is an impulsive genius in a new and marvelous land where everything attains extraordinary proportions; where nature, creatures, and passions are different; where man himself seems to move with a new purpose and a new rhythm. The novelists of this country have turned their eyes to the soil, with the feverish impatience of gold miners or the serene movements of harvesters, in order to show the world new products of beauty. Brazilian culture is enhanced by these vivid regional works, and never before have the writers of this country displayed such ardent nationalism.

The most interesting of these regionalists is José Lins do Rego (1901–57), who was, at the early age of forty, the leading fiction-writer of Brazil. The novelist of the sugar plantations in the northeast, he is a great writer because he has created his own world of experiences, imagination, and emotions—a world in which he lives continually, and into which the reader follows him to take part in his drama. Lins do Rego describes the life of the *engenho*, rural tasks, the habits and customs of the people, their conflicts and sufferings and passions; all this, with an organic style, a sensuous approach to literature and to life, a truly poetic realism. Few writers can give a more vivid impression of rural life in Brazil than he has evoked in *Plantation Lad* (1932), *The Queer Lad* (1933), *Banguê* (1934), *The Moleque Ricardo* (1935), *Factory* (1936), *Purity* (1937), *The Stories of Old Totonha* (1936), and *Pedra Bonita* (1939).* And none can surpass him in the vivid evocation of his own past. For all his novels are the recreation of his own childhood and youth, brought to life with such a rich background of memories and suggestions that the reader is held spellbound, as in the novels of Dostoevski.

In contrast, Erico Veríssimo (1905-) is the sophisticated writer of the city, the novelist of Porto Alegre. Well versed in foreign literature, he has learned much from English and

---

* Lins do Rego, *Menino de Engenho, Doidinho, Banguê, O Moleque Ricardo, Usina, Pureza, Histórias da Velha Totonha, Pedra Bonita.*

American novelists; at the beginning of his literary career, Veríssimo was exceedingly fond of Oscar Wilde, Bernard Shaw, Anatole France, and Ibsen, but in his present technique he shows rather the influences of Aldous Huxley, Ernest Hemingway, and John dos Passos. He himself gives full credit to his masters. Thus, he confesses that just before writing his first novel of consequence, *Clarissa* (1933), he had read Rosamond Lehman's *Dusty Answer*. Again, before undertaking *Cross Roads* (1935), Veríssimo translated Huxley's *Point Counterpoint*, an influence which shows even in the title of the Brazilian's novel. This technique learned from Huxley—that of the 'cross roads' of lives that meet briefly—has remained dominant in all of Veríssimo's intense novels, *Faraway Music* (1934), *A Place in the Sun* (1936), *Behold the Lilies of the Field* (1938), *Saga* (1940).* He takes pleasure in showing characters that are drawn together for a while, in a school, a boarding house, a hospital, only to be separated by some fatal command; in studying lives of people crushed by domestic tragedy, some fighting heroically while others surrender easily to the force of destiny. This technique is admirably suited to Veríssimo's special province as a novelist—the metropolitan scene, the agitated life of the city, the cross roads of everyday occurrences.

Closer to the earth is the work of José Américo de Almeida (1887–   ), another of those novelists of the Brazilian northeast, that part of the nation which seems to bear all the misery of an unbalanced economy. The relatively prosperous central and southern regions of Brazil find it hard to understand the frightful conditions of the poor souls who drag themselves through poverty and sickness in the northern *Sertão*—conditions which Almeida has described remarkably in his best novel, *The Bagaceira* † (1928). The first draft of

* Veríssimo, *Clarissa, Caminhos Cruzados, Música ao Longe, Um Lugar ao Sol, Olhai os Lírios do Campo, Saga.*
† Almeida, *A Bagaceira.*

this book, which deals exclusively with the misery of a northern settlement, was vigorous but crude. Fortunately, Almeida sent the manuscript to Plinio Salgado, a São Paulo writer of distinction; Salgado discovered in *The Bagaceira* a work of great promise, and suggested that Almeida rewrite it according to the tenets of the new school; the result is an excellent and very modern novel, free from the exaggerations so typical of Vanguard literature. Indeed, *The Bagaceira* initiated the series of authentic Brazilian novels. Its influence is easy to understand, for Almeida is not only a good sociologist, but an artist who knows how to cover ugly reality with a veil of poetry. He himself was born in the *Sertão*, and hence knew from childhood the drama of that poverty-stricken people who still had enough heroism to continue the desperate struggle for existence; and he has described their life with startling veracity, in a vernacular idiom full of color and vigor.

Even more earthy is Jorge Amado (1912-), the most distinguished of the socialist-minded writers of northern Brazil. Amado is primarily a regional novelist, but his work gives expression to universal emotions and aspirations. Through his cycle of six novels of Bahía, he has interpreted the daily existence, feelings, and hopes of the suffering masses of his native state, in a style that throbs with intensity. Each of these works deals with a different phase of Bahía life: *Carnival Land* (1932) shows the reader an interlude in the intellectual life of Brazil; *Cocoa* (1933) describes the lot of the plantation workers in the south of Bahía; *Sweat* (1934) depicts the wretchedness and hopelessness of dwellers in the slums; and *Jubiabá* (1935) relates the adventures and picturesque ways of the black race. Amado continued these pictures with *Dead Sea* (1936), a novel that won the Graça Aranha prize; and, according to his own statement, closed the series with his *Captains of the Sand* (1937)—a story of the urchins of Bahía, the 'dead-end kids' who roam the streets and wharves of the city.* Amado's earlier books seem fragmentary and unfinished, but his later ones are increasingly skilful propaganda for the social amelioration of the underprivileged.

Graciliano Ramos (1892–1953) likewise feels sympathy with the poor; for this reason he has been considered communistic and has been persecuted—though in his works he is primarily a stylist interested in psychological reactions. Ramos wasted his youth in the *Sertão;* there he wrote his first novel, *Caheté* † (1933), which exhibited a better command of language than that of most contemporary Brazilian fiction writers, a fact that caused critics to compare him to Machado de Assis. As a protest against this comparison, Ramos wrote his second novel, *Saint Bernard* (1935), revealing himself once again as a true stylist, a master of short dialogue and psychology. In his latest books, the novel *Anguish* (1936) and a collection of short stories, *Dry Lives* (1938), he has carried his deep analysis of human lives and his constant introspection a step further— adding to his stylistic merits a strange new note of bitterness and profound skepticism.‡

These five writers—Lins do Rego, Veríssimo, Almeida, Amado, and Ramos—are perhaps the best-known novelists of modern Brazil.[30] There are others somewhat less renowned, but no less important. Among them one should mention Amando Fontes, Lúcio Cardoso, and Rachel de Queiroz, all of whom belong to the realistic and nationalistic school. Thus, Amando Fontes (1899–   ) excels in lifelike descriptions of city slums, though his work lacks psychological insight. In *The Corumbas* § (1933), he tells the story of three girls who come from the hinterland to live in the city, only to sink into a life of misery and degradation; what irks him is not the fate that changes human destiny without purpose, but the injustice

* Amado, *O País do Carnaval, Cacau, Suor, Jubiabá, Mar Morto, Capitães da Areia.*
† Ramos, *Caheté.*
‡ Ramos, *S. Bernardo, Angustia, Vidas Sêcas.*
§ Fontes, *Os Corumbas.*

of society which drags these girls downward. In his search for reality, Fontes scorns literary style, to write in a simple though intensely dramatic prose. On the other hand, Lúcio Cardoso (1913-), one of the youngest and most realistic of Brazilian novelists, is constantly struggling for a greater perfection in his style. Yet he too fills his pages with a wealth of documentary material. In his earlier novels Cardoso was strictly a regional writer, painting the *Sertão* with all the misery of its inhabitants and giving excellent pictures of the *caboclo*. Later, in *Subterranean Light* * (1936), he tried to sketch a wider horizon but failed. Lúcio Cardoso was received by Brazilian critics as the Dostoevski of his country, because of the strange atmosphere of his narration, and his dialogue suggestive of mystery; and much can be expected from this abnormal writer, who exhibits a constant preoccupation with ghosts and esoteric themes. Promising also is the work of Rachel de Queiroz (1910-), a precocious young lady who at the age of eighteen had already published her first novel, *1915*—a narrative dealing with that year's drought, a strong sober concise work, somewhat under the influence of Almeida. Rachel has a very strong personality, and her subsequent novels—*John Michael* (1935), *Stony Roads* (1937), *The Three Marys* (1938)—are written in a prose tinged with emotion, yet retaining a serenity of form and content.† All her work stresses the need for considering the rights of women, and (appropriately enough) she occupies the first place among the feminine writers of Brazil.

Somewhat different tendencies mark the work of two other novelists: Cruls, a physician who has kept himself aloof from literary circles, and Oswald de Andrade who has deliberately chosen to represent foreign tendencies in the midst of a nationalist era. Gastão Cruls (1888-) is a writer of unbridled imagination, as may be seen in his extraordinary work *The*

---

* Cardoso, *A Luz no Subsolo*.
† Queiroz, *O 15, João Miguel, Caminhos de Pedra, As Três Marias*.

Amazons (1925), in which he writes of the Indians and the landscape of the Amazonian region, combining description with dramatic adventure very much in the manner of André Maurois.* Still farther removed from current trends is Oswald de Andrade (1890–1954), the *enfant terrible* of Brazilian letters. Andrade is fond of an eccentric way of living, and he is no less eccentric in his writings. He has imitated every well-known contemporary European writer—Wilde, Huysmans, Gide, Joyce, Lawrence, and Freud—in a series of artificial and shocking books: *The Damned* (1922), *The Star of Absinthe* (1927), *The Vermillion Ladder* (1934), and so on.† Among contemporary Brazilian novelists [81] who are sincerely endeavoring to interpret their native land, Oswald de Andrade must be classed as a writer who has betrayed his mission, one who has used his undeniable gifts merely to become a literary sensation.

For the contemporary Brazilian novel, like the regional novel of the rest of Latin America, is remarkable above all for its representation of the native scene. These novels, whether they deal with the *Sertão*, or the life of the gaucho, or the mysterious and frightful tropical forests, or the struggles of the Mexican Indian, form perhaps the best and most sincere contribution of Latin American literature. They represent a new form of expression, attuned to the reality and the genius of a New World. They are, to put it succinctly, a monument to the present and a promise for the future of literary Americanism.

* Cruls, *A Amazônia Mysteriosa.*
† Andrade, *Os Condenados, A Estrêla de Absinto, A Escada Vermelha.*

APPENDIX

NOTES AND BIBLIOGRAPHY

CHAPTER I

Notes

1. MacLeish, Archibald, *Remarks on the Occasion of the Dedication of the Hispanic Room in the Library of Congress*, Oct. 12, 1939.

2. *Historia General y Natural*, edition of the Real Academia de la Historia, Madrid, 1851, vol. I, p. 460; translated by A. T.-R.

3. *The True History . . .*, English edition, New York and London, 1928, pp. 90-91; translated by A. P. Maudslay.

4. Ibid. 489-90; translated by A. P. Maudslay.

5. *First Part of the Royal Commentaries*, English edition of the Hakluyt Society, London, 1871, vol. II, pp. 457-8; translated by Clements R. Markham.

6. Translated by S. Griswold Morley.

7. Cf. José Toribio Medina's edition of *La Araucana*, Santiago, 1910, for details on Ercilla's life.

8. Translated by S. Griswold Morley.

9. For Ticknor's judgment of the *Araucana* cf. *infra*, p. 18. Ticknor's unfavorable opinion is not accepted by critics today.

10. Translated by S. Griswold Morley.

11. Translated by S. Griswold Morley.

12. Translated by S. Griswold Morley.

13. Translated by S. Griswold Morley.

14. Translated by S. Griswold Morley.

15. Leonard, Irving A., *Colonial Society* in *Colonial Hispanic America*, George Washington University, 1936, pp. 253-4.

16. Ibid. p. 254.

17. Ibid. p. 255.

18. Schons, Dorothy, 'The Influence of Góngora on Mexican Literature during the Seventeenth Century,' in *Hispanic Review*, vol. VII, no. 1, January 1939, p. 30.

19. Menéndez y Pelayo, Marcelino, *Obras*, Madrid, 1911, *Historia de la Poesía Hispano-americana*, vol. II, p. 191.

20. Sor Juana Inés de la Cruz, *Respuesta a Sor Filotea*, edited by Ermilo Abreu Gómez, Mexico, 1929, p. 12.

21. Ibid. p. 13.

22. Ibid. pp. 13-14.

23. Translated by Elizabeth Selden.

24. Translated by Muna Lee.

25. Menéndez y Pelayo, op. cit. p. 81.

26. Sor Juana, op. cit. pp. 27-8.

Bibliography

Barreda Laos, Felipe, *La Vida Intelectual de la Colonia*. Lima, 1909.
García Calderón, Francisco, *Latin America*. London, 1913.

Gutiérrez, Juan María, *Estudios Biográficos y Críticos sobre algunos Poetas anteriores al Siglo* xix. Buenos Aires, 1865.

Henríquez Ureña, Pedro, *El Teatro de la América Española en la Epoca Colonial*. Buenos Aires, 1936.

Medina, José Toribio, *Biblioteca Hispanoamericana*. 7 vols. Santiago, 1907.

Menéndez y Pelayo, Marcelino, *Historia de la Poesía Hispanoamericana*. Madrid, 1911.

Moses, Bernard, *Spanish Colonial Literature in South America*. New York, 1922.

Pirotto, Armando, *La Literatura en América: El Coloniaje*. Montevideo, 1937.

Quesada, Vicente, *La Vida Intelectual en la América Española durante los siglos* xvi, xvii, *y* xviii. Buenos Aires, 1910.

CHAPTER II

Notes

1. Spell, J. R., *Rousseau in the Spanish World before 1833*, Austin, 1938, p. 255.

2. Ibid. p. 255.

3. On some of this pamphleteering literature, cf. Rojas, Ricardo, *Historia de la Literatura Argentina: Los Proscriptos*, Buenos Aires, 1925.

4. *El Periquillo Sarniento*, Mexico, 1830, vol. ii, p. 142; translated by A. T.-R.

5. Hills, E. C., *Hispanic Studies*, Stanford University, 1929, p. 118.

6. Ibid. p. 117.

7. Translated by A. T.-R.

8. Hills, op. cit. pp. 126-218.

9. *Autores Americanos Juzgados por Españoles*, Paris, n.d., Menéndez y Pelayo, 'Bello,' p. 239.

10. García Calderón, *Latin America*, London, 1913, p. 230.

11. Lastarria, J. V., *Recuerdos Literarios*, Santiago, 1878, pp. 65-6.

12. *Mercurio*, 27 April 1842.

13. *Mercurio*, 19 May 1842, quoting the remarks made by Bello in the *Semanario*, under the pen-name of 'Un Quidam.'

14. *Mercurio*, 22 May 1842, again quoting 'Un Quidam'; Sarmiento was fond of repeating his adversaries' most biting remarks, in order to refute them.

15. The reader who is interested in reading Sarmiento's articles in this historic battle-of-wits will find them reproduced in handy form in Donoso, Armando, *Sarmiento en el Destierro*, Buenos Aires, 1927.

16. This sketch was first published in 1871, after the author's death; the incomplete manuscript is barely legible, and exhibits the haste with which it was composed.

17. For a sketch of Sarmiento's life, cf. *infra, Romanticism rampant*, p. 60.

18. *Facundo*, Madrid, 1917(?), p. 49; translated by A. T.-R.

19. Ibid. p. 106; translated by A. T.-R.

20. *Facundo* was one of the earliest Spanish American books known abroad. The reader is referred to the still-excellent English translation by Mrs. Horace Mann, *Life in the Argentine Republic in the Days of the Tyrants, or Civilization and Barbarism*, London, 1868. When Mrs. Mann made her translation, *Facundo* was not then accorded the position that criticism gives it today: first place in Spanish America's classics.

21. Prologue to *Facundo*, p. xxi.

22. *Siete Tratados*, with *Introducción* by R. Blanco-Fombona, Paris, n.d., vol. II, pp. 350-51; translated by A. T.-R.

23. Ibid. vol. II, pp. 148-50; translated by A. T.-R.

24. Cf. Meléndez, Concha, *La Novela Indianista en Hispanoamérica*, Madrid, 1934.

25. *María*, Madrid, 1899, p. 28.

26. Ibid. pp. 419-20.

27. The authors of these novels are, respectively, Darío Salas, Pedro Castera, Emilio Constantino Guerrero, Rafael Delgado. One should add *En el Cerezal* (*In the Cherry Orchard*) by Daniel Samper Ortega, to the list of imitations of *María*.

28. Space does not permit the discussion of all these poets in the text. In addition to the ones named above, the following may be mentioned: In Cuba, Gertrudis Gómez de Avellaneda (1814-73), who is usually classed with the literature of Spain, because of her long residence there; and 'Plácido' (Gabriel de la Concepción Valdés, 1809-44), the revolutionist patriot. In Mexico, Guillermo Prieto (1818-97), a writer of popular inspiration, author of *El Romancero Nacional* (1885). In Argentina, Carlos Guido y Spano (1827-1918), who represents an early reaction against romanticism; and 'Almafuerte' (Pedro Palacios, 1854-1917), a virile writer of not always good taste. In Uruguay, Juan Carlos Gómez (1820-84), romantic poet, revolutionist, and soldier; and Alejandro Magariños Cervantes (1825-93), an early cultivator of 'literary Americanism.' In Colombia, José Eusebio Caro (1817-53), a religious poet; Julio Arboleda (1817-62), author of the unfinished modern epic *Gonzalo de Oyón;* Rafael Pombo (1833-1912), who represents the philosophic tendency in romanticism, and who found inspiration in topics ranging from love to nature, patriotism, and religion; and Diego Fallon (1834-1905), who represented the more exquisite phase of romanticism in his famous poem *A la Luna*. In Venezuela, José Antonio Maitín (1814-74), a singer of rustic themes; Abigail Lozano (1821-66), who wrote mainly love poems; and José Antonio Calcaño (1827-94), who became, under the influence of English and German poets, a romanticist of wide appeal. In Ecuador, Numa Pompilio Llona (1832-1907) was more modern in form, and from the elegance of his sonnets might be classified as a Parnassian. In Peru, Carlos Augusto Salaverry (1831-90), Clemente Althaus (1835-81), and Pedro Paz Soldán y Unanue (1839-95) are the representatives of a romanticism that has likewise already evolved towards more modern patterns.

29. Cf. the Introduction to the Official Peruvian Government edition, Madrid, 1924, of the *Tradiciones Peruanas*.

30. Ibid. vol. I, p. 42.
31. Ibid. vol. I, p. 46.

Bibliography

Barrera, Isaac, *Historia de la Literatura Hispano Americana*. Quito, 1935.

Blanco, Fombona R., *Autores Americanos juzgados por Españoles*. Paris, 1912.

Cañete, Manuel, *Escritores Hispano Americanos*. Madrid, 1884.

Coester, Alfred, *The Literary History of Spanish America*. New York, 1916.

Cometta Manzoni, Aída, *El Indio en la Poesía de América Española*. Buenos Aires, 1939.

Estrella Gutiérrez, F. y Suárez Calimano, E., *Historia de la Literatura Americana y Argentina*. Buenos Aires, 1940.

García Calderón, Francisco, *Latin America*. London, 1913.

García Calderón, Ventura, *Del Romanticismo al Modernismo*. Paris, 1910.

García Calderón, Ventura, *Semblanzas de América*. Madrid, n.d.

Ghiraldo, Alberto, *El Romanticismo en América*, in *Antología Americana*. Madrid, 1923.

Hills, E. C., *The Odes of Bello, Olmedo and Heredia*. New York, 1920.

Menéndez y Pelayo, Marcelino, *Antología de la Poesía Hispanoamericana*. Madrid, 1892.

Ospina, Eduardo, *El Romanticismo*. Madrid, 1927.

Piñeyro, Enrique, *Biografías Americanas*. Paris, n.d.

Spell, J. R., *Rousseau in the Spanish World Before 1833*. Austin, Texas, 1938.

CHAPTER III

Notes

1. Thus, for example, the date of 1820, when Lamartine published his *Meditations*, is generally assigned as the beginning of the romantic period in French literature; this, despite the fact that romantic tendencies were strongly marked in earlier writers, as in Rousseau and Chateaubriand.

2. Translated by Arthur Symonds.

3. Henríquez Ureña, Pedro, Introduction to *Eleven Poems of Rubén Darío*, New York and London, 1916, p. v.

4. Darío, in a letter written in November 1899.

5. Craig, G. Dundas, *The Modernist Trend in Spanish-American Poetry*, University of California, 1934, p. 3.

6. Translated by A. T.-R.

7. Translated by Isaac Goldberg.

8. Translated by Isaac Goldberg.

9. Translated by Muna Lee.

10. Translated by G. Dundas Craig.

11. Translated by Muna Lee.

12. Craig, op. cit. p. 278.

13. Translated by A. T.-R.

14. Translated by G. Dundas Craig.

15. Translated by Alice Stone Blackwell.

16. For details on the life of Darío, cf. *Rubén Darío: Casticismo y Americanismo*, Cambridge, Mass., 1931, by A. T.-R., pp. 3-121.

17. Henríquez Ureña, op. cit. p. vii, summarizing. The reader who is interested in a detailed and technical study of some of Darío's verse innovations is referred to *Rubén Darío* by A. T.-R., pp. 134-60.

18. Translated by Thomas Walsh and Salomón de la Selva.

19. Translated by G. Dundas Craig.

20. Translated by Thomas Walsh and Salomón de la Selva.

21. Translated by G. Dundas Craig.

22. Translated by Muna Lee.

23. Translated by Muna Lee. Miss Lee wrote, 'To get himself in silence to his tree,' which has been emended here.

24. Translated by G. Dundas Craig.

25. Translated by G. Dundas Craig.

26. Translated by Muna Lee.

27. Translated by Muna Lee.

28. Zaldumbide, Gonzalo, *José Enrique Rodó*, Montevideo, 1933, p. 49.

29. Barbagelata, Hugo D., 'Rodó (silueta que podrá servir para un retrato futuro),' in Rodó's *Cinco Ensayos*, Madrid, n.d., p. 12.

30. *Ariel*, Boston and New York, 1922, pp. 61-4; translated by F. J. Stimson.

31. Ibid. pp. 123-6.

32. Zaldumbide, op. cit. p. 144.

33. Translated by Alice Stone Blackwell.

34. Translated by Muna Lee.

35. Translated by Muna Lee.

36. Translated by A. T.-R.

37. Cf. Alonso, Amado, 'Algunos Símbolos Insistentes en la Poesía de Pablo Neruda,' in *Revista Hispánica Moderna*, Julio 1939; and Alonso, *Poesía y Estilo de Pablo Neruda*, Buenos Aires, 1940. The illustrative verses from Neruda quoted here were translated by A. T.-R.

38. Cf. the *Antología de Poesía Negra Hispano Americana*, compiled by Emilio Ballagas, Madrid, 1935, for other compositions illustrating these tendencies. This poem is by José Zacarías Tallet, translated by Joseph Leonard Grucci.

39. Poem by Alejo Carpentier; translated by A. T.-R.

40. Translated by Joseph Leonard Grucci.

41. Translated by Joseph Leonard Grucci.

42. Translated by A. T.-R.

43. *Orbita de la Poesía Afrocubana*, Havana, 1938.

Bibliography

Blackwell, Alice Stone, *Some Spanish American Poets*. New York, 1929.

Blanco Fombona, Rufino, *El Modernismo y los Poetas Modernistas*. Madrid, 1929.

Contreras, Francisco, *Les Écrivains Contemporains de l'Amérique Espagnole*. Paris, 1920.

Craig, G. Dundas, *The Modernist Trend in Spanish-American Poetry.* Berkeley, Calif., 1934.

Goldberg, Isaac, *Studies in Spanish-American Literature.* New York, 1920.

Henríquez Ureña, Max, *Rodó y Rubén Darío.* La Habana, 1918.

Henríquez Ureña, Pedro, *Horas de Estudio.* Paris, n.d.

Machado, Manuel, *La Guerra Literaria.* Madrid, 1913.

Mapes, Erwin K., *L'Influence française dans l'Oeuvre de Rubén Darío.* Paris, 1925.

Marasso, Arturo, *Rubén Darío y su Creación Poética.* La Plata, 1934.

Marinello, Juan, *El Modernismo, Estado de Cultura,* in *La Literatura Hispano-Americana.* Mexico, 1937.

Onís, Federico de, *Antología de la Poesía Española e Hispanoamericana.* Madrid, 1934.

Rodó, José Enrique, *Cinco Ensayos.* Madrid, 1915.

Sanchez, Luis Alberto, *Balance y Liquidación del 900.* Santiago de Chile, 1940.

Torres-Ríoseco, Arturo, *Precursores del Modernismo.* Madrid, 1925.

Torres-Ríoseco, Arturo, *Rubén Darío, Casticismo y Americanismo.* Cambridge, Mass., 1931.

Valera, Juan, *Obras Completas,* XLI. Madrid, 1915.

Walsh, Thomas, *Hispanic Anthology.* New York, 1920.

CHAPTER IV

Notes

1. Sarmiento, Domingo Faustino, *Life in the Argentine Republic in the Days of the Tyrants, or Civilization and Barbarism;* translated by Mrs. Horace Mann, London, 1868, pp. 1-4.

2. On this subject, cf. Nichols, Madaline, 'Colonial Tucumán,' *Hispanic American Historical Review,* Vol. XVIII, No. 4, November 1938; 'The Gaucho,' *Pacific Historical Review,* March 1936; 'The Spanish Horse of the Pampas,' *American Anthropologist,* Vol. XLI, No. 1, January-March 1939; 'El Gaucho Argentino,' *Revista Iberoamericana,* Vol. I, No. 1, May 1939.

3. Lugones, Leopoldo, *El Payador,* 1916, p. 43.

4. Cf. Costa Alvarez, Arturo, 'Las Etimologías de "Gaucho,"' *Nosotros,* Buenos Aires, October 1926.

5. From this same word *guacho,* which in Chile is a contemptuous word much as gaucho was to the citizen of Buenos Aires, comes the Chilean term *huaso* for the cowboy or peasant. The word *huaso* also carries the implied meaning of 'uncultured person.' Incidentally, society has taken two quite different attitudes towards *huasos* and *gauchos:* for the former, scorn at their barbaric ways of living; for the latter, admiration of their courage and virility.

6. Quoted by Sarmiento, op. cit. p. 12.

7. For descriptions in English of gaucho garments, cf. the notes to Walter Owen's translation of *Martín Fierro;* for this material in Spanish,

cf. Eleuterio Tiscornia, *Martín Fierro, comentado y anotado*, and *La Lengua de Martín Fierro.*

8. Bunge, C. O., 'La Literatura Gauchesca,' Introduction to the 1919 edition of *Martín Fierro.*

9. Sarmiento, op. cit. p. 21.

10. Ibid. pp. 27-8.

11. Translated by Muna Lee.

12. Sarmiento, op. cit. pp. 42-3.

13. Ibid. pp. 43-4.

14. Owen, Walter, Introduction to *The Gaucho Martín Fierro.*

15. Holmes, H. A., *Martín Fierro, an Epic of the Argentine*, New York, 1923, p. 50.

16. Holmes, op. cit. p. 72.

17. Lugones, op. cit. p. 159.

18. Translated by Walter Owen.

19. Translated by Walter Owen. All the subsequent quotations from *Martín Fierro* are likewise from Owen's admirable English translation of Hernández' epic, *The Gaucho Martín Fierro*, Oxford, 1935.

20. The reader who desires further acquaintance with Sánchez' work, is referred to the Cervantes edition of his plays, *El Teatro del Uruguayo Florencio Sánchez*, 3 vols., Barcelona, 1917, which contains an excellent introductory essay by V. A. Salaverri.

21. The relation of the gaucho novel to the Spanish American novel in general is not stressed here; for this relationship, the reader is referred to Torres-Ríoseco, *La Novela en la América Hispana*, Berkeley, 1939, 'III. La Novela Criolla,' pp. 210-43.

22. The works cited are, Zavala Muniz' *The Chronicle of Muniz, The Chronicle of a Crime;* Lynch's *Raquela, The Romance of a Gaucho;* Rodríguez Larreta's *Zogoibi;* and Reyles' *The Gaucho Florido.*

23. Other gauchesque novelists in Uruguay are A. Montiel Ballesteros (1888-   ), author of *La Raza* (1925), and *Castigo'e Dios* (1930); Vicente Salaverri, with his *Este era un País* (1920) and *El hijo del León* (1922); and the extremely promising Francisco Espínola, a writer of powerful gaucho short stories in *Raza Ciega* (1926).

24. Cf. Torres-Ríoseco, 'Benito Lynch,' in *Novelistas Contemporáneos de América*, Santiago, 1939, pp. 151-210.

25. Lynch, *Raquela*, edition of 1926, pp. 109-10: translated by A. T.-R.

26. Cf. Torres-Ríoseco, 'Ricardo Güiraldes,' in *Novelistas Contemporáneos de América*, pp. 123-49.

27. Güiraldes, *Don Segundo Sombra*, edition of 1927, p. 26.

Bibliography

Bunge, Carlos Octavio, *La Literatura Gauchesca.* In *Martin Fierro.* Buenos Aires, 1919.

Cunninghame Graham, Robert B., *The Horses of the Conquest.* London, 1930.

Furt, Jorge, *Lo Gauchesco en la Literatura Argentina de Ricardo Rojas.* Buenos Aires, 1929.

Furt, Jorge, *Arte Gauchesco.* Buenos Aires, 1924.

Holmes, H. A., *Martín Fierro, an Epic of the Argentine.* New York, 1923.

Hudson, William Henry, *Far Away and Long Ago.* New York, 1924.

Lehmann-Nitsche, Robert, *Folklore Argentino, Santos Vega.* Buenos Aires, 1917.

Lugones, Leopoldo, *El Payador.* Buenos Aires, 1916.

Nichols, Madaline, *The Gaucho: Cattle Hunter, Cavalryman, Ideal of Romance.* Durham, N. C., 1942.

Owen, Walter, *The Gaucho Martín Fierro* (English Translation). Oxford, 1935.

Page, Frederick Mann, *Los Payadores Gauchos.* Darmstadt, 1897.

Quesada, Ernesto, *El Criollismo en la Literatura Argentina.* Buenos Aires, 1902.

Reyles, Carlos, *El Nuevo Sentido de la Narración Gauchesca.* Montevideo, 1930.

Rojas, Ricardo, *La Literatura Argentina.* Vols. I-II. Buenos Aires, 1924.

Sarmiento, Domingo Faustino, *Life in the Argentine Republic in the Days of the Tyrants.* Translated by Mrs. Horace Mann, London, 1868.

Salaverría, J. M., *El Poema de la Pampa.* Madrid, 1918.

Tiscornia, Eleuterio, *La Lengua de Martín Fierro.* Buenos Aires, 1930.

Tiscornia, Eleuterio, *Martín Fierro Comentado y Anotado.* Buenos Aires, 1925.

Tiscornia, Eleuterio, ed., *Poetas Gauchescos: Hidalgo—Ascasubi—Del Campo.* Buenos Aires, 1940.

CHAPTER V

Notes

1. Cf. the classification in Torres-Ríoseco, 'La Novela de la Ciudad,' in *Novelistas Contemporáneos de América,* pp. 211-307, and the reservation in ibid. p. 5. As with any literary movement, it is impossible to draw hard and fast lines of demarcation; thus, Gálvez, while primarily a city novelist, has also attempted the rural novel, and Barrios has used a city background for only one of his three best-known works.

2. Cf. Torres-Ríoseco, 'Manuel Gálvez,' in *Novelistas Contemporáneos de América,* pp. 251-70.

3. Cf. Torres-Ríoseco, 'Joaquín Edwards Bello,' in *Novelistas Contemporáneos,* pp. 271-307.

4. Cf. *infra,* 'The Novel of Artistic Escape,' pp. 191-92.

5. Cf. *infra,* 'The Psychological and Philosophical Novel,' pp. 197-98.

6. In Chile, for instance, Alberto Romero (1897-), in *La Viuda del Conventillo* (1930), and J. S. Gonzalez Vera (1897-), in *Vidas Mínimas* (1923), have written realistic studies of the city and its suburbs; while Manuel Rojas (1896-), in his *Lanchas en la Bahía* (1932) has described life in the seaports.

7. Cf. Torres-Ríoseco, 'José Eustasio Rivera,' in *Novelistas Contemporáneos,* pp. 45-90.

8. Rivera, *La Vorágine*, eighth edition, New York, 1928, pp. 240-41; translated by A. T.-R.

9. Rivera, *The Vortex*, translated by Earle K. James, New York, 1935, pp. 222-3.

10. Cf. Torres-Ríoseco, 'Rómulo Gallegos,' *Novelistas Contemporáneos*, pp. 91-122.

11. Gallegos, *Doña Bárbara*, edition of 1929, p. 50; translated by A. T.-R.

12. Cf. Campa, D. (unpublished Ph.D. dissertation), *La Novela de la Revolución Mexicana*, Berkeley, 1940, which discusses some hundred novels.

13. Cf. Torres-Ríoseco, 'Mariano Azuela,' in *Novelistas Contemporáneos*, pp. 11-44.

14. Azuela, *The Underdogs*, translated by E. Munguía, New York, 1929, pp. 70-71.

15. Azuela, *The Underdogs*, translated by E. Munguía, pp. 220-22.

16. For the earlier romantic phase of the *novela indianista*, cf. Meléndez, Concha, *La Novela Indianista en Hispanoamérica*, Madrid, 1934; for the more modern novel on Indian themes, cf. Torres-Ríoseco, 'La novela de tema indígena en Bolivia y Perú,' and 'La novela de tema indígena en el Ecuador,' in *La Novela en la América Hispana*, Berkeley, 1939.

17. Among these Peruvian followers of Valdelomar, one might mention Augusto Aguirre Morales, author of the Inca novel, *El Pueblo del Sol* (1924), Ernesto Reyna, for his *El Amauta Atusparia* (1930), and especially Luis Valcárcel (1891-), who has attempted to capture the native spirit in his *De la Vida Inkaica* (1925). Other Peruvians have followed the more sombre and realistic example of Clorinda Matto de Turner—notably César Falcón, in his *Pueblo Sin Dios* (1928), and Enrique López Albujar (1872-), author of the widely read *Cuentos Andinos* (1920), *Matalaché* (1928), and *Nuevos Cuentos Andinos* (1937).

18. Cf. the discussion of the term *modernistas* as applied to these novelists, Torres-Ríoseco, *Novelistas Contemporáneos*, pp. 5-6.

19. 'Alone' [Díaz Arrieta, Hernán], *Panorama de la Literatura Chilena Durante el Siglo XX*, Santiago, 1931, p. 130.

20. Cf. Torres-Ríoseco, 'Carlos Reyles,' in *Novelistas Contemporáneos*, pp. 311-51.

21. Reyles, *El Embrujo de Sevilla*, p. 41; translated by A. T.-R.

22. Cf. *infra*, 'The Psychological and Philosophical Novel,' p. 196.

23. Cf. Torres-Ríoseco, 'Manuel Díaz Rodríguez,' in *Novelistas Contemporáneos*, pp. 353-78.

24. *El Cojo Ilustrado*, founded in 1892; and *Cosmópolis*, founded in 1894.

25. Díaz Rodríguez, *Sangre Patricia*, undated Madrid edition of the *Sociedad española de librería*, p. 128; translated by A. T.-R.

26. Cf. Torres-Ríoseco, 'Rafael Arévalo Martínez,' in *Novelistas Contemporáneos*, pp. 411-22.

27. From a letter of Arévalo Martínez to A. T.-R.

28. Arévalo Martínez, *El Hombre que Parecía un Caballo*, Guatemala edition of 1927, pp. 17-18.

29. Cf. Torres-Ríoseco, 'Eduardo Barrios,' in *Novelistas Contemporáneos*, pp. 213-49.

30. Barrios, *El Niño que Enloqueció de Amor*, Cervantes edition, pp. 11-12; translated by A. T.-R.

31. Cf. Torres-Ríoseco, 'Pedro Prado,' in *Novelistas Contemporáneos*, pp. 379-409.

32. Prado, *Alsino*, edition of 1928, p. 296.

Bibliography

Ayala, D. C., *Resumen Histórico-crítico de la Literatura Hispanoamericana*. Caracas, 1927.

Barrera, Isaacs, *Historia de la Literatura Hispanoamericana*. Quito, 1935.

Coester, Alfred, *The Literary History of Spanish America*. New York, 1916.

Edwards Bello, J., *El Nacionalismo Continental*. Madrid, 1925.

Henríquez Ureña, Max, *El Retorno de los Galeones*. Madrid, 1930.

Henríquez Ureña, Pedro, *Apuntaciones sobre la Novela en América*. Buenos Aires, 1927.

Meléndez, Concha, *La Novela Indianista en Hispanoamérica*. Madrid, 1934.

Sánchez, Luis Alberto, *América, Novela sin Novelistas*. Lima, 1933.

Sánchez, Luis Alberto, *Balance y Liquidación del 900*. Santiago, 1940.

Sánchez, Luis Alberto, *Historia de la Literatura Americana*. Santiago, 1937.

Torres-Ríoseco, Arturo, *La Novela en la América Hispana*. Berkeley, 1939.

Torres-Ríoseco, Arturo, *Novelistas Contemporáneos de América*. Santiago, 1940.

CHAPTER VI

Notes

1. Peixoto, Afrânio, *Noções de História da Literatura Brasileira*, São Paulo, 1931, pp. 47-8.

2. Vieira, *Sermão pelo bom sucesso das armas de Portugal contra as da Holanda;* translated by A. T.-R.

3. From *bandeira*: ensign, banner, flag, band of men.

4. Translated by Frances Ellen Buckland.

5. Translated by Frances Ellen Buckland.

6. Translated by Frances Ellen Buckland.

7. The *Cartas Chilenas* (published in 1845) have also been attributed to Alvarenga Peixoto and to Claudio Manoel da Costa. There is evidence for believing that da Costa was the real author.

8. Cf. *Poesías Avulsas de 'Américo Elysio'* (José Bonifacio), Bordeaux, 1825.

9. Cf. Souza Caldas, *Obras Poéticas*, Paris, 1820-21; *Poesías Sacras*, Río, 1872.

10. Translated by Frances Ellen Buckland.
11. Translated by Frances Ellen Buckland.
12. Translated by Frances Ellen Buckland.
13. Translated by Frances Ellen Buckland.
14. Peixoto, op. cit. p. 161.
15. Translated by Frances Ellen Buckland.
16. Translated by Frances Ellen Buckland.
17. Translated by Frances Ellen Buckland.
18. Translated by A. T.-R.
19. Translated by Frances Ellen Buckland.
20. Translated by Frances Ellen Buckland.
21. Translated by Frances Ellen Buckland.
22. Translated by Frances Ellen Buckland.
23. Translated by Frances Ellen Buckland.
24. Cf. *supra*, 'The Romantic Upheaval in Spanish America: María," pp. 75 ff.
25. Cf. the English translation by Isabel Burton: Alencar, *Iracéma, the Honey-lips: A Legend of Brazil*, London, 1886.
26. Cf. the English translation, *Inocencia: A story of the Prairie Regions of Brazil*, by 'Silvio Dinarte' (Taunay), London, 1889.
27. Cf. *supra*, 'The Spanish American Novel: The Realistic Novel,' pp. 168 ff.
28. Cf. English translation by Mariano Joaquin Lorente: Graça Aranha, *Canaan*, Boston, 1920.
29. Cf. *supra*, 'The Spanish American Novel: The Novel of the Land,' pp. 178 ff.
30. There are evident similarities between these novelists and their contemporaries in Spanish America. Thus, Lins do Rego might be compared to Gallegos; Erico Veríssimo (for his subject matter) might be compared to the city novelists; and Almeida and Amado might be compared to Ciro Alegría. Ramos, of course, is related rather to the artistic and psychological novelists.
31. Contemporary Brazilian novelists, in addition to those discussed in the text, include the following—most of them promising young writers who have not as yet developed the full force of their genius: João Alphonsus, José Geraldo Vieira, Marques Rebello, Plinio Salgado, Cornelio Penna, Cyro dos Anjos, Domingos Olympio, Yan de Almeida Prado, Telmo Vergara, Luiz Delgado, and Vianna Moog.

Bibliography

Andrade Muricy, José Candido de, *A nova Literatura Brasileira*. Pôrto Alegre, 1936.

Carvalho, Ronald de, *Pequena Historia da Literatura Brasileira*. Rio de Janeiro, 1919.

Denis, Ferdinand, *Resumé de l'Histoire Littéraire du Portugal, suivi du Resumé de l'Histoire Littéraire du Brésil*. Paris, 1826.

Fernandes Pinheiro, J. C., *Resumo da Historia Litteraria*. Rio de Janeiro, 1873.

Ford, J. D. M., *A Tentative Bibliography of Brazilian Belles-Lettres.* (In collaboration with Arthur F. Whittem and Maxwell I. Raphael.) Cambridge, Mass., 1931.

García Mérou, Martín, *El Brasil Intelectual.* Buenos Aires, 1900.

Goldberg, Isaac, *Brazilian Literature.* New York, 1922.

Lima, Jorge de, *Dois Ensaios.* Rio de Janeiro, 1930.

Montenegro, Olivio, *O Romance Brasileiro.* Rio de Janeiro, 1938.

Motta, Arthur, *Historia da Litteratura Brasileira.* São Paulo, 1930.

Oliveira Lima, Custodio de, *Aspectos da Litteratura Colonial Brasileira.* Leipzig, 1896.

Peixoto, Afrânio, *Noções de Historia da Literatura Brasileira.* São Paulo, 1931.

Romero, Sylvio, *Compendio de Historia da Literatura Brasileira.* (In collaboration with João Ribeiro.) Rio de Janeiro, 1909.

Romero, Sylvio, *Historia da Litteratura Brasileira.* Rio de Janeiro, 1888.

Taunay, Affonso d'Escragnolle, *Escriptores Coloniaes.* São Paulo, 1925.

Varnhagen, Francisco Adolpho de, *Florilegio da Poesia Brasileira.* Vols. I-II, Lisboa, 1850; Vol. III, Madrid, 1853.

Veríssimo, José, *Historia da Litteratura Brasileira.* Rio da Janeiro, 1929.

Wolf, Ferdinand, *Le Brésil Littéraire.* Berlin, 1863.

INDEX